Kent Rivers

in

The Story

By

Anthony K. Benefield

Kent Rivers – The Story

Kent Rivers – The Story
by Anthony Benefield

Copyright © AKB Publishing and Marketing 2017

ISBN: 978-0615969725

Published by AKB Publishing and Marketing Cleveland, Tennessee USA

Revised 2017

Cover Design: SelfPubBookCovers.com/quentin_designs

Acknowledgments

I am thankful for the many officers, deputies, and detectives that I have worked with over the years. I cherish the good times and some of the painful lessons we shared.

I want to thank those who had a direct impact on my career, the judges, district attorneys, sheriffs, and detective partners.

To all the deputies and officers I have worked with over the years at: Longwood, FL PD, Carroll County Virginia Sheriff's Office, Bradley County Tennessee Sheriff's Office, Tenth Judicial District Drug Task Force, and the State of Tennessee, Thank you for your friendship, your cooperation, and your backup.

Sending a special, "thank you", to my brother Gary and his wife Corinne, for their willingness to put up with me and share their land. It gave me a place to think, reflect, and write. I enjoyed it more than I can say.

To my sister Karen Benefield Ward: Thank you for your help and your insight.

To my wife, Angie. I love you.

Dedication

When I was a young boy, a tall, handsome Orange County, Florida deputy sheriff pulled his patrol car into my grandmother's driveway. It was probably the first time I had been up-close to a law officer.

He walked into the house, sat at the dining table, and ate lunch with those of us in the house. It may have been his first day on the job. I couldn't help but stare at his gun, the uniform, and the silver star on his chest. He was bigger than life.

Through the years I saw that deputy sheriff regularly as he came to our house or some family outing. There were many family outings during those days. He changed his looks from time to time. But it was the same tall deputy sheriff.

Once, a big Harley chopper pulled into the yard driven by a man with long hair and a long beard. It scared me at first until I heard him speak. It was the tall deputy sheriff. He put me on the back of that bike and took me for a fast ride. I'm sure it was only about 25 miles per hour, but at age nine, everything is bigger and faster. I remember hearing the rumble of a Harley motorcycle coming up the road when this deputy sheriff was assigned to the motorbike unit. He pulled the "Hog" onto the carport, shut off the engine, and dismount.

His tall black motorcycle boots, his baggy motorcycle pants, the uniform, and the white helmet with the big star, always made my day. He looked down at me, smile, and say, "if you hear them say, Orlando 124 (or some number), come get me," before he walked into the house to visit my mom and dad. I listened intently for that number, worried all the while that I would miss it. It was the most important assignment I could have at that young age.

Sometimes, the deputy came by the house to pick me up and take me to get a strawberry milkshake. Then we went to his house and hung out. It was fun just to be around him. He was bigger than life. I grew up and became a deputy sheriff myself.

On my first opportunity to work in an undercover operation, I called the deputy and asked him for his advice on how to operate. He gave me some quick, but solid, guidelines that proved to be valuable through the years. The tall, handsome deputy became well known for his work against organized crime and political corruption. He received commendations by three Florida governors for his work.

In later years I described this deputy to my friends as a cross between Charlton Heston and Clint Eastwood. But he was much more than an action figure. His words were few and soft-spoken but always had meaning. If he had been in western movies, he would have been one of the good guys that rode into the sunset after saving the day.

Beside his photograph should be the words, "there are few like him," because, truly, there are few like him.

This book is dedicated to the best lawman, and one of the finest Christian men, I ever knew;

Wayne Bird
June 29, 1942 – March 28, 2014

Kent Rivers – The Story

CHAPTER ONE

Bright Lights

Sunday night – June 20th

Up and dressed in just minutes, he still obtained a high from the rush of knowing he was about to jump into some unknown situation that called for his particular skills and unique talents. He would do this!

As Rivers was pulling out of his driveway, he remembered he was to meet Diane for breakfast early the following morning. She was a lovely woman and treated him well, but they both knew that they didn't have that much in common. He did, however, enjoy her company, and she seemed to enjoy his.

When a woman started looking beyond the next date, Kent graciously stepped away. He had no plans for marriage, so he saw no need for a long-term relationship. He hated to call her so late on a Sunday night, but he knew it might be the last chance to let her know. She understood.

It's not that he didn't think about marriage, he did. But it was the marriage he had once known that besieged his mind at times. He never came to terms with losing the love of his life. For that reason, he never allowed himself to go much beyond a dinner, a glass of wine, and hopefully good conversation with a woman.

As he turned onto Interstate 75, he could see the blue and red lights illuminating the horizon more than a mile away. As a kid, when Rivers went on long trips with his family, they traveled mostly at night. He figured it was to beat the heat of the day since none of the cars his dad owned had air conditioning.

Sometimes, as he lay on the back of whatever old station wagon his dad had at the time, he heard the sound of the wheels and engine slowing down. He raised his head half-asleep to check out what was happening. He wondered to himself why the change in the sounds didn't wake any of his siblings. On more than one occasion, he saw bright lights flashing in the road ahead and wondered what horrible thing had taken place during the black of night.

His mind reflected upon those childhood days as he pulled up to a light bonanza with the patrol units, rescue units, and a few of the detectives that had already pulled onto the side of the interstate. What horrible thing has taken place during the black of night? He wondered.

He got out of his car and took a few steps toward the bright lights and met Detective Jesse Hawkins.

"Hey, Chief," Hawkins said as he shook Kent's hand.

"Hey, what do we have, Jesse?" Rivers asked the detective.

"Well, there is a white male lying right on the white line of the road. The victim was shot in the head. It is a wonder that he wasn't run over since he is just over the white line," Hawkins replied.

"Is there ID? Do we know anything about who he is?" Rivers inquired.

"No. None, Chief. He is wearing a pair of red shorts, and that's it. No wallet, no shirt—nothing," Hawkins answered."He could be from anywhere," Hawkins added.

"No clue about this guy," Rivers thought. They had to figure out the victim's identity, where he was from, where he had been, and where he was going. After that, hopefully, the killer could be tracked down.

Detective Hawkins's description was right on target—a white male with a bloody face and neck area. Blood had time to dry somewhat but was still wet at the openings of the skin. There was more than one entry wound. There was not a lot of blood on the road, but what was there had pooled in one place.

To Rivers, the face of a dead victim made a statement; it was usually a horrid comment. What did the victim have to say about their last moments? His mission was to find the ones who forced that unwitting proclamation.

Since he couldn't go back in time physically, he knew he had to go back in time through the portals of evidence. One piece after another, he traveled back in time until finally the portal closed around the murderer's neck. He needed to find a way to bring that gift of time to the person he was working for—for the dead.

The first responding deputies did a good job of slowing traffic and directing the vehicles around the scene on this night. Typically an officer could count on a truck driver to use proper care when approaching a traffic stop or accident scene, but there is nothing more unnerving to a cop than to look up and see a speeding driver headed right for him or her.

"Jesse, would you see if Kevin was called and his ETA?" Rivers asked.

Rivers was a pie plate spinner. He understood investigating. He knew how to keep things rolling. He often thought of himself as an air traffic controller. The information was collected and analyzed, and decisions made. If he or his team didn't have the knowledge or skills needed, he knew someone who did.

Kevin Dalton was the one he counted on to take charge of the crime scene processing. Dalton was the most detailed crime scene investigator that Rivers knew. When it came to processing a crime scene, Rivers wanted Dalton to take the lead. Dalton lived in the next county west of Chattanooga. The distance made it difficult when he was needed, but Rivers felt he was worth the wait.

"I was just talking to Kevin on channel two. He said he would be here in 15," Hawkins replied.

"Thanks, and how 'bout Dek, Don, and Pete?" Asked, Rivers.

"I heard Dek and Don check in on the main channel about five ago. I'll check on Pete," said Hawkins.

"Great! I want to get things rolling," Rivers stated.

"Anyone else, chief?" asked Jesse.

"I'll let you know."

Rivers never liked flipping a body. He had only told Dek about his queasiness in this area and swore him to silence. In this case, the body had only been there a short time, so touching it was not going to cause any damage to the body itself. When a body has been lying in the same spot for days or longer, depending upon the surrounding temperature, it can be very ripe.

One time, Rivers pulled an arm off a badly decomposed body. Since then, he tried to avoid that task without others realizing what he was doing. Nothing else about a crime scene seemed to bother him, but that task did. Others would have thought it was funny. So, he never let them know.

Rivers was looking at the victim's hair. He noticed that it was short but full and fairly well kept. He saw the route the blood had taken as the body lay in the road. The right cheek was touching the pavement with the nose turned slightly downward. The hair had caused some of the blood to pool just a few inches into the scalp from the wounds in the face. Whoever did this was looking this man in the face, and the victim was watching his killer.

The face was clean-shaven with no noticeable stubble. The blood must have pooled in the victim's hair, as the body was being dumped or turned because the nose was pointing more toward the ground. Once the head turned downward, the majority of the blood had oozed from the wounds onto the pavement where a large, thick circle of blood had pooled.

The left knee was touching the white line on the right side of the road. The rest of the body was away from the line. Rivers thought that it was a wonder someone hadn't run over the body after it was left there.

The head was pointing north, perpendicular to the road. His right arm was mostly under the body. The left arm was lying across the body. There were no other visual marks on the body. There was some blood on the chest and neck areas.

Much of the blood had dried on the face, but there was still some oozing at each of the wounds. There appeared to be five wounds in the face. Rivers guessed that the shooter was no more than three to four feet away as the gun discharged.

There was no blood splatter or signs of blood around the body other than what was directly under the body. There was no blood smeared on the body, which indicated that the body was not dragged or moved through any blood. There was a very light amount of blood on the left forearm. There was no blood on either of the hands. That lack of blood caused Rivers to believe that someone had a small amount of blood on his hand and could have possibly touched the body on the left forearm. Was that where the victim was grabbed after the shooting and put on the ground? It could explain the small amount of bleeding into the hair on the left side of the head.

Kevin Dalton walked up behind Rivers and stood there as he took some mental notes and decided the best approach to start collecting evidence. Dalton gathered the tools he needed to collect what was before him. Of course, he had help from other investigators, but Dalton was in charge. There had never been a problem in a court situation with the evidence when Dalton was handling the scene.

"Hey Chief, anything you think I should know before I get started?" asked Dalton.

"Hey Kevin, just a few things that are interesting. Notice the small amount of blood on the left forearm? Also, I couldn't find any blood around this area other than right here at the body. What is your initial take on just how the body got here?" asked Rivers.

Dalton looked around the body for anything that stood out to him. "Well, my first thought, before actually looking into it, is he was pulled out of a car. But that is obvious, I guess. If he were pulled out of a car, either the car stopped in the middle of this lane, and someone pulled him out of the passenger's side, or the car was already pulled over, and someone pulled him from the driver's side. If that is true, then it could have been someone hitchhiking that he stopped to pick up. Other than that, I don't know quite yet," Dalton concluded.

"Yeah, that's pretty much what I was thinking," Rivers responded. "The other team members that are coming should be here soon, and I want them to see the scene as it is. I know you will probably start with a video, and that will give them time to get here. I appreciate you coming out so quickly, Kevin."

"No problem, Chief. I hadn't gotten to bed yet, so I was already pretty much ready," Dalton said as he cleared the point.

"Okay, Kevin. I'll let you get started. I'm going to make a few notes while they are fresh on my mind," Rivers responded.

While Detective Dalton began to take the crime scene photos and video, a couple of the other detectives arrived on the scene. Detectives Don Blackman, Detective Lieutenant Dek Bates, and Pete Sanchez were talking with Rivers as he gave them what they had so far. Shortly after, they began discussing the case. Detective

Jen Rogers arrived. Rogers was well trained in crime scene technology. As she got out of her car, Rivers caught her eye and simply pointed toward Detective Dalton. Right away she knew her assignment. She walked over to Kevin Dalton and let him know she was there.

"Hey, Jen, ready to do another one?" Dalton asked.

"Does it really matter if I am or not, Kevin? These things never come at a good time. I was just getting out of the shower and ready for a restful night's sleep. I was so tired from driving most of the day from my mom's in Spartanburg. When I got back, I had to go over any last minute thoughts on the Mallory case. I have to have the file ready for the district attorney by morning. Glad I had the shower though, feel better anyway," Jen replied.

"I'm glad you got that case and not me. That guy turns my stomach just to look at him."

"Yep, I plan to watch him when his stomach turns as the judge gives him life."

Dalton laughed just a little as if to say, yeah, I understand.

"The chief wants us to go ahead with the photos and video. He will be back in a few with the others for a look," Dalton explained.

Rogers got the camera out of her trunk and started taking photos from the outside, then moving inward. The entire scene was to be photographed in a circle while moving closer to the center with each completed circle. Dalton felt that the coverage was better that way, and things that may not seem so important while on the scene could be critical later.

Rivers and the other detectives walked over to the crime scene but stayed back so not to contaminate the area around the body. The scene benefited from all the lights, so it was not difficult for the others to get a good look at the entire scope.

"Were any spent rounds found yet?" Sanchez directed his question toward Rivers.

"Not unless there are some under the body, there are none in plain view. We will have to check the grassy area after the sun comes up and maybe use some metal detectors," Rivers said as he looked around in the rough areas.

"Could you tell how many times he was shot?" asked Detective Bates.

"Of course I can't be sure, but it appears to be at least four and maybe five. But several," Rivers answered.

"Dek, I want to use some reserve deputies as soon as it gets daylight, enough to walk both sides of the northbound lanes along the road. Be sure they have some patrol deputies to help keep traffic off of them. I want them to start about a mile south of here, and walk at least one mile north of here. Have them look for anything that could be interesting. I don't care how big or small or insignificant they think it is unless it's obviously old, I want it photographed in place and collected. Be sure they call you to come collect anything they find. Also, be sure they understand their mission completely. We are looking for anything that may help us figure out who this guy is or what happened here," Rivers ordered.

"Okay, I'll go ahead and start making phone calls and lining up people," Dek responded.

It was about two in the morning by now, and it would be almost five hours before daylight. But Rivers wanted that team in place when there was sufficient daylight.

"Dek, I don't have a clue just how long it will take, but let them know they may be here most of the day. But yeah, go ahead and get that in motion. Also, you are going to need at least ten reserves. Get a hold of Captain Taylor and see if he can get some patrol help to keep the traffic off of them," Rivers concluded.

After working almost two hours in the area around the body,

Detective Dalton was ready to roll the body over and continue with the crime scene investigation. Flipping or moving a body could reveal new evidence. Sometimes nothing new was discovered, but some discoveries would send investigators in an entirely different direction.

"Hey chief, we are about ready to turn the body," Jen told the trio. "Kevin wants to know if you want to be there when we do,"

"Yes," replied Rivers. "Just give me a couple of minutes to go over something with these guys,"

"Okay, it will be a few before we are ready. He just wanted to give you a heads up," Rogers advised.

Rivers told Sanchez and Blackman to start talking with the deputies and EMTs that arrived first so they could get their statements. They decided to divide that task up to make better time. Everyone knew that when a case started to break, the pieces could come flying by, and you had better be in a position to retrieve them.

Rivers headed back over to the body. Dalton and Rogers had completed the photographing and videoing of the crime scene. They were now working on collecting any evidence that may be on the road or the body. They videoed each step of the collection of proof. Since this crime scene was on the roadside of a major interstate highway, they were looking through various items that may or may not have anything to do with the murder. They carefully went through each item found on the road and adjoining ground. Even the things that were not thought to be from this crime were collected and labeled. Elements such as trash thrown from vehicles or debris from a passing truck were all placed in the bags. Nothing was left out. If there was a bottle top near the body, it was marked, photographed, videoed, and collected. It was better to rule something out later and discard it than to miss a piece of critical evidence.

After photographing everything in place, they labeled and numbered each piece of proof. Each piece, no matter how seemingly insignificant, was in a separate container. The technician then made a list of the evidence with its corresponding number.

At a crime scene people usually kept the task they started. If someone started the photography, they did all of the photographing. The same went with the videoing and other aspects of the process.

Jen Rogers had been doing the videoing and photography. But now it was time to roll the body over to see what was beneath. It was the norm to have both a photograph and video of this process. Rivers decided that he would video, and Rogers could continue with the photography. Doing it this way allowed Dalton to roll the body slowly so to not miss a clue.

"Ready chief?" asked Dalton.

"Yeah, go ahead, Kevin. I'm rolling," replied Rivers as he smiled ever so slightly, realizing that he had avoided grabbing and flipping the body.

Detective Dalton took the left wrist of the victim, and slowly lifted it off the ground. Earlier, Rivers had requested that one of the detectives set up the generator and lights around the crime scene. The lighting was perfect on this particular gloomy night. Under the hand of the victim was blood from where it had pooled near the head.

They carefully examined the bloody hand and then wrapped it in a paper bag to protect anything under the nails or on the skin for later examination. They viewed the left hand, but only saw blood with the naked eye.

Next, Dalton took a grip on the left shoulder of the victim and gently rolled the body, enough to see some of the ground under the left arm and in the stomach area. There was only a little blood in this area and no foreign matter that could be detected, so it was photographed and videoed as Dalton kept his hold on the shoulder.

After completely turning the body, they found nothing new under the body or no new marks on the face and neck areas. The body was checked thoroughly by Dalton and Rogers. Nothing else noteworthy. There were just the shorts, white ankle socks, and white Nike's.

"I was wondering if there would be any spent rounds under the body," Rivers told Rogers and Dalton. "But there or not, it's a clue."

"How could not finding anything under the body be a clue?" asked Detective Rogers, immediately realizing the rookie sound of her question. Of course, it is a piece of the puzzle; it's all a piece of the puzzle, she thought. She was a little miffed at herself for asking the question but marked it up to being tired.

"Well, I said a clue, not evidence."

"I know Chief; I wasn't thinking. It was a stupid question. Of course, it is a clue either way or at least a small piece of the puzzle."

"Yep," Rivers said with a smile.

"I know, I know," Rogers admitted.

"I guess he was shot inside of a vehicle and thrown onto the road. That is because of the way the body is laying, the area of the bleeding, and the fact there are no spent shells. What do you think Jen?" Asked Rivers, realizing she was a little embarrassed.

"Sounds right to me."

Rivers started walking away from the body. As he got a few yards away, Rogers looked at Dalton and said, "don't you say a word! I feel stupid enough as it is. You just need to let it ride."

"Hey, I wasn't gonna say a word. What could I add to that?" Dalton said and started laughing.

"I know my job, but sometimes the Chief just makes me nervous or something, and I come out sounding like a dork!"

"Don't worry about it. He knows you are not a dork. Even if he did think you were a dork, he picked you to be on the team. So, he must see something in you. You will get used to it in a year or so." Dalton said, maintaining his smile the whole time.

"A year or so huh?"

"He has that effect on a lot of people until they get to know him. Then they realize that he is just another guy with a job to do. Actually, he is a pretty good guy to have on your side. Trust me on that one."

"Okay, let's forget it okay?"

"Okay with me, rookie," Dalton said, changing his smile to a short laugh.

As he was walking away from the body Rivers noticed Detective Carl Howe had arrived and was talking to Detective Blackman. When Howe saw Rivers, he met him half way.

"Hey, Carl, did Don catch you up on what we have and what we are doing so far?" Rivers asked.

"Yes, but I was wondering if anyone told you about a car just north of here that looks abandoned?" asked Howe.

"North of here?" Asked Rivers.

"Yeah, about a mile or so at the rest stop. I heard one of the patrol units call in the tag number. It's not stolen, but it doesn't come back to that car. But with it being north of here, it may not have anything to do with this case since the victim was a mile from making it that far," Howe surmised.

"Yeah, you didn't think it had anything to do with it since we are south of there. Which deputy called it in?" Rivers questioned.

"432, Mitch Davidson, I think," Replied Howe.

"4-0-3 to 4-32," Rivers called on the radio.

"Go ahead 4-0-3," deputy Davidson replied.

"Go to tact three," Rivers ordered.

"4-32, to 4-0-3, go ahead on tact three," Davidson called.

"On that vehicle, you ran at the rest stop, what was the situation with it?" Rivers asked.

"1983 yellow Toyota. Florida tags, but they didn't come back to the vehicle. The trunk was open, and the back passenger door was open. Some clothes were on the ground outside the car," said Davidson.

"Okay, thanks!" Replied Rivers.

"Let's go, Carl!" Rivers said to Detective Howe while moving quickly to his car.

"Where are we going," Howe asked as he walked to keep pace with Rivers'.

"That car! I want to see it!" said Rivers.

CHAPTER TWO

Kenny and Lisa

Tuesday, June 8th somewhere in Desoto County, Florida.

It was in the middle of the day in the heat of Florida. Things were as normal as any other day for Kenny Saxton. He had just left the house of his girlfriend, Lisa Angel and was walking home. He had lived with some friends for the past two months. He didn't seem to be able to get things quite put together in his life, and his friends were not much different.

Bo Dixon and JoBeth Davis were in their earlier twenties and had lived together for about two years, but this was the first time they had their own place. It wasn't exactly their place; it belonged to JoBeth's stepfather. It was an old single-wide trailer at the edge of a run-down trailer park, but to them, it was home.

Lisa's apartment, where she lived with two other young women, was about four miles from the trailer where Kenny was staying. Sometimes he walked the entire distance, but that was mostly at night and not in the humid, 90-plus degree Florida summer days.

It was not as hot has it had been the previous days, but it was hot enough. It was late that evening and Kenny was going to try to catch a ride. When he heard a car coming, he looked to see if it was someone he knew. Several cars and pickups had passed, but not one he recognized. Finally, he decided to hitch a ride. He put out his thumb as each car passed while turning and walking backward as they approached. He was hot and tired. He hoped for an air-conditioned ride, but he would settle for the back of a pickup.

A few cars passed, but people just looked at him as if he was covered with dirt or carrying a sign that read something weird. Hitching a ride was not nearly as popular as it had been in previous years. To most people, anyone walking along the roadside with their thumb in the air had to be of questionable character, but Kenny had done this since he was fourteen. In his mind, he was the one taking the risk; he had hitched rides with quite a few characters.

At last, an old yellow Toyota stopped in the middle of the road just past Kenny. The driver, a young man about Kenny's age, yelled out his window.

"Hey, come on!"

Kenny ran to the passenger side door and tried to pull it open, but it wasn't open.

The driver, who had seemed a little impatient earlier with his tone said, "Oh, my bad," and unlocked the door.

Kenny jumped into the seat after moving a few Coke cans and a half-eaten honey bun. As he was moving the honey bun, he looked at the driver and held it in the air for a second as if to ask, are you still eating this?

The driver caught the look and said, "Just chunk it out the window."

Kenny looked out the open window but decided to place it on

the floor—somewhere he wouldn't step on it.

"How far ya going?" asked the driver as he pressed the gas pedal, releasing a plume of white smoke behind him.

"Just about three miles up this road," responded Kenny.

"That's cool," the driver said, "because I'm only going up to the old pawn shop on Baker Dairy Road. If you were going very far, you was out of luck with me," the driver said while looking at Kenny with a half grin.

"I'm Mark, by the way."

"Kenny," Kenny answered back.

"Kenny?" Mark asked. "Not just Ken?"

"Nope, Kenny, but some people do call me Ken," responded Kenny.

"Do you live here?" asked Mark.

"Yep," Kenny promptly replied.

"Me too," Mark continued. "Well, not in the city, but out near Lake Bonnet. My uncle has an old camper he lets me stay in. But I'm leaving this hellhole soon. I hate this damn place."

Kenny responded by laughing, "It can be the pits sometimes, I've had it worse!".

Kenny had lived in several places in his short twenty-four years and mostly in Central Florida. He had lived in Arcadia for almost a year now. Before moving in with Bo, he lived with his girlfriend's brother, David Angel, for several months. That's how he met Lisa. But after he and Lisa got hot and heavy, her brother decided he didn't like Kenny. They had just about come to blows once, so Kenny decided it was time to find another place.

Mark Manning was 26 years old and by most people's standards had lived a difficult life. However, most of his difficulties came at his own hands. He grew up in an area outside of Dayton, Ohio. His dad was an alcoholic and abusive, but Mark always talked about his father in friendly terms. He never told anyone what happened to his dad. All he told them was that he left when he was twelve. By the time Mark was 19, he had been arrested four times for petty crimes, including shoplifting and drug possession. When he was twenty, he was charged and convicted of robbing a man outside a bar in Muncie, Indiana.

The man he robbed was later accused of child sex abuse and was in the court system the same time that Mark's case came to trial. Mark's attorney managed to get him three years probation with 60 days in jail due to the high profile child abuse case of his victim. The prosecuting attorney's office felt it was the best they could get, considering the circumstances. Mark served his time in the local jail and was even made a trustee in the kitchen the last 30 days of his sentence.

Making trustee could have easily been the highlight of Mark's life. He was always a rebel, and for the most part, a loner. There were times he seemed to fit in with a group, but he always did something to pull away from the crowd. His conflicts usually began with small issues. Someone laughed at the wrong time or make a joke that he thought was aimed at him, and he went into fight mode. It really didn't matter what the topic was about or whether it was aimed at Mark or not, he found a way to make it about him. He was the kid in school that messed things up for the entire class.

As an adult, Mark made friends quickly. He had a way about him drew a person in when they first met him. He had an almost offensive boldness, yet he was somewhat engaging.

The problem for Mark was he didn't know how to give or feel for others. He had been in some relationships, and a few ended well—but they all ended. He made friends quickly, but enemies more quickly. The friendships seldom lasted but his opponents endured. He did, however, have a faithful friend or two in the dark world of the occult.

Mark had gotten involved in the occult when he was 16. It was mostly out of curiosity and to rebel against his church-going Mom. Early on, he just dabbled somewhat. He met a girl, Katie Bells, who was a couple of years older. He followed her into the darkness he later called his religion.

While Mark never went to an actual occult service, he considered himself a true believer. He was a talented artist and drew many of the signs and symbols of the occult. He had the downward pointing pentagram tattooed on his right forearm and a bigger one between his shoulder blades. A few other tattoos were representing his belief, but they were from his imagination. Some tattoos he did himself, and some were done from his drawings by a tattoo artist. Katie Bells introduced him into this dark world and was still considered one of his few real friends. She was passionately involved in Wicca and had shared that passion with Mark.

When Mark first got involved with his new religion, he didn't hide the fact from his Christian mother. Mark's mother, Delores Shelton Ward had to grow up fast and hard. Her dad and mom were both sent to jail for 20 years when she was eight. She never saw either one of her parents after they went to prison.

Delores lived with her mom's sister until she was 14 when her aunt died in a motor vehicle accident. The state put her in a foster home, but she left after the foster parent's son tried to rape her. She got a job in a small restaurant in Dayton and lived in a room in the back of the place. That's where she met Mark's dad.

He had a job and a place to live. It looked like a good situation for her at the time, so they stared living together. By the time she was 17 Mark was born. Mark's dad married his mom just before he was born.

His dad had always been a heavy drinker, but his mom overlooked it in exchange for a place to live. A home came at a high price for her and Mark at times. His dad became more and more abusive when he drank and his drinking became more frequent.

To cope with her home life, Delores started going to a small church not far from their apartment. It became her refuge and a place she could take Mark to see another side of life. She became a regular member at the church. She sang in the choir and taught the younger children who came to mid-week services.

At first Mark's dad was angry with her going to church. But after a short period of time, he no longer gave her a hard time about going. Once he even walked to the church to let the pastor know that she was sick. Even then he didn't enter the church but knocked on the door until a couple of older ladies who were cleaning the church came to see why someone was knocking on an unlocked door.

Once when Katie was at Mark's house, Delores' pastor was there. Mark's mother asked the pastor to talk with them about the occult while they all were in the living room. Her pastor was not a college graduate and had only studied some about the occult. However, he did know the Bible and was convinced that it was the truth. But now matter how much the pastor knew about the Bible, Katie was not going to change her mind. She even felt she could convince the pastor of his errant faith.

After a two-hour encounter, they both decided they were wasting their breath. Katie looked at Mark, rolled her eyes, and then looked back at the pastor. "You believe what you want to, Mister, I'm not spending my time on earth debating something I don't believe. Are you ready to go Mark?"

"Yep," Mark said, as they walked out of the room. He glanced at his mom briefly, without any expression or sound.

★

"You get high?" Mark asked.

"Only when I can get it," Kenny replied with a smile.

"Well, I got it. Wanna smoke one?"

Kenny had smoked pot since he was 13. He once even sold it to be able to afford it himself.

"Sure," said Kenny.

Mark pulled about 100 feet onto a dirt road and stopped in the middle of the road.

Kenny glanced back to see if there were any cars or people around and saw nothing but an old house with broken windows. He decided the house was empty. Kenny had been arrested twice for possession. He wasn't looking to get arrested anytime soon, and certainly not today. He smiled just for a moment while thinking about Mark's boldness to stop in the middle of the road and light up.

The two finished the skinny joint, and Kenny was soon dropped off in front of the trailer park. "Thanks, man!" Kenny said as he opened the car door.

"Hey, maybe I'll see ya around sometime," Mark yelled as Kenny got about six feet away from the car.

Kenny responded by a single upward nod, thinking that it probably would never happen.

It would not be dark for another couple of hours. Ordinarily, Bo and JoBeth didn't see Kenny until late at night or late mornings when he got up. To see him walk through the door at this time of day was a little surprising.

Their bedroom door was open, and their room was straight down the hall from the living room with the front door in plain sight. Kenny quickly figured out what was happening and walked into the kitchen instead of going down the hall to his room. Soon he heard the bedroom door close. Kenny went to his room and played his video game the rest of the day.

☆

Wednesday, June 9th

Bo and JoBeth were already up, watching TV when Kenny woke up the next morning and walked into the kitchen. He looked for his cup to rinse out so he could get some coffee.

"What happened to my cup?" Kenny asked.

"The green one?" responded Jobeth.

"Yes," replied Kenny.

"Bo broke it yesterday," she informed him.

"Is there another one somewhere?" Kenny said with irritation showing in his voice.

"Not that I know of; you may have to use a glass," responded Jobeth.

"Great! Holding hot coffee in a glass," Kenny said.

"Sorry," Bo finally spoke.

"I'm going back to bed," Kenny said in a tired voice. He heard Bo laughing in the other room. "What?!" Kenny snapped.

"Like going back to bed is gonna help you wake up," Bo said in a laughing voice.

"Screw you!" Kenny snapped back. Bo continued laughing.

"Either of you going anywhere this morning?" Kenny asked as if wanting them to make up for their earlier insolence. It was almost noon, but to them, it was still morning for a while after getting up.

"You need a ride to see Lisa?" Jobeth queried.

"Yes."

"I can drop you off. I need to go by Ben's anyway," JoBeth answered.

In reality, JoBeth was not going to Ben's or anywhere. But she had been drawn to Kenny since he had been staying in their trailer. She never acted on it but thought about him a lot when Bo was gone.

"Okay, thanks," Kenny replied.

Kenny suspected that JoBeth enjoyed taking him places a little too much. She leaned over when he got out of the car and touch his hand and tell him to be good, but Lisa was the love of his life no matter what JoBeth's motives may have been. Besides, he thought, she had been with Bo for a pretty long time. He decided it was just his imagination.

Lisa and Kenny had a special relationship for being so young. Kenny treated her well, and she responded in kind. They had talked about getting married but realized that they needed more money to make it.

Lisa worked at a local grocery store. She had been working there for three years, and everyone loved her. Lisa was always friendly to the customers and got along well with co-workers and the management. She worked any shift, so she was an asset to the store. Lisa had only missed two days in three years. She had been very sick both of those days.

Kenny picked up odd jobs here and there and bought her simple gifts now and then. She loved the gifts because she knew that he didn't have much money.

Lisa was off work and at home when Kenny knocked on the door. "Hey girl!" Kenny said when Lisa opened the door.

"Hey!" Lisa responded, as she opened the door wider and stood behind the door to allow room for Kenny to come inside.

"Did ya just get up?" Kenny asked.

"No, I've been up for about an hour. I have things to do, I'm not sleeping in all day on my day off!" Replied Lisa.

"What kind of things?" Kenny asked.

"Just things. Nikki and Sari and I are going to Wal-Mart in a little while to get some hair coloring for Nikki's hair," Lisa said.

Lisa's two roommates Nikki and Sari were the same age as Lisa. They had all known each other since 4th grade, but none of them finished high school for one reason or another.

"Hair color again? She just changed it last month. Damn!" Kenny resounded.

Lisa laughed. "Silly man, that's what girls do! Why should that bother you? You can hang out here with us. It won't take long. Besides what else are you gonna do?" She questioned as she laughed out loud.

Lisa had a fun personality. She was one of those people whose life may have been entirely different if she had been born into a different family. She was smart, witty, cute, and enjoyed people. Her stepfather abused her while her mother basically looked the other way to have a place to stay. It was a very high price that Lisa paid for her mother's dry roof and a full stomach. For the most part, Lisa had put all of that behind her. She was working a full-time job, enjoying life, and feeling for the first time that she had a future.

"Okay, but I'm not going to Wal-Mart with Y'all!" responded Kenny. "I'll watch TV until you get back. When are you going?"

"As soon as Nikki gets back. She went to her sister's to pick up some curlers to do her hair. Her sister was about to leave so she had to run get 'em."

A few minutes later Nikki pulled into the driveway. Lisa and Sari grabbed their purses and headed for the car. Lisa stopped by the couch where Kenny was watching TV, kissed him on the forehead, and started to leave.

"Whoa!" said Kenny. "I want more than a dang kiss on the top of my head. I ain't no damn puppy," he said, laughing, as he stood up and kissed Lisa on the mouth for several seconds. "There, that may hold me until you get back," he continued as he walked Lisa to the door. "I love you."

"I love you, Baby; see you in a few. We won't be gone too long!" responded Lisa.

Kenny grabbed a beer out of the refrigerator and went back to watching TV as they left.

CHAPTER THREE

Dynamic Duo

Kent grew up in Central Florida in the early. When he was a teen in high school, he sometimes attended the morning classes and then grab his cycle and a friend to head to the beach. Kent didn't feel comfortable with a guy hanging onto his waist while he rode his bike. For this reason, his friend was always one of his female friends.

It was about a 45-minute drive from the school, but he enjoyed both the beach and the ride. This was mostly done his senior year but not during football season. The beach always remained one of the places Kent loved to be, no matter his age. He always planned his vacations around a beach somewhere. His favorite beach was New Smyrna Beach on the east coast of Florida. That's where he usually went when he was a teenager, but sometimes he went further north to Daytona Beach.

Once, toward the end of the school term his senior year, one of Kent's teachers caught onto the fact that he was at school in the morning, but miss her class in the afternoon.

"Mr. Rivers," she said, as she walked up to his desk. "You have missed my class for the last time." She showed him the attendance record. "What do you have to say for yourself?" The business law teacher looked at him sternly.

Stunned at her ability to solve the case of the missing student, Rivers looked at her and swallowed hard. He was seldom at a loss for words, but when Mrs. Culbertson confronted him, he could only come up with two words, "Uh-me?" he asked.

"Come with me young man," she said as she grabbed him by his left ear and lifted him out of his seat. The entire class broke out in hysterical laughter as she pulled him by his ear out of the classroom and down the hallway. His back was bent over, and his head turned, as she dragged him like a dog on a leash.

Resigned to the fact that he was caught, he reflected on the many afternoon trips to the beach with his favorite girlfriend at the time. Was it worth it? He thought as she pulled him down the hallway past other students, as they pointed and laughed. He just waved at them. Yes, he decided, it was worth it.

As she entered the main office with this tall, tough football player held by the ear, the attention of all the staff was immediately upon them.

"Where is Mr. Eldridge?" she asked. "This young man needs to meet with the principal."

The office clerk, wide-eyed, pointed toward the principal's door. His teacher continued to lead him by the ear to the principal's office. "You need to talk with Mr. Rivers about skipping school and my class!" She ordered the principal.

Astounded by what he saw, he stood up and came almost to attention, as she walked in with Rivers. Perhaps his reaction was out of fear that his ear was next.

"Uh, Okay, Mrs. Culbertson, leave him here, and I'll speak with him about the matter," the principal advised.

"Thank you," Mrs. Culbertson said.

All eyes in the front office were on her, as she walked out about as fast as she walked in. It was as if their lives had been temporarily interrupted by a brief storm. They were surprised to see it come and glad to see it go.

The principal, who knew Rivers because of his outstanding football talents, told him to have a seat in another room where he served a period of in-school suspension.

When the class period was over, the principal came into the room and asked Rivers, "Have you learned anything today?"

"Yes sir. Don't skip Mrs. Culbertson's class," Rivers responded.

"Exactly," the principal agreed. "Now get out of here!"

★

Kent played wide receiver and returned punts on the high school football team. He didn't start playing football until he was in the ninth grade.

In his junior and senior years, Kent led the district in pass receptions. He also scored more touchdowns his senior year than any receiver had in school history. By the end of his high school career, he was well known as a local sports hero.

Bruce Rider, the team quarterback, and Kent had become well-known in the area as a great duo in pass and catch. Kent received several offers from top college teams for scholarships to play football. But because of his height or the lack of it, the only major college offer for Bruce was from the Minnesota Golden Gophers. Bruce didn't feel like he was a good fit for the cold weather that far north. So he took an offer from the Chattanooga Mocs which were part of the University of Tennessee system. Kent had leaned heavily toward Ole Miss because he had loved watching Archie Manning and considered him the best college football player of his time.

As signing day came closer, Kent decided to go with his best friend since fourth grade, Bruce, to the University of Tennessee at Chattanooga. Kent always said that Bruce had nothing to do with his going to Chattanooga. But it was because UTC wore the same colors as his high school team, and he could wear some of his same clothes. But everyone, including Bruce, knew it was because Bruce had committed to Chattanooga.

There were never any better friends than Bruce and Kent. To say they were close was an understatement. In some ways, they were an odd pair. Kent was tall, olive complexioned, and handsome. He was also very fast. Bruce was several inches shorter than Kent. Bruce had red hair and freckles, and as a young kid, was sort of portly. However, as he got into junior high school, he began to lose weight and put on muscle. By the time Bruce was in tenth grade he was a lot slimmer, built well, and quicker than anyone on the team for 10 yards. He could change directions on a dime and throw the football through a hoop 30 yards away.

★

When Bruce and Kent arrived on campus at UT Chattanooga, they were excited about the possibilities of becoming the dynamic duo once again. With Bruce passing and Kent catching, it was a cinch that they would impact the team. But as freshmen often do, they overlooked the fact that most of the team had one-to-three years of college playing time ahead of them.

During their freshmen year, they were mostly relegated to some highlights at practice. Kent did some playing time as a backup kickoff returner. He returned four kickoffs for a total of 42 yards. Bruce was always encouraging Kent. Whenever Kent was down on himself, Bruce always tried to bring back his confidence through his cheerful words. In their senior year, they would reminisce about their first season together and the hopes they had envisioned and laugh about it.

Half way through their junior year, the starting quarterback was injured and was out for the rest of the year. Bruce Rider stepped in and filled the injured player's shoes very well. Bruce threw for over 1,400 yards in the second half of the season and the Dynamic Duo, as they were called, connected on more than 400 of those yards, scoring five touchdowns. In the last game of that season, Bruce scored on three touchdown passes and ran in one from the seven-yard line.

By their senior year, they both were starters, and the DD was in full operational mode. Bruce set one conference record for the most passing yards in a game with 493 yards. He threw for four touchdowns that game and ran in one from the 19-yard line.

Kent set a conference record in the total yards received in one season. He caught 117 passes for 1,634 yards. By the end of their college football careers, they both felt that they had accomplished what they set out to do. But more importantly, they were able to be together those four years. After those years, life changed dramatically for them both.

Kent Rivers had his share of ups and downs, just like everyone else. He was married to Michelle Morgan for a short time after he graduated from college. It wasn't a story of high school sweethearts or anything like it. It was a story of two people making the wrong choice because of physical attraction. She was nineteen and thought that Kent Rivers was the best-looking thing that she had ever laid eyes on. She loved that Kent was tall, dark and very handsome. Rivers thought she was the cutest girl he had ever met. That was about the extent of their relationship.

They met at a restaurant near the campus in the last half of his senior year in college. Michelle was in her first year of college at a local community college, studying nursing. She had met some friends who went to UTC at the restaurant for dinner when they noticed Bruce and Kent and a couple of other guys at the next table. The flirtation was thick, spirited, and funny between the tables, but only Kent and Michelle decided to make more of it.

They were married a month after he graduated. They lived in a downtown apartment. He worked at a nearby warehouse moving packages on the night shift. She continued school and worked part time as a hostess at a fancy downtown restaurant.

Within six months they both knew they had made a mistake, but because of their families, they tried not to let anyone see their struggles. But soon everyone knew their problems, and within a year they had filed for divorce. Kent was now 24 and single, again. It was a scar that he tried to cover time and again until he realized that he was actually okay with it and he moved on with his life.

After the divorce, Kent decided to join the Army. Bruce and Kent's family questioned his decision since he had just finished college. Bruce was looking at several different places to become a police officer. He had applied at Atlanta, Miami, Jacksonville, and Nashville. Now he just waited for the process to begin.

Bruce felt that Kent could do an excellent job as a cop, but he also knew Kent wanted more than just a regular job. He wanted a career that was always exciting and challenging.

Kent felt that the change and experience in the Army would do him good.

He went through basic training and applied for the Criminal Investigations Division of the Army. With his college degree in criminal justice, he thought he might have a chance. He was accepted and began his CID training. He became a warrant officer one and soon went to work on investigating felony cases at Ft. Knox, Kentucky. He soon moved up to warrant officer two and considered making it a career.

Kent and Bruce didn't get to see each other as much as they wanted, but they both seemed happy with their choices. Bruce was with the Atlanta, Georgia Police Department as a street officer and Kent was happy as an Army investigator.

Kent called Bruce when he needed a little advice about a girl or an investigation, but really it was just to connect again. Kent always felt good after talking with Bruce, no matter what was happening before the conversation.

Bruce had gotten married about two years after graduation from college. Bruce met Tia Kingston through a friend from college who lived in Atlanta. She was a beautiful, Afro-American woman, with a smooth dark bronze skin tone. Kent was his best man and planned the honeymoon for him. Kent had asked Bruce and his fiance if he could do this as a wedding present. He got approval from the two to have their honeymoon at Montego Bay in Jamaica. Kent even paid for the lodging at the resort and their flight. Kent told Bruce that was the last help he was getting from him concerning his marriage.

CHAPTER FOUR

Bruce

Two years had passed since the wedding and Kent had just returned from lunch when he found a message on his desk to call his dad. He talked with his parents quite often, but seldom did his dad call him at his office or during the week. He felt a little anxious when he read the note. Kent didn't want to seem apprehensive on the phone, so he went to the restroom to wash his hands and calm down before making the call. He never liked to start back to work after eating without washing his hands. Kent remained standing when he made the call.

"Hey, Dad! I found your message when I got back from lunch. What's up?"

"Hello, son." His father paused for what seemed like minutes.

"What is it dad? Is everything okay?"

"Well… I'm afraid I have some bad news. I don't really know how to tell you this other than just come out and say it. Bruce Rider was shot and killed during a robbery in Atlanta last night."

"What?!" Kent interrupted his dad.

"I got a call from his brother, Ted, and he knew you would

want to know. I am so sorry, son. I know how much you both meant to each other," his dad said with a sad voice.

Kent was bewildered and dismayed. He couldn't even think about Bruce being dead. It wasn't something that he could even consider at this moment. He thought if he had more details he could take his mind off of the reality and focus on it from a different direction.

"How did it happen? Did Ted give you any details?" Kent asked in an almost demanding voice.

"Ted really didn't have anymore that he could tell me. He did say he would let us know when any more news came in."

Both Kent and Bruce had received their degrees in Criminal Justice. Neither one of them really knew what they wanted to do with their degrees even after graduating. But in less than a year after graduation, Bruce had applied and had been accepted by the Atlanta Police Department. He was assigned to the night shift patrol from the time he completed the police academy and was in no rush to be moved. He liked the action that he found working at night.

Kent was in shock as his dad hung up the phone. He moved slowly as he sat down at his desk. He looked across the room with the phone receiver still in his hand. They had been best friends since Mrs. Robinson's fourth-grade class. They fought together, ran together, double dated together, and were always seen together at all the high school events and parties. They were the "DD" and would always be there for each other, or so Kent thought.

Kent had Ted's number in his desk draw. He decided to call Ted as if that would somehow give him some connection to Bruce.

"Hello, Ted? This is Kent. My dad just called. This can't be true! Tell me something different, Ted. How did it happen?" Kent asked.

"I know. I'm broken into a thousand pieces and Mom had to be taken to the hospital because she collapsed after Dad told her. I'm here with the kids, or I would be at the hospital with Mom," Ted replied.

"When, how?" Kent ordered.

"I called and talked to his captain just a few minutes ago. They will have all the details soon, but they are still investigating. What he said was that Bruce was on patrol and received a call to back up another unit at a hotel. Someone tried to rob the place, and the first officer had the suspect cornered near the hotel," Ted explained.

"Yeah, and Bruce went to help the other officer?" Kent questioned while already knowing the answer.

"Yes, and when Bruce arrived, the two of them ran toward the area where the first officer thought the suspect was hiding. Apparently, there was a second suspect who jumped from behind a building nearby and started shooting at them. That's when the first suspect came out from somewhere and shot Bruce. The other officer shot the first suspect, but he got away somehow. They think that Bruce shot and killed the second suspect before the other guy shot Bruce, but they are still working on it."

"Please let me know what you find out, Ted. I'm sorry for your family. You know what Bruce meant to me," Rivers said as he began to understand that it actually did happen. Bruce was gone.

After the funeral, Kent went back to Fort Knox a different man. He had never known such pain as losing Bruce Rider. Kent could not remember a time when Bruce was not part of his life. Never in his wildest nightmares did he ever consider that he would not be around somewhere.

Kent took a ten-day leave from his Army assignment, but he

stayed at his apartment instead of visiting with family or taking a vacation. He went to the base Class VI store and bought three bottles of Bruce's favorite wine. He wanted one for now and the others for some date in the future when he felt like looking back on their times together.

A few months after Bruce was killed, Kent took a flight back to Atlanta to see Bruce's wife, Tia, and perhaps talk to someone who had been at the scene that night. Tia and Kent never really became close. They had known each other for a brief time before she married Bruce. It didn't really matter, though, because both were connected because of their mutual love for Bruce.

Kent had called and checked on Tia several times since Bruce had died, but this was the first time they got together and talked. Tia had an Afro-American mother. She was dark skinned and beautiful. A white, red-headed man and a black woman drew the eyes of some people, but neither of them ever cared nor let it bother them in the slightest. They were in love and the best of friends, and that is all that mattered to them and their family and friends.

Tia picked Kent up from the airport, and they took the short drive to her home in Morrow, Georgia. Tia was an insurance actuary for a large company in the Atlanta area. They lived in a beautiful area in the suburb of Atlanta.

It was too early for dinner and too late for lunch, but they decided to stop for a drink and some conversation before going to the house. As they exited the SUV Tia was driving, Kent walked around to Tia's side of the car and gave her a hug.

"It certainly is good to see you, Tia. You are looking very well. I know that it has been hard. It's been difficult for everyone. God, I still can't believe it most of the time," Kent told her.

They talked as they walked toward the door of a restaurant.

"There are times I just collapse into a little ball, Kent," Tia said. "Other times I just get up like everything is normal and go for a day or two without getting depressed or being haunted by it. But each day at some point, my eyes will water just a little when thinking about him being gone. Do you think that's bad, that I sometimes go a few days without it haunting me?"

Kent started to answer her question when she continued talking.

"I loved Bruce with everything in me. We were just getting things started in our lives. We bought our house, I got a raise at work, we were planning a vacation back to Jamaica," she said as she allowed a little smile to come to her face while remembering the honeymoon and the fact that Kent had paid for most of it.

"Hell no, it isn't bad for you to have some good days! I hope the number good days increase. You have to move on, Tia. I hope no one is making you feel sorry about that!" Kent growled.

"No, no one is, Kent, I guess I'm just hard on myself. I don't know what I'm supposed to feel. If I feel sad and depressed about it, I start thinking that he wouldn't want me to do that. If I feel good on some days, I feel a little guilty, because I don't remember it so vividly," She replied.

"I understand, Tia, I do, but I think you should just feel what you feel on any given day and not worry about feeling guilty either way. You loved Bruce, we both did. I know for a fact that he loved you. You are all he talked about when we would get together or even talk on the phone."

The waiter took their drink order. They both decided to have a Long Island Tea in memory of Bruce. It was his favorite drink. They talked some more about their wedding, Bruce's job, and their home. Kent talked a little about how things were going at Ft. Knox and his job. They had their drinks, ate a salad, and decided to go to her house.

While at the house Tia brought some papers and other things that she had wanted Kent to look over. Tia had been a foster child and didn't have any real family. She had met a brother about five years ago, but they were not close. Tia knew that Kent would come by, so she put aside some of the legal papers and other documents. She was certainly capable of understanding the documents, but she had wanted Kent's advice on a few things. Plus, she knew she wasn't thinking all that clearly since his death and felt it was better to have someone else opinion. There was no opinion worth more than Kent's to Bruce, so she felt the same way.

"Listen, it is getting late. If you don't mind, I'm going to call a taxi to run me over to the Hilton. We can talk again tomorrow," Kent stated.

"No way am I letting you take a cab or stay at the Hilton! You will stay right here in the guest room. It is all ready for you. It is the only bedroom downstairs so you will have your privacy and free run of the TV room and kitchen," Tia replied insisting.

"Tia, thank you very much, but I couldn't stay here. I wouldn't feel right," Kent responded.

"Feel right? What are you talking about, feel right?" Tia said indignantly.

Kent realized how silly he was sounding and possibly even suggestive that something would happen between them, so he immediately recanted.

"Well, I just don't want to put you in a position where you feel you have to entertain me," Kent said, hoping it was good enough to smooth over his half-witted comment.

"Hey Kent, I'm not gonna entertain you. Don't be silly," Tia said laughing out loud. "You are one funny man, Kent. Do you know that?" she said smiling.

"I guess I am sometimes. Wasn't trying this time, though," Kent replied while smiling big.

"Oh my, that is the best laugh I've had since the funeral. Thank you, Kent!"

"In that case, I'm glad I was silly, then."

"Get your stuff out of the car. The keys are on the counter in the kitchen. I'm not helping you there either!" she said laughing a little more.

"Okay, you talked me into it. I'll be right back." He wondered why he made such a big deal out of staying at his best friend's house. Even without Bruce there, it was still where he had lived with this beautiful woman.

"Hey, I put your keys back where I got them. Where do you want me to put my things?" Kent asked as he returned to the house.

"Okay, it's the last room down the hall; it's on your right. You can get to the bathroom from your room," Tia responded. "You make yourself at home. I'm going upstairs to change clothes. I'm tired of these dress clothes and shoes."

Kent felt guilty for even thinking that he shouldn't stay, but at the same time, he still felt a little odd, especially after hearing her say she was going upstairs to change. It just sounded like an old movie black and white movie playing in his head. He laughed at his conjectures and changed clothes himself.

That night they talked about Bruce, high school, growing up in the Orlando area, college, football, girls, and almost everything in between. They laughed some, and they both cried some. Kent realized that this was a mission of closure for them both. Other than his parents, no two people knew Bruce any deeper than the two sitting in this room together.

The next morning, Kent got up before Tia. He always got up early and never seemed to be able to sleep-in, even when he was off work. After several years in the military, he woke up early and his internal clock was set. He had made some coffee and had opened the front door to see if by chance there was a newspaper. He knew that Bruce would always read a newspaper in the morning, even during college.

He got the newspaper and sat at the kitchen table drinking his coffee. It was quiet, and he reflected on the last time he had come to this house. The three of them had watched the college national championship game. He smiled as he remembered how excited Bruce would get during a game. The excitement about football never left Bruce, and he loved college football the best.

The smile was still on his face as Tia stepped into the kitchen. "Well, aren't you the early riser and all smiles in the morning. I hate people like you, you know!" She said not cracking a smile as she passed him heading for the coffee pot. "Although I could get used to having my coffee ready in the morning," she said this time with a little grin.

"Yeah, well I also run four miles every morning, could you get used to that?" Kent said without even a hint of a smile.

"Oh Honey, you can run all you want to, it will not bother me one bit! Just run on, big man! Run on!" Tia replied with a little southern accent thrown in for effect.

Kent laughed and said, "Not this morning, Tia, not this morning."

"Don't you have to get to work?" Kent asked.

"Get to work? You Army guys may work on Saturday, but we suburban people take off on weekends," Tia replied laughing.

The two finished their coffee together and had a few more laughs. Kent said he was going to rent a car for the day and ride around. She knew he was going to the police department to see if anyone would talk with him about Bruce's death.

"Would you feel bad driving Bruce's car?" Tia asked.

"Bruce's car?" Kent asked back.

"Yes, the Mustang in the garage. Did you think they were both mine?" Tia asked with a smile.

"Well, to be honest, I didn't even think about Bruce still having that car," Kent replied.

"I'm selling the pickup. A guy from work already wants to buy it." Bruce kept it outside the garage, and I parked my SUV in the garage. But I didn't want either of his outside until I did something with them," Tia told Kent.

"I don't know Tia, that Mustang is one in a thousand. Me, driving that around Atlanta may be risky," Kent said.

"In fact, Kent, I want you to have that car," Tia said looking straight at Kent's face.

"No, Tia, no way! Don't even go there!" Kent responded immediately.

"Kent, shut up a minute and let me talk!" Tia said resolutely. "Who in this whole wide world would be the only person that Bruce would give that car to?"

"I don't..." Kent started to say when Tia interrupted.

"Kent! Let me finish!" Tia said once again looking Kent straight in the eyes. "I miss Bruce every moment of every day. I loved him more than I can tell you. My heart hurts every time I think of him not coming through those doors, but this is not about me missing him. Whether I like it or not, though, life goes on. I have to go on, too. It's not easy, but I'm thinking about him and what he would want. So don't fight me on this! Every time that car was mentioned in a story, you were in the story—every time Kent! So, you just figure out how you are gonna get that car back with you, because you are taking it!" Tia proclaimed firmly to Kent.

Kent sat quietly for a few seconds and didn't know how he felt about the car. There were a lot of memories in that car, and he wondered if he could ever drive it without being sad.

"Can I think about it, Tia?" Kent requested.

"Sure, Kent," Tia said with a softer voice. "But you are still taking it with you when you leave."

Kent ended up canceling his flight back to the base and drove the car back. He had checked on getting it hauled by a trucking company back to Kentucky, but it cost more than the return ticket had cost him. Besides, he thought, it would be a chance to relive a lot of memories on his drive back.

Kent and Tia said their goodbyes and committed to being brother and sister for life. Neither of them ever forgot that pledge either. They kept in touch and were like kin from that day forward. Even after Tia remarried, Kent went to the wedding and gave her away. Kent always felt Bruce was smiling on him and saying, "You can do this Kent. You have it in you." Then laughing a little and saying, "Just don't fumble." Kent smiled as he drove the old Mustang down the highway.

Not long after Kent returned to base, he turned in his papers to start the process of leaving the Army. Within a few months, Kent Rivers was no longer CW2 Kent Rivers but was private citizen Kent Rivers.

A friend from UTC, Dek Bates, knew Kent and Bruce in college and had kept in contact with Kent over the last few years. He was aware that Kent was leaving the Army and asked him to come to Chattanooga for a class party they were having, sort of a reunion.

But he had an alternative reason for asking him to come back to Chattanooga. He was a Hamilton County, deputy sheriff. They were hiring, and he wanted Kent to apply. Dek Bates was a second generation Hamilton County deputy, and a third-generation lawman. Dek's Granddad was an officer in Atlanta for nineteen years before dying of cancer. His dad was the first black deputy to become a detective at the sheriff's office.

The reunion was thrown together at the last minute by a group of former students. They just happened to run into each other at one of the football games the previous fall on campus and decided to do it. It was planned for that July. They sent out notices to those graduates whose addresses they knew and had asked them to pass the word.

It was late May, so Kent decided to go home to Longwood, Florida before making the trip to Chattanooga. He decided to make reservations for July at the Chattanooga Choo-Choo. He had always enjoyed visiting the Choo-Choo while in school. Going home was a little difficult for Kent. It was the first time he had returned home since Bruce was killed.

He had mixed emotions as he drove Bruce's car down the same streets they had driven years before. He slowed down as he passed their Alma mater, Lyman High School.

The school was out for the day, so he decided to pull into the parking lot. He pulled up to the football field in back of the school. He got out of the car and walked down the sidewalk to the stadium. It was smaller than he had remembered. Then he remembered he had played at a bigger stadium in college, so no wonder it looked smaller.

The gate was unlocked, so he walked passed the dressing rooms and onto the field. It was the first time he had been on the field since Bruce, and he had played their final game there. Flashbacks were popping up left and right with each yard he walked.

A few people were walking the track around the field, but he hadn't noticed them. He was in is own world at the moment. It was a world that once again included Bruce for a short, few minutes.

As he walked away, he saw the people walking on the track and wondered how they had gotten there without him seeing them. That's odd, he thought. He left the school and drove on into Orlando to a place he had loved as a kid—Lake Eola. The beautiful fountain in the middle always dazzled him. At night the colors would totally mesmerize him.

He parked his car and started walking around on the sidewalk that circles the park. He stopped in front of the amphitheater and took a seat. Nothing was showing but he just wanted to take in the whole experience. Somehow he knew it might be a long time before he ever got back to this park—this iconic place of his childhood.

Soon he left the park and drove around a few more places in Orlando, Longwood, and Altamonte Springs. So many memories of fun, it was a grand time and place to grow up, he thought.

In years to come, he would revisit his hometown and realize that it was not the same place. It was as if it had been invaded and changed into a new country. To him, his homeland was gone forever. His roots were transplanted to Tennessee.

He visited with his parents and saw a lot of other family members and old friends. He stopped by Bruce's parent's house for a visit. It wasn't an extended visit, and he couldn't call it a good visit. Somehow seeing Kent brought back the loss of Bruce new in their minds and hearts. They were very nice to him and asked him to stay for dinner, but Kent sensed that it was the right thing to leave them with their thoughts. They did express their gratitude that Tia had given Kent Bruce's Mustang. It was home, they told him.

★

Dek insisted that Kent stay at his home during the time before and after the reunion. He had a four-bedroom home. It was only Dek, his wife, and a small child. Kent was comfortable with Dek and his wife, so he agreed.

During the reunion, Kent saw lots of his old teammates, and they laughed and shared the good times. Some of them were not sure how to approach the subject of Bruce's death, so they avoided it all together. But Kent wasn't going to let Bruce's memory die nor was he going to revisit the funeral.

Kent talked about Bruce like he was in Europe or some other place that was too far to travel back to this little event. Once everyone saw that Kent was comfortable talking about Bruce, they opened up with their own stories. After all, for a lot of them, he was their quarterback, their captain, and their team leader. Bruce meant a lot to so many people. He had touched the lives of these teammates; he would never be forgotten.

After the reunion, Dek talked Kent into applying at the sheriff's office. With his background with Army CID, his degree in criminal justice, and his recommendations, he was one of the first one's chosen.

He attended the police academy like every other law enforcement officer in most states. Once it was over, he went through some department orientation and was assigned a training officer. His training officer was Nick Taylor.

Nick had moved from Miami six years earlier. His looks were above average, and his style was laid back, but that didn't stop him from the occasional outburst of profane words. At times, his friends wondered if this mild-mannered man was one day explode and take out a city block.

Nick appeared to have some pent-up anger issues. Most of the time, though, Nick was a calming influence for those around him. Most things just didn't bother him or get him emotionally fired up.

Before Nick left Miami, he and his wife split up. In fact, the loss of his marriage was pretty much the reason he left. He had worked in the aviation business in Miami for a few years. He and a friend, Jake Long, had managed to purchase a Beechcraft King Air C90 twin turboprop airplane. They would often laugh at what they named the vessel. They called it Collateral; because of the amount, they had financed to make the purchase.

Jake and Nick had gone into business flying executives around Florida, Georgia, and other parts of the south. They traveled to Nassau, Bahamas and Kingston, Jamaica. It was a business that kept them busy.

Nick was an instrument rated flight instructor. Between plane trips, he gave flying lessons. That kept him away from home a lot, but he was building a business, and that meant commitment. His wife, Nancy, had encouraged him and told him that she understood what it took to build a business. She said that she appreciated his commitment to their future. He loved Nancy and was glad she understood and was on his side.

With those words in mind, Nick never learned or really got over how he lost his wife to an affair. It was an affair with his best friend and business partner—Jake. The affair was damaging enough, since Nick and Nancy were high school sweethearts and had grown up only a block away from each other in Hialeah.

But as affairs sometimes happen, it was Nick's partner that had stolen this piece of his heart. He lost his business and both of his associates, but it was the loss of his life's partner that sent Nick to a depth he could not have previously imagined.

Maybe Nick was a little too trusting, but to him marriage meant trust. He had never worried about Nancy cheating on him. He believed that they were the closest of kin and nothing or no one could ever break that bond. But it was Nancy herself that broke it.

Nick was left with his mind running between hurt and anger, and the two seemed to run together most of the time. He went to sleep crying and woke up thinking that it had to be just a nightmare, but by the time the coffee hit the bottom of his cup, he knew that the ugly dream was his reality.

Nick had a friend that worked at the local airport in Chattanooga. Nick was given a job helping with some flights, working on the planes, and other odd jobs around the company. It didn't pay much, but he was looking for a new life, not a fortune.

Within a few months, Nick had made a lot of friends and was well liked by a growing number of people. He was outgoing, charming, and had an infectious laugh. He had flown the sheriff of Hamilton County to several meetings in Nashville over several months.

The sheriff liked Nick and asked him to apply at the sheriff's office. Nick did, and he excelled. His goal was to be part of the air team at the sheriff's office. The team was small, and turnover was almost never heard of, but he decided he would wait patiently.

CHAPTER FIVE

Shots Fired

Nick was a good deputy and had solved several felony crimes while on patrol. He had been a training officer for a year and Kent was his third pupil. Roll call was over. Nick walked over to collect Kent and thus began their sometimes-tumultuous relationship.

"You ready for your first day on the streets?" Nick asked Kent.

"Ready as can be at this point," said Kent.

"Good. Now I will see if you are," replied Nick.

"That's okay with me, " retorted Kent.

"Okay, let's go." Nick looked at him squarely.

Nick drove, and Kent was in the shotgun seat. The two were assigned north side zone, which included a lot of rural countryside along with some parts of the suburbs of Chattanooga.

"I heard that you were from Florida." Kent tried to break the ice and have a conversation with Nick.

"That's right, but let's get something straight here. I'm not your friend. I'm here to see that you understand how this works. I don't want to be your friend. I don't want to know about your life, and I'm not going to talk about mine. Let's work and keep it business, Nick demanded.

"That's fair, I was just friendly."

"I have all the friends I need. What I need is for you to pay attention and not gab."

Kent looked at him and acknowledged by nodding his head. He had seen his share of hard-asses. He didn't know what made them so, but he learned not to care.

"Echo Four," the communications center called on the radio.

"Echo Four," Nick responded without giving Kent the opportunity to reach for the radio.

"10-65?"

10-65 was a code asking if you were ready to copy down some information. Nick looked at Kent and lifted one eyebrow. Kent reached for his pad and was ready to write.

"10-4, go ahead."

"Area 12, 2-1-8-8 Branch Drive, domestic disturbance."

"In route," Nick advised.

A domestic disturbance could be anything from a juvenile giving his mom a hard time to a full-blown fight between husband and wife. Since the communication center did not clear them for emergency traffic, it was probably just an argument of some kind. The problem was that you never knew until you came up to the scene.

"Don't do anything until I tell you to. Got that?" Nick barked.

"Yep," Kent responded.

Nick looked briefly at Kent to see if he thought he understood what he was saying. When they got to the scene, there was no one outside. It was a mobile home, and there were car parts and assorted junk in the yard. A large barking dog met them as they pulled onto the scene. Nick got out of the car and didn't even look at the dog. Kent followed but kept glancing at the dog to see where it was and what it was doing. He didn't want to get bitten on his first day on duty. "Knock on the side of the trailer," Nick told Kent. Kent stood back from a window and knocked as loudly as he could hit with his bare knuckles. Nick walked over to the other side of the trailer with the front door between him and Kent.

No one came to the door, so Nick nodded at Kent to knock again. Kent beat again this time a little harder and this time on the window glass closest to him. Still, no one came to the door. The storm door was closed, but the front door to the trailer was open. Nick motioned Kent to go to the back and check it out.

As Kent rounded the back end of the trailer, he saw the head of a man standing behind a shed. He had a cap on, and his head seemed to be moving around rather rapidly. Then Kent noticed a foot in a woman's shoe behind the shed. The foot was where he thought the man's foot should have been.

The man didn't see him, so he backed around to the front of the trailer and made eye contact with Nick. He motioned to let Nick know something was going on in the back. Then he proceeded back to his position in the rear of the trailer.

Nick went to the other side of the trailer, but the shed blocked his view. There was also an old junk car between him and the shed. The dog that had been barking the entire time, quit barking, and followed Nick to the rear of the trailer. Nick could see Kent at the opposite end of the trailer. Kent pointed to the back of the shed and held up two fingers and pointed again.

Nick walked around the junked car and make his way to the back of the shed. After Nick had got about half way to the shed, the man noticed Kent and bolted from the side of the shed in plain view of Kent but out of the view of Nick.

The man had a woman in a choke hold with his left arm and a small handgun in his right hand. Kent immediately pulled his semi-automatic pistol and pointed it at the two as they slowly made their way to Kent's right; still out of the view of Nick.

"Stop right there!" Kent yelled out to the man. Seeing Kent's actions, Nick took off running toward the front of the shed jumping over car parts and batteries as he pulled his firearm. Kent remained focused on the man and woman.

"I will kill her!" the man shouted back.

"No, you are not gonna kill her. You are gonna stop and not let this get worse," Kent responded.

"Echo four, send back up. Man with gun. Possible hostage situation." Nick called on his portable radio in a hushed voice.

"Echo Four 10-4," the communication's officer replied.

The man took another step to Kent's right but was still about twenty yards in front of him. Nick had made his way in front of the shed, but the couple was still to the right side of the shed. Nick didn't want to give his position away until he was ready.

"Sir, drop your gun!" Kent yelled out again. "Do it now and stop this here."

By this time Nick was ready to let the man see him, so he slid out a little at the front edge of the shed with his weapon pointed right at the man.

The woman was on his front side between the man and Kent, but Nick was in a wide open area. That's when man noticed Nick at the edge of the shed and turned toward him. He took the aim of the gun off the woman's head and pointing it at Nick. He had pulled the woman around between him and Nick, which caused his left side to be open to Kent.

When the man had the gun to the woman's head Kent was in no hurry to shoot the man or cause the situation to escalate. Kent didn't believe the man would shoot the woman unless he saw no way out. He was using her as a shield. He needed her alive to be that shield.

But now everything had changed. The gun was no longer

pointed at the woman with her between him and Kent. The gun was pointed at his trainer. "Damn!" Kent said loud enough so only he could hear it. With the weapon pointed at his training officer and the woman between his training officer and the perpetrator, it became a dangerous scenario for the deputies and a hard decision for Kent.

Kent felt that time was running out. What were the chances of this situation happening on your very first call of your career? Kent briefly wondered. Kent could faintly hear the clock of doom ticking in his head. Perhaps this could end without Nick getting shot. Perhaps the man would get scared and just shoot Nick. "Tick Tick," went that damnable clock! Perhaps the man didn't think he would shoot since they had been in a standoff for several minutes without incident. "Wrong!" Kent said barely audible, as he squeezed the trigger. The bullet struck the man in the neck and knocking him to the ground immediately. The clock stopped ticking. Kent knew in his heart he did what he had to do to possibly save his trainer's life. At that moment everything seemed so surreal.

The woman fell to the ground across the injured man's legs but quickly crawled over to a woodpile and sat on the dirt screaming. The wounded man lay flat on his back almost perfectly still with his eyes opened and focused on the gray sky looming through the openings in the trees above. He didn't blink or move his eyes. Blood was oozing rapidly from the wound in his neck. The bullet had struck him about three inches below and behind his left ear. Blood had started to pool under his neck on the ground, and his t-shirt's collar was now stained with the dark blood.

"Echo Four, shots fired, suspect down; request EMT and supervisor," Nick called on his portable radio as he ran over to kick the gun away from the injured man's hand.

Sirens were blasting in the background as backup came rushing to the scene, but neither Kent nor Nick heard them. They were surprised when their sergeant came rushing toward them. Kent still had his weapon drawn. Nick had his put back in its holster.

Everything seemed to go from light speed before the shot was fired to slow motion after the man was struck by the single blast from Kent's firearm. Kent walked over to the woman who was still crying loudly.

"It's okay ma'am. Settle down. Are you hurt?" Kent asked.

She didn't even look at him but kept her eyes on the injured man lying a few feet away from her. Finally, she glanced at Kent, held her crying for about a second, then looked back at the hurt man and started crying loudly again.

"Ma'am, are you hurt anywhere?" Kent repeated.

She looked at Kent, sobbed a little, and held out her left arm. Under her left arm, just a few inches below her armpit was a large mark that looked like a bad burn. There were some small circles inside the boundaries of the large dark-red injury.

As more backup deputies arrived, the sergeant had two deputies remain at the front of the trailer and told the rest they could go back in service.

Soon two lieutenants and a captain were on the scene along with four paramedics. A detective arrived after about twenty minutes. Three of the paramedics worked with the injured man while one tended to the woman. The wounded man was taken from the scene with the ambulance running red lights and sirens. The woman was placed in the back of the other ambulance and soon left the scene without fanfare. A deputy was dispatched to meet the ambulance carrying the injured man at the hospital.

Kent and Nick were asked to go to the front part of the property after they separately gave the detective a brief account of what had just transpired. There was no time for Kent to reflect on what had just happened, and he had not formed a judgment on whether he could have handled it differently. There would be plenty of time to reflect and second-guess his actions later.

Kent and Nick didn't talk much about what had just happened. They just glanced at each other as they were standing outside their patrol car. Nick took out a cigarette, lit it, then raised the blue box of smokes in Kent's direction. Kent nodded no. Nick was looking toward the trailer and then across the street at an open pasture. There were about six cows total in the field and a small pond. There wasn't much to look at, but Nick kept looking back at the pasture like he was searching for something. Once in a while, Kent browsed the field himself just to see what had caught Nick's attention, but there were just a few cows and a pond, nothing more.

"You okay?" Nicked asked

"Yeah, I guess. You?"

"Yeah, all right here."

"Wow, what a way to start a day."

"Yeah," Nick said, and then paused for a few seconds. "It is."

Other than a few more occasional glances in each other's direction, there was no more communication between them until they left the area. They realized the magnitude of what had just happened and didn't want to diminish it with idol chat.

In about an hour, two agents from the Tennessee Bureau of Investigations and an assistant district attorney pulled up. One of the county's detectives saw them and met them halfway between the trailer and the shooting scene. Then the four of them walked over to where Kent, Nick, and their sergeant were standing.

There were a few questions the ADA and the TBI agents asked the two deputies. They briefly walked the agents through the scenario step by step. The officials asked a few more questions, and the ADA asked a couple of questions about the woman, any statements she made, and her general condition.

Nick and Kent left the scene after the questioning and drove back to the sheriff's office where they both made a report and wrote down a complete statement of the morning's event.

About two hours, after they arrived back at the sheriff's office, the chief deputy, Sal Dillard, came into the report room where the two were still writing. He told them that the man had died on the way to the hospital. He also told them that the man had just been paroled about two months previously. The man had been serving twelve years for robbery and aggravated assault. Before that sentence, he had served nine years for stabbing a man in a fight. He had several other convictions for drugs and resisting arrest. They had also found several ounces of meth in his back pocket. A blood test later revealed that he had meth in his system at the time of the shooting.

The communication center's tape of the call made was from the woman at the scene. The voice was calm on the date of the call and just said that someone needed to come there because her boyfriend was cussing at her and she didn't want it to get out of hand. There was never a mention of a fight, a gun, or of a physical altercation. It was discovered that the woman's injury was by an iron. She had been ironing when the boyfriend went out of control and grabbed the iron from her. She tried to keep him from getting the iron, but he forced it out of her hand. Her arm was still in the air from the momentum of the struggle. That's when he pushed the hot iron against her arm.

The TBI and district attorney's office did a complete investigation that took about three months and called the shooting justified. After the shooting, the deputies were off on administrative leave for a short period of time until the sheriff's office internal affairs unit classified the shooting as warranted.

Nick and Kent continued to work together for the next sixty days until Kent Rivers had completed his training period. The two never became friends during his training time. The shooting wasn't talked about much after it was ruled justifiable by the district attorney, but Nick did give Kent less grief about being a rookie than he had intended or than he had the other trainees. Kent had done well under difficult circumstances. It was long remembered by everyone at the sheriff's office.

Kent continued in the patrol unit another year and a half until he was promoted to detective. He felt right at home in the group from the very beginning. While it was different from his days with Army CID, it was still investigating, and he knew it was in his blood.

CHAPTER SIX

Yellow Toyota

Late Sunday Night, June 20th

Rivers and Howe pulled into the northbound rest area. Deputy Davidson had just arrived. The rest area was really just a parking lot—there were no facilities and no buildings. A yellow older model Toyota was sitting in the middle of the parking area with the trunk and both the driver's side door and the right rear passenger door open. A single shoe was lying just outside the passenger door, and a shirt was hanging halfway out of the trunk over the bumper. The tag was a Florida plate about to expire, but it did not belong to the car.

In a few days the plate would be reported stolen by the registrant. It was clear that someone had left this vehicle in a hurry. There were a couple of other cars in the parking area, so Rivers asked Davidson to make contact with those people to find out if any of them had noticed the car when they pulled into the parking area or had seen anyone around the car.

Rivers and Howe continued to look through the vehicle. There was a fishing box in the trunk with the initials KS and a few tools with the same initials.

"Let's get this car processed, Carl," Rivers said.

"Okay, do you want me to do it?" Carl Howe replied.

"Yeah, if you don't mind."

"Photos, prints, everything?"

"Treat it like a suspect's car. I think we may have something here. I'm not sure just how it fits yet. Even though the body is south of here, I can't help but feel it's somehow connected."

"Want it towed?"

"Yeah, go ahead, after it's photographed here. But be sure to follow the tow truck all the way into the compound. You know, chain of custody."

"Oh yeah, sure will."

"Let's see if Davidson can stay here with it while I run you back to your car. I also want Dek to start from this area and work north, looking for things along the road. But I'll tell him."

Davidson remained with the Toyota to maintain a chain of custody in case the vehicle became part of homicide investigation. Kent took Carl back to the crime scene to get his vehicle. Each detective was fully trained and equipped to work and collect evidence at a crime scene. It helped when everyone was on the same level while discussing physical evidence during investigative meetings.

Detective Mike Zinkovich had just arrived on the crime scene when Rivers and Howe returned from the Toyota. Rivers asked Zinkovich to help Howe with processing the car. They both drove to the rest area and began the long task of processing the car. Since it was being treated as a suspect's vehicle they would need to go over it with a fine-tooth comb. That meant looking for fibers, hairs, and other trace evidence, as well as possibly preserving items for the DNA fingerprint. In addition, Luminol testing would be done to show any presence of blood that might not be seen with the naked eye. The vehicle would get a complete examination.

★

The morning sky started to peek over the hills, and the flashing blue and red lights started to yield way to the brilliance of the sun. The body was removed from the scene and taken for an autopsy. Detectives Rogers and Dalton followed the ambulance carrying the unknown body unceremoniously to the morgue.

Lieutenant Bates, with the aid of Detective Grayson organized a group of reserve deputies to comb the shoulders of the interstate for any possible clues and evidence. With the sun now shining and the night giving way to the day, the deputies were in place and ready for their task. There were six teams and they worked in teams of two. A patrol unit was put behind the teams to warn oncoming traffic and protect the teams. A state road department crew put out traffic cones diverting traffic to the outside lanes.

The team also set up flashing warning lights where the crews started their work. Each team was placed about 500 yards apart, and a traffic cone was used to mark the beginning and end of each team's area. When the teams had covered half a mile, the entire project could be moved to the next point, and they walked another half mile trek. The teams were given evidence markers and a radio to communicate with Lieutenant Bates. They were prepared to continue the task all day, if necessary.

They planned to cover the areas up to five miles. After that the plan was to use patrol units driving slowly on the shoulder of the road to see what they might find. The reasoning Rivers utilized for the task was simple. If this unknown victim had any personal belongings or identification prior to the shooting he didn't have it now. If the perpetrators had taken something, they was probably want to discard the items before traveling too far up the road in case they were stopped by police at some point.

★

The news media had been waiting since early morning to get the story. The first camera crew on the scene was from Channel 5 News. Felix Dobbs had been with Channel 5 News for thirty-three years. Rivers had known Dobbs since his first day on duty as a Hamilton County Deputy when he and his training officer, Nick Taylor, had been involved in the shooting of an armed suspect.

Tricia Ledford was the Hamilton County Sheriff's Office's public information officer. She had already spoken with Lieutenant Bates about the basics of the case, but she needed the okay from Rivers before releasing any information.

When Rivers returned from looking at the Toyota at the rest area, she spoke with him briefly and was able to make a release from the information given. Rivers knew that the media wanted the information, and he had noticed on his return from the rest area that Dobbs had pulled over on the shoulder. Rivers knew that having the right information in the right hands of the media could help a case. However, the wrong information in the wrong hands could hamper a case.

Tricia told Dobbs that Rivers would try to get with him later if possible and that she would have the press release faxed to his station within the hour. Dobbs was satisfied. He got the footage from the scene and returned to the TV station so his producers could match the video with the press release. Tricia drove back to her office in downtown Chattanooga to hammer out the press release and get it to the surrounding news outlets.

The finished release was short and pithy.

From the Public Information Office Hamilton County Sheriff's Office Chattanooga, Tennessee For immediate release: At approximately 9:30 PM yesterday evening, a 911 call was received reporting a possible body lying along Interstate-75 in the northbound lanes. Our patrol units responded and did find a body at the location reported by the caller. Investigators have been on the scene since the body was discovered. It was apparent to the investigators that foul play was involved. There is no information at this time on the identity of the body other than it was a white male. Investigators are currently working on the case, and details will be released as it becomes available. Please direct all questions to this office. Thank you, Tricia Ledford, PIO

★

Monday, June 21st 9:30 A.M.

One of the reserve deputies working along the interstate called Lieutenant Bates with a possible finding. Bates immediately went to the location of the find and learned that they had most likely hit the jackpot. Reserve Deputy Dale Mason had recovered a Tennessee driver's license belonging to a man that lived in a neighboring county. It was their first substantial lead, and Bates jumped on it quickly. He advised the others to shrink their search area and concentrate in the mile just north of the find.

The license belonged to Alexander Fisher. The address showing on the license was 1134 Trumpet Road Cleveland, Tennessee. Cleveland was the county seat of Bradley County, the next county northeast of Hamilton County.

The address was located in a rural section of Bradley County. Bates called Rivers and then met him back at the scene. By this time there was not much of a scene left other than searching the nearby wooded areas and the median for any further clues.

Rivers was in the command post vehicle that had been brought to the scene earlier that morning. He had closed his eyes for a few moments trying to steal a little sleep. He knew that they were at the beginning of this case and in the next forty-eight hours, there would be little time for sleeping.

Rivers and Bates both had been through enough investigations to know that finding the license didn't mean it had to belong to their victim. Many times in a case something popped up and seem like a decent lead, only to be discovered later that it had nothing to do with the case. However, they both felt that the license was the break they had needed. They would have to prove it, but they both felt they had their victim. Until they proved it, however, the find was just a license that was found along the interstate. They would hate to declare someone a victim, only to have them show up looking for their license.

Rivers and Bates were soon headed to the address in Bradley County. Rivers called his counterpart in Bradley County, Captain Brian Sutherds. He and Rivers had worked together since Rivers first made detective. Sutherds had been with Bradley County for 27 years. He knew just about every convicted criminal around, including those in Hamilton County.

Sutherds was out of pocket at the time, but he had Detective Lieutenant Bryant give him a call, and they were able to hook up and locate the address. The house was a wood-frame house, white with green shutters and a full screened-in front porch.

There was an older model Chevrolet Impala in the driveway. Lieutenant Bryant knocked on the door. It was only a few seconds until someone opened the door.

"Hello ma'am, my name is Barry Bryant, and I'm an investigator with the sheriff's office. These two men are also investigators. They are from Chattanooga."

"Hello," replied a lady who looked to be in her mid-seventies.

"The reason we are here is to see if you know Alexander Fisher?" Lieutenant Bryant asked.

"He is my son, why"

"Well ma'am, these investigators from Hamilton County sheriff's office in Chattanooga would like to speak with you about Alexander," Lieutenant Bryant replied.

The lady nodded and opened the door wider to indicate that they may come in the house.

"Ma'am, I am Chief Detective Kent Rivers, and this is Lt. Dek Bates. As Lt. Bryant told you, we are from Chattanooga. May I get your name please so I'll know who I am speaking with?" Rivers asked.

"My name is Gloria Fisher," the woman responded.

"Ms. Fisher, I would like to see if you know who this driver's license belong to," Rivers said as he looked at Bates.

Bates pulled the license out of his shirt pocket and showed it to the lady.

"That belongs to my son, Alex, where did you find it?"

"Does your son live here with you Ms. Fisher?" Bates asked as if he didn't hear her question.

"Yes, he does. Is he in trouble? He has never been in trouble in his life," she replied.

"When did you last see Alex?" Rivers asked.

"I saw him yesterday morning before he left for work."

"Did he come home last night? Rivers continued.

"No, but he sometimes stays with a friend and doesn't come back. I know if I don't hear him come in or see him the next morning that he stayed there."

"Where does he work ma'am? We would like to talk to Alex and see if he could help us on a case we are working," Bates asked.

"Waffle House in Ooltewah."

"Do you know how we might get in touch with his friend?" Bates continued.

"His name is David Williamson. He lives in Cleveland, I think, or he did. I have his number here somewhere, I'm sure."

"Oh, that is great Ma'am if we could get that from you" Rivers said.

Ms. Fisher walked over to a small, antique desk and lifted a tiny piece of paper off the top of the bureau.

"Here it is."

"That's great Ma'am, do you mind if I copy down that number?" Rivers asked.

"You can have that paper. I have it wrote down in my address book, too."

"Thank you!" Rivers said.

"Alex isn't in any trouble is he?" The mother asked once again, looking for assurance. "It's just him and me here. His dad died about six years ago. So he is all I have. Lord, I hope he hasn't gotten into trouble."

"Ms. Fisher, as soon as we figure out what is going on, I promise I'll tell you." Rivers spoke firmly but compassionately to the lady as he stood up and got ready to walk out the door.

"Thank you, sir. And what is your name again?" She asked.

"My name is Kent Rivers, ma'am. Here is my card. I promise I'll let you know what is going on very soon. I should be back today sometime. Thank you so much for your help!"

"Okay, but I didn't do anything but give you a name and number on a slip of paper," she replied.

"That was a lot ma'am, thank you," Bates responded as he walked out the door.

Rivers and Bryant followed Bates out the door as Bryant turned and nodded to the lady while pulling her door closed. The three stood by their vehicles for a few moments but didn't want to stay too long and force Ms. Fisher to wonder what they were saying.

"What do you think?" Bates asked Rivers.

"Without being able to see the face better, I'm just not sure, but if I had to bet, my money is on this guy being our victim."

"Yeah, me too."

"I could have asked about red shorts and some other things, but I didn't want to say anything until we are sure."

"Yeah, I understand. Same here."

Rivers and Bates thanked Lieutenant Bryant and told him they may need him again depending on what they come up with on David Williamson.

Bates called and asked Kathy Meadows, one of the office assistants back at the detective office, to run a cross-reference on the phone number and the name they were given by Ms. Fisher. They also had her look up the number for the Waffle House in Ooltewah.

The number was not listed in the cross reference, but there was an address for a David Williamson. They were just hoping for time sake that it was the same guy. The address came back to a trailer park in Ooltewah, a small community on the north end of Hamilton County.

They went directly to the trailer park and tried to find David Williamson. Rivers called Waffle House on their way to Ooltewah in hopes of saving some time. Someone at the Waffle House told him that Alex left work at the usual time of 7:30 the previous night. No one had seen him today, and he was not expected back to work until the following Thursday.

"I hate trailer parks," Bates said, as they were driving to the newly found address. "Numbers on trailers in trailer parks are usually out of order—someone moves a trailer to a different spot, and it keeps the same number, or a new trailer is added between two existing trailers, and it gets a number not even close to the other two. So, I hate them. You might as well just start knocking on the first trailer to see if anyone knows the person you are looking for. It's faster," Bates concluded.

Rivers' mind was on what he might learn when they found Williamson. He didn't even hear what Bates had said.

"What?" Rivers asked.

"Never mind," Bates replied as he flipped through some notes he had jotted down from earlier.

Bates was a prophet. The trailer park was scattered with various numbers in seemingly random order. But sometimes a little luck goes a long way. One of Rivers favorite quotes that he borrowed from baseball great, Lefty Gomez, "I'd rather be lucky than good any day." Today, they had double luck. Not only did they find the right David Williamson, but he was home. With just a little more luck they could identify their victim soon.

CHAPTER SEVEN

The Casket

"Good afternoon," Bates said as the door opened before they even knocked.

"Hello!" A little man with a deep voice that certainly didn't fit the body spoke back.

"I'm Lieutenant Bates with the Hamilton County sheriff's office, and this is Chief Rivers. We are investigators, and we would like for you to help us identify someone if you can."

"I don't know too many people. I doubt that I can identify anyone. Besides, I stay at home a lot and don't see much of anything happen."

"No sir, we are not asking you to be a witness to anything. We just need to know if you know Alexander Fisher."

"Why do you need to know?"

"Well, to be honest, we are trying to make sure he is still alive."

"Alive?!" The man yelled and this time in a higher pitch that matched his small frame.

"Yes, we are working a homicide, and we need to locate Mr. Fisher to rule him out as the victim," Rivers said.

"May we come in?" Bates asked. "Sure," the little man said as he swung the door open wide. "What makes you think that it could be Alex?"

"We found his driver's license not far from the crime scene," Bates spoke up.

"Let me ask you a few quick questions," Rivers said.

"Okay."

"Is this the Alex you know?" Rivers asked as Bates showed the license.

"That's his license alright. That's the Alex I know."

"Do you know where he is right now?" Bates asked.

"No. I haven't heard from him since the night before last. He stopped by for a few minutes on his way home from work," Williamson answered.

"Does Alex sometimes stay here after work instead of going home?" Bates asked.

At this point, the detectives have to consider that Fisher is their victim and that Williamson could be a suspect. This caused them to be careful with their questions because it may be the only time they get to question him so freely and without his asking for an attorney.

"Yes, Alex does stay here, quite a bit, to be honest," Williamson stated.

"When was the last time he was here?" Rivers asked.

"He was here a couple of nights ago, but he went home and didn't stay here," Williamson replied.

"You say that he stays here quite a bit," Rivers said, "Does he keep any clothes here?"

"No, not really. Maybe a pair of shorts or a t-shirt, something to sleep in," Williamson answered.

"Do you know if he had a pair of red gym-type shorts?" Bates asked.

"Oh my lord, yes! That's all he likes to wear are those worn out red shorts, but I think they are here."

"Would you mind checking?" Rivers spoke up.

"Sure," Williamson said as he stood to retrieve the shorts.

Williamson walked down the hall to a bedroom, turned to his left and disappeared for a moment. Bates knew that it doesn't take a cop worth his salt very long to know that you do not let anyone who could even remotely be a suspect out of your sight So Bates followed Williamson down the hallway and into the bedroom.

Williamson opened a top drawer in an old dresser and searched for the shorts.

"Hmm, I don't see them. That's strange," Williamson said while looking around on the floor and in the connecting bathroom.

The two walked back out of the room.

"What about this room." Bates put his hand on the knob to open the door to the only other room in the trailer.

"No! Please don't open that door!" Williamson yelled loudly in high pitched voice and grabbed Bates' hand.

Williamson was only a couple of feet behind Bates so when he yelled so loudly and grabbed his hand, it startled Bates and caught the attention of Rivers who started walking toward the two men.

Bates yanked his hand away from the doorknob and free from Williamson grip. Bates stepped back a couple of steps and looked right at Williamson. Bates' jaw clenched tight as yelled, "What?! Don't grab my hand!"

"I'm sorry I yelled, but you scared me."

"I scared you? What in the hell was that all about?" Bates yelled, letting his anger show.

Williamson sighed for a moment then said, "I might as well tell you."

"Tell us what?" Rivers asked, while Bates just glared at Williamson.

78

"There's a casket in there."

"A what?!" Both Bates and Rivers said at the same time.

"A casket. Let me show you."

Williamson slowly opened the door and stepped back so Bates could see inside the room. Bates saw the coffin and a room full of old artificial flowers. He stepped back just a little and looked down the hall at Rivers and just nodded his head.

"Why do you have a casket?" Asked Rivers.

"It's a long story, but it's mine. It's not stolen or taken out of a graveyard or anything," Williamson replied.

"What were you planning to do with it? Bates asked.

"Just keep in the room for when friends come over. We like to take new friends back there after we hide someone in it, without them knowing of course. Then the person in the casket opens the lid and pops out," Williamson said while chuckling. "It scares the hell out of most of them," he continued as he laughed even harder.

"Looks like it has been in there a while," Bates said.

"Oh yeah, about two years now. A friend of a friend owned a funeral home at one time. He went out of business. I heard that he had a couple of caskets, so I gave him two hundred dollars for one," Williamson said as he started laughing again.

"Two hundred dollars, huh?" Bates said.

"Yeah, I just didn't want to scare you when you opened that door and saw that in there. I should have told you it was in there," Williamson said.

Williamson couldn't help but snicker one more time at the thought of possibly scaring Bates.

"Thanks, but screaming in my ear probably scared me more than the casket would have," Bates said in reply.

"Did you say that sometimes Alex stays all night with you here?" Rivers asked.

"Yes sir, he stays here a lot, actually."

Rivers briefly turned his head to look for any other rooms in the small trailer.

"Where was he sleep?" Rivers asked.

"In that bedroom."

"So you shared your room?"

"Yes, sir. Alex and I aren't dating or anything. We just like each others company."

"Okay, I understand," Rivers responded.

"So the famous red shorts are not here?" Bates asked.

"I don't know where they are. I guess he wore them home. He has done that before, but usually, he just leaves them here. I wash them and put them up for him. I've been tempted more than once to just throw them away and put some new red shorts in there," Williamson said laughingly.

"Okay, we may be back in touch. What is your phone number?" Rivers asked even though he already had a number for him.

Williamson gave him his phone number, and it was the same one on the piece of paper Ms. Fisher had given Rivers. The two detectives thanked Williamson and left the trailer. They didn't even look at each other until they got back into the car and pulled away.

"Are you believing that?" Bates asked.

"What? That they are gay?" Rivers asked.

"No, the casket! Weird."

"Yes, it is. Very strange."

"I think Alex is our guy, Dek," Rivers said after a moment or two of silence.

"Me too."

"Let's head over to the morgue and see if we can see his face any better with it cleaned up," Rivers finished.

They got about a mile from Williamson's trailer when Rivers

did a u-turn in the middle of the road.

"I just thought of something," Rivers said, whirling the car around.

"What?" Bates asked while holding onto the handle above the window.

"Do you remember a while back, someone talking about the rest area being a place where gay prostitutes sometimes hang out?"

"Yeah, a few months ago. I don't remember who, though. And your point is?"

"Okay, if Fisher is our victim, and the Toyota has something to do with it, and Fisher happened to be a gay prostitute, then the puzzles start to fit!" Rivers said as he quickly changed lanes to turn into the trailer park again. "We are going to have a serious talk with Williamson about possible activities at the rest area. If he and Alex were just casual partners, then he may know if Fisher ever went to the rest area."

The door opened once again before they knocked.

"Back already? I'm not in trouble am I?" Williamson asked.

"Yes, we are back. I don't know if you are in trouble or not, but we need to talk," Rivers responded.

Williamson left the door open and walked back into the trailer. Rivers and Bates follow.

"I want to talk about something, and I need you to be very honest. I'm not here to embarrass you or cause you grief. I'm working a homicide, and I need some facts," Rivers told Williamson.

"O-k-ay," Williamson said, drawing out the word slowly.

"You and Fisher are gay."

"Yes."

"Do you know anything about the rest area near here on the interstate?"

"I know where it is if that's what you mean."

"No, that is not what I mean, and I think you know that."

"Are you asking me if I've been there?"

"I'm asking you if you know anything about what goes on there sometimes?"

"I'm not sure what you are talking about."

"David, do you know anything about gay prostitutes hanging out at the rest area?" Bates cut into the conversation.

"Gay prostitutes? Good Lord, no! How would I know about gay prostitutes?

"You are telling us that you have never heard of gay prostitutes hanging out at that rest area?" Rivers said leaning forward in his chair and looking right into Williamson's eyes.

"Well, I may have heard things, just like anybody hears things, but I'm not a prostitute! Good Lord, no!"

"I'm not saying that you are a prostitute. I'm asking you for any information that you may know about the rest area. I need your help, David. To be honest, Alex may want your help."

"Why would Alex need my help? Where is he?"

"We think he may be dead, David." Bates said and sat back in his seat and watched for Williamson's reaction.

"You think that Alex is dead?"

"There is a good chance," Rivers added.

"Who would, why would anyone want to kill Alex? He doesn't bother anyone!"

"That's why we are here, David. We are looking for answers, and you may have a piece of that puzzle," Bates inserted.

"A very vital part," Rivers said. Williamson sat back in his seat and looked around the room like he was looking for a reason to say or not say what he knew.

"Do you think Alex ever went to the rest area looking for some kind of action?" Bates asked.

Williamson took a long breath then took just as long to release it. "You guys are gonna ruin me aren't ya?" Williamson asked.

"How so?" Rivers responded.

"If I say that he did, and he is not the one dead, then I will have thrown him to the wolves."

"David, I'll be honest with you. The more I think about it, the more I believe that Alex is dead. He is our victim. Help us out here," Rivers replied.

"Okay, yes. We have both been there looking for a little fun, but we aren't prostitutes. Sometimes people will meet up there and just talk, and then sometimes people will hook up, but nobody pays anybody nothing."

"Do you know if Alex was going there yesterday? Last night?" Bates asked.

"He did ask me if I wanted to go hang out there. I told him no and asked him why not just stay here with me, and we could watch a movie or something. He said he was tired of movies and just needed to get out. So, yes, he might have gone there. Yep, he probably did." Williamson's hands rubbed his face harder and harder as he spoke. "Sweet Lord! I can't take this! Do you really think Alex is your victim?" Williamson asked.

"It looks like it to me, David," Rivers spoke back softly. "Now, I need to ask you to do something that may be tough.

"What is harder than this?"

"I understand, but I need someone who was close to Alex to look at the body to identify it for sure, or rule it out."

"No way!" Williamson yelled as he stood up. "No way, no way, no way!"

"I didn't say that you had to, David; I was asking you. We can probably get Alex's mother to do it," Rivers said, knowing that he was laying a guilt trip on him.

"Not Alex's mom. That would kill her."

"Well, we need someone to identify him, David. Someone who knew him pretty well." Bates said.

"Oh good Lord, no, I just couldn't. That would be awful! What if it was Alex? Then I'll be there with him being dead! Good Lord, no. I don't see how I could do it, but I can't let his mom. I would never forgive myself."

"Do you know anyone else that knows him like you and his mom?" Bates asked.

"Not anymore. He used to have another friend before he met me, but he moved to New York."

"Why don't you ride with us and we will bring you back," Rivers suggested while standing up and walking toward the door.

Williamson just sat in his chair. He didn't look at Bates or Rivers and didn't look up. Both hands were on the armrest of the seat, and he didn't move them. Rivers and Bates walked to the door and Rivers put his hand on the doorknob.

"You coming?" Rivers asked while leading him with every move.

Finally, Williamson stood up and walked toward the door. He picked up his sunglasses and keys as he passed the bar between the living room and kitchen.

"Let's go," Williamson said, as he got closer to the investigators.

Williamson still wasn't sure that he was going to do it when he got there, but he was willing to see how he might feel when the time came. When they got to the morgue, Williamson backed out twice. But when Rivers told Bates to go get Ms. Fisher and take Williamson home, he was brave.

They walked into the morgue. The autopsy had been delayed in the slim hopes of getting identification before the cuts were made. It's hard enough for a family member to see the ones they love dead, but to see them cut up by the autopsy procedures makes it worse. However, it had to be done soon. A body may be identified by fingerprints, but it could take weeks to get results, and that is if there are any to get. Fisher had a three-inch scar on the left side of his chest. When Williamson saw the scar, he became weak and almost had to vomit.

Williamson looked at the scar and said, "Oh my God, Alex, what did they do to you?!"

Williamson put his hand up to his mouth and gagged a couple of times.

The face had been cleaned of all the blood. There were five shots apparently embedded into the face. Two shots hit Fisher about an inch from each other in the middle of the forehead. A third shot was just to the right of his nose. The fourth shot hit him just below the bottom lip and had knocked out most of his front teeth. The final shot was in his throat just below the jaw, a little on the left side.

There was a towel covering Fisher's face. Bates pulled the cloth back briefly for Williamson to see. He didn't look long at Fisher's face, but he did recognize him, even though his face had been shot to pieces. He looked at Rivers and told him that he was positive it was Fisher. It was indeed Alexander F. Fisher.

They would get a call from the lab later that .25 caliber bullets killed Fisher. Williamson had made a positive identification.

When they walked out of the morgue, Williamson fainted on the front lawn. Bates managed to catch him before he hit the ground. They drove him the short distance to the hospital so he could be checked out. They told him someone would come back to take him home once he was able to leave. They thanked him for his help and let him know they would be in contact with him soon.

The case now had a name for its victim. It became the Fisher case. Rivers kept his promise to Ms. Fisher and returned to tell her what had happened. This time he did it alone. Her brother was there when Rivers came back. He was glad that someone was there with the mother. The mother didn't know where any papers were on her son's vehicle, and Rivers didn't asked her to find them.

Rivers contacted the Department of Safety and inquiries were made at DMV of any vehicles that were in Fisher's name. There was one. It was a Blue 1987 Chevy Monte Carlo. Rivers was given the license plate information as well as the vehicle identification number.

Rivers had the communications center enter all the information on the car into the NCIC data system and listed it as a stolen vehicle and to use caution. If the vehicle was stopped by another agency and they ran the numbers through NCIC, the case could take a quick turn toward getting it solved. Rivers knew that first the car had to be stopped by police and then the officer had to check the vehicle on NCIC, but it was the best thing they had going at the time.

CHAPTER EIGHT
Adelicia

Kent had dated some since his divorce, but there was nothing that came close to a serious relationship. He remained single for five years, but then he met Adelicia Winegate. To Kent, Adelicia was a sweet, southern lady who just happened to be beautiful.

They met on the Fourth of July at a political function where the governor spoke on his re-election promises. The event was held at one of the largest homes on Lookout Mountain, the home of a wealthy banker.

Lookout Mountain was a small town outside Chattanooga and is known to have an abundance of rich people. Adelicia came with her father who was a big donor to most Republicans running for office. He had built a plastic container business from the ground up and then sold it for millions to a big rubber company.

Adelicia wore the best clothes and looked the part of beauty and refinement. But what caught Kent's eye and heart was how she treated those around her, her smile and her laugh. But her beautiful looks and features were not lost on Kent.

Kent was thirty-one when he met Adelicia. She was twenty-five and a recent graduate of the University of Georgia, where she had played in the Red Coat Band and received her Master's degree.

When they met for the first time, she looked at him with her big blue eyes. They grew a little bigger the longer she looked at him. When she noticed that Kent was looking back, she quickly looked away, hoping he hadn't noticed her briefly admiring him.

Kent didn't miss many details as an investigator, and he didn't miss that little expression she exhibited. He tried to hide his smile, but a terse grin slipped onto his face. He was used to people looking at him. He was 6'3", had a well-cut physique, gorgeous green eyes, dark hair, an olive complexion, and a very handsome face. His green eyes seemed to look straight into the windows of a gal's heart. He was a head turner for sure, or as some females say, eye candy. When Kent spoke, his voice was deep yet soft. He could have easily gone into broadcasting. Tonight, in his black Gucci suit, he looked exceptional. Kent wasn't extravagant, but he believed in spending his extra money on nice clothes and of course, a nice car.

Adelicia recovered quickly from her astral gaze at Kent. She returned promptly to her usually shy demeanor.

"Miss Adelicia Winegate, may I present Mr. Kent Rivers. Mr. Rivers is a local detective," a mutual friend said as she introduced them to each other. "Adelicia is recently returning from her studies at the University of Georgia."

"Hello Kent, you are in a very exciting profession," Adelicia said while taking the opportunity to look straight into his eyes.

"Hello, Adelicia, it's nice to meet you. Yes, sometimes the job is exciting, but most of the time it is just a matter of following the lead in a dull, methodical sequence. There is no magic wand," He said with a serious look, but then smiled.

Kent was smitten by her voice, beauty, and poise, but he too, tried to not show how enamored he was with her.

"I noticed that you are not drinking anything, may I get you a drink?" Kent continued.

"Thank you, but no, I'm fine right now."

"The band is about to play. Would you like to find a better place to listen?" Kent asked feeling that if she took him up on his offer then maybe she had already enjoyed his company.

"No, I think I'm going to go talk with some old friends that I haven't seen in over a year. I noticed that they came in a few minutes ago."

Although he was a little taken back by the early rejection by this fascinating woman, Kent kept his own poise.

"Well, seeing old friends should always trump listening to a band. The night is young, and perhaps we will run into each other again before we leave," Kent responded, knowing that he would see her again, even if he had to do surveillance on her the rest of the night.

They both became engaged in conversations with others throughout the evening. Each of them tried to capture a peek at the other during the night without being noticed. Kent observed that some of the crowd was slowly leaving. He knew that time was beginning to be a factor in having a future conversation with Adelicia.

Adelicia also noticed that the crowd was starting to thin and was wondering why Kent had not yet approached her. Kent decided to take the direct approach and not waste whatever time was left. His attitude toward asking for dates was nothing ventured, nothing gained.

Kent spotted her across the room talking to some older men and women. He knew this was the right time. He didn't want to be rude by interrupting them while they were talking, so he walked across the room and stopped where a group of older men was talking. He was about ten feet from her group. He looked her way a few times to see if he could catch her eye.

The older men seemed to catch on quickly what Kent was doing. One guy patted him on the back and smiled like they were long-lost friends. Kent winked at the man.

"Oh the joys of being young, the older man said. "But son, I'm glad I've already sailed those seas."

Kent laughed as he spoke back, "I think I understand sir."

"I'm not sure you can yet, but it's good to see that some things haven't changed."

"Yes sir," Kent said, smiled and gently nodded his head.

Adelicia was keenly aware of Kent's nearness, and was wondering how and when he would finally make his move. Kent was a polite gentleman and knew proper etiquette, but he also was a fairly aggressive person who knew how to take charge.

Earlier in life, Kent had been a little shy and backward but decided that didn't get him very far with the opposite sex and ensured that he left parties alone and hungry.

As Adelicia took a brief stroll of the eyes to see what Kent was doing, she noticed him looking right at her. Her eyes froze in place momentarily, which felt a little odd to her, so she made a quick frown at him. One of the ladies in the group did notice and turned to see where she was looking. She smiled at Kent and went right on with her conversation. Kent just smiled and made a slow but deliberate motion with his head inviting her to leave the group and join him. She gave him another look in the eyes as if to say, "I can't just walk off." Kent made the same head motion again, this time raising his eyebrow just a little as if to say, "Yes you can." Finally, she decided to excuse herself from the group and walked toward Kent.

Kent slowly turned and walked toward the punch bowl. At first Adelicia wondered why he was walking away. But when he stopped at the bowl she followed.

"Would you like a little of what's left from the punch bowl? Kent asked Adelicia while barely raising his head and lifting his eyes to find her.

"Maybe just a little," Adelicia replied.

She really didn't want punch but decided to take it since she had walked to the bowl to meet him.

"Here you go," Kent said as he walked around the table to her side. "One of these days I'm going to go to one of these events and there will be green or purple punch. It's always red." Kent said, looked at Adelicia and grinned.

"I guess red is the color for these events. It does match Tennessee, a red-state map," Adelicia said referring to Tennessee's republican leaning.

"Come to think of it, you are right. I guess I need to go to a Democrat event to see if they have blue punch," Kent continued with the topic.

"Are you an actual Republican Kent or just like hanging out with the rich folks?" Adelicia said with a little smile.

"I guess I will have to pass on both of those," Kent replied with a little chuckle. "I'm not that politically minded. There just seems to be a lot of people I know that are Republicans, and I get invited to these events once in a while. I guess rich folks need friends too, right?"

Adelicia's smile grew a little with his response.

"Oh, so you are not prosperous, Kent? I'm not sure I should be hanging out with you then."

"If rich means having lots of money, then, no, I'm certainly not rich, but I think I'm a rich man. I have lots of friends, a great job, and season tickets to the Atlanta Braves games. What more could a man ask for?" Kent finished.

"Not a thing," Adelicia replied. She was almost tempted to say, Other than someone to share it with, but she refrained.

"Is your daddy one of the rich people?" Kent asked.

Adelicia frowned then changed to a smile. "Yes, he is," she said with an exaggerated arrogance. "We come from a long line of money." Adelicia laughed as those last words left her mouth. She felt proud that she had done a perfect job of sounding like a snob.

"Well, your daddy has done well in the daughter department also," Kent countered.

"Ah, I think you were attempting to sound sweet with that comment,"

"That was my full intention. Did I fall short?"

"You did okay." She faked taking a sip of her punch to control any smile that may have popped out at that moment.

By this time Kent had stepped a little closer to her but stayed just outside her personal zone.

"Since I did okay with that one, I'll push my luck and ask you to go to dinner with me," Kent said softly while looking right into her blue eyes.

Kent's softer tone caused Adelicia to have to lean in just a little to hear what he was saying. She quickly realized that was probably his plan. Unknowingly, she made a very slight pucker while searching for her answer. Kent saw the cute expression and cracked a smile.

Unaware that her expression caused his smile she responded, "Sure of yourself, aren't you?"

"No, I'm just sure I want to spend more time with you."

"Since you put it that way how could I say no? Okay, when would you like for this to happen?" She asked.

"I do have some things going on this month." "How about tonight?"

"Tonight?!" She exclaimed and laughed. "I don't even know you!"

"Sure, you know me. I am Detective Kent Rivers of Hamilton

County Sheriff's Office and a really nice guy. Just ask your friends. Besides, the night is still young and we can get some real food and maybe take a walk downtown. Have you been there at night?" Kent asked. "It's a beautiful city."

"I haven't been there at all. Would it be safe at night?" Adelicia responded.

"Safe? I think I can manage to keep you safe. It's only nine thirty and I promise to have you home before daylight," Kent said with a straight face.

"I'm sure you will, Mr. Rivers!" Adelicia answered energetically while wearing a half smile. "Okay, let me tell my dad. I rode with him."

"I would love to meet your father," Kent insisted.

"You do know all the right things to say don't you, Detective?" Adelicia started walking toward her dad who was standing with a few other men. "Well, come on!"

"Right behind you."

"Dad, I would like to introduce you to Kent Rivers. He is one of the city's detectives. Kent, this is Herb Winegate, my dad." Adelicia stepped back just a little so Kent could step toward her dad.

"Good evening sir," Kent said confidently as he stepped toward her father and stuck out his hand.

Her father looked at him a moment before responding with his hand.

"Actually, I'm with the sheriff's office here," Kent said.

"Oh, that's right, sorry Kent. Anyway Dad, he would like to take me to get some real food and then walk the streets of Chattanooga," Adelicia said as she moved almost under her dad's arm and smiled at Kent.

"Just the beautiful areas downtown Mr. Winegate," Kent added.

"Tonight Adelicia?" Her dad questioned.

"Detective Rivers insisted and said I'll be safe, Dad. And the night is still young. I think I will be okay, Dad." Adelicia looked up at her dad and smiled.

Her dad gave her that look as if to say, What are you up to?" But he told them to have fun.

"I'll be back before daylight," She said with a smile as she turned to walk away.

Her dad just shook his head and smiled.

"We will not be too late, Sir. It was nice meeting you," Rivers said in a comforting voice to her dad.

"Thank you, you too, Kent," Her dad said as he acknowledged Kent's polite words.

Adelicia waited in the foyer while Kent pulled his vehicle around to get her.

Kent owned a metallic gray Porsche 968 CS. He enjoyed getting out on the road in a nice car and putting the world behind him. Being single and living in a modest apartment allowed him the luxuries that mattered to him. He had saved a considerable amount of money while in the Army. He had lived on base and socked away about sixty percent of his pay during his four-year hitch.

As they left, they didn't get into the usual back and forth conversation of a new date trying to decide where they wanted to go. Kent took charge, and all he told her was, "I think you will like this place."

Adelicia sat back and enjoyed the ride and began to have a warm feeling about the evening. Kent pulled in front of an old motel on the edge of downtown. It was just a moment, and a young lady walked up to his car.

"May I park it for you tonight sir?" asked the valet parking attendant.

"Yes, you may," Kent replied.

Kent got out of the car and walked over to open Adelicia's door. Before he could get to it, she had it opened and started to get out.

"I am not so old-fashioned when it comes to letting a man do things for me," she stated.

"Well, that's a shame. You just demoted me to average Joe."

"You'll get over it," Adelicia said while laughing.

"You are wrong there, mainly because I don't want to get over it. But for this night, we will do it your way. After all, you are my guest."

As they started to walk up the steps to the front door, they heard squalling tires behind them. They turned to look as the young lady valet waved and smiled as she passed. Kent laughed.

Adelicia was impressed as they walk into the main room to see the stage full of musicians coming back from their break.

"Oh! It's the old Big Band sound! Wow!" She said as she laughed out loud, almost embarrassing herself.

Suddenly the band started back up with a booming blast of the trombones playing a fast tune that made them both want to snap their fingers to the beat.

"I love it already!" Adelicia shouted with a huge smile on her face, grabbing Kent's arm to be sure he heard her.

Kent smiled and nodded like he knew it all along.

"This is one of my favorite places in the world and it is right in my back yard!" Kent said as he pulled her a little closer to speak into her ear to overcome the loud music.

Kent spotted a corner table near the back. He wanted to be able to talk with Adelicia without yelling or having to read lips. They ordered a couple of drinks and sat back to listen to the band while tapping their toes for a few minutes.

During the evening they talked about their schools, his jobs, different events in their lives, and a whole host of noteworthy topics of interest. They both were pleased that this night had happened. They both wanted more just like it. Kent never discussed losing his best friend, Bruce. He didn't want the conversation to get on a sad note.

By the end of the evening, she knew how much Kent loved his career. She was excited because she had never personally known a cop, and Kent was a detective. Kent asked Adelicia about her name. She explained that she was named after a very wealthy Nashville woman from the 19th century. When the woman's first husband died, she was twenty-seven and had inherited a fortune. She talked about the fact that she had wanted to change her name when she learned that the woman had owned almost 800 slaves, but she said her dad told her to keep the name and rehabilitate it. She decided that was a worthwhile goal.

Adelicia had just graduated from the University of Georgia. She told Kent that she loved marching on the field during football games and that was what she would miss most after college. She majored in marketing but was not in a real hurry to find a job. She said she would find something she liked or she would just wait.

Kent asked her why a Tennessee woman with a rich Tennessee heritage was go to the University of Georgia. She told him that when she thought of a true southern belle, she thought of Georgia. She thought it was a great campus and one of her best friends also went there.

"Besides," She said, "I enjoy doing the unpredictable."

The two laughed and talked until almost two in the morning. Kent drove her to her hotel, which was less than a mile away. He walked her to the lobby and then on to her room.

"Tonight was fun, thank you, Kent," Adelicia said as she stopped several feet from the door to her room.

"Yes, it was nice Adelicia," replied Kent while moving a little closer to her. "It just seemed that we ran out of time. I would like to do this again."

"I'll only be here one more night. I don't have a clue what Dad has on his agenda for us tomorrow or tomorrow night. What is your idea of soon?" Adelicia said.

"Soon is a relative word. In this case I think soon is before you leave, if it fits into your schedule. May I call you tomorrow?" Kent inquired.

"I would like that, let me write down my number," she replied.

Kent took the small piece of paper with the number on it. He folded it without looking at it and placed it in his shirt pocket. He gave her a hug. She clung to him a little longer after his grip had eased.

"Goodnight, Adelicia."

"Night, Kent."

CHAPTER NINE

The Funeral

Saturday, June 12th 2:30 P.M.

The funeral for Kenny's girlfriend, Lisa was held at Pine Level Church of God, a small Pentecostal church outside of Arcadia, Florida. Several of Lisa's friends came, along with most of her co-workers who could get off, including the manager and two of the assistant managers.

Lisa didn't have much of a family left. She never wanted to see anyone that was connected with her abusive upbringing.

The Mother of one of the other girls killed in the accident came in and sat on the back pew. She sat without emotion during the entire funeral. At the very end of the service, after Lisa's casket was taken out, the woman made her way to the pastor.

The pastor didn't look like the pastor of a church. He was in his fifties and looked like he had worked hard most of his life outdoors. His face was dark, and his features looked chiseled in stone. He was one of those men who had lived a tough, troubled, younger life but found God and his softer side as he grew older.

The brokenhearted mother spoke briefly with the pastor. Before she walked away, he put his hand on her shoulder, bowed his head, and began to pray. He raised a small black Bible into the air above his head with the other hand. Those near him could hear him but not well enough to make out the words. He finished the prayer by saying, "In the name of our Lord and Savior, Jesus Christ, Amen."

When he finished praying, he pulled a white handkerchief out of the inside pocket of his jacket and handed it to the woman. She took the cloth and dabbed her eyes a few times, put it back in his hand, turned and walked away.

A man was sitting in an old white Buick Park Avenue in the parking lot. As she approached, he got out of the car, put out the cigar that he was smoking, and put the butt in his pocket. He opened the car door for her. She reached to him, and they hugged for a moment. He backed away a few inches while still holding on to her and kissed her on the forehead. They got into the car and left. Only a few people there, other than the preacher, even knew who she was and why she had come to the funeral.

The people at the store where Lisa worked had collected some money for Lisa's burial. The manager went to the funeral home director and told him that his business would raise the money for the services and burial if he would give them some time. The deaths of the three young women had an impact on the entire community. The director told the manager that he would do his services for free and only charge him his cost on the casket. Someone from the church donated a plot that was previously purchased for the family. Various florists from the small community gave flowers for all the services and gravesides. A person from the next county overheard about the story and donated a headstone for each family.

The community held a memorial service for all three women at the high school where they had attended a few years earlier. Only one of them had actually graduated, but they all were well known at the school.

Kenny was totally lost after Lisa's death. He would stay in his room for hours and go days without eating. He would hitch a ride to where Lisa had lived and sat out in front of the trailer, remembering her smile as she opened the door to greet him. For a person who had such a rough start in life, Lisa had begun having things go her way. Without many friends in the area, Kenny went from day to day, wandering around town like a lone wolf that had lost its mate.

About 3:00 P.M. Friday, June 18th,

Kenny had only been at Lisa's trailer about ten minutes before deciding that it was his last time there. As he was starting to hitch a ride, Mark came down the road in his yellow Toyota. Kenny knew from the moment he saw the car that it was Mark. He had seen Mark around town at some of the stores and fast food places but hadn't caught a ride with him again. There was no mistaking it was Mark. No one else around had a yellow Toyota like that one.

"Hey, where are you going?" Mark asked as he pulled alongside Kenny; stopping in the middle of the lane.

"Home, I guess."

"You still live where I dropped you off last?"

"Yep."

"Wanna 'another ride?"

"Hell, yeah!"

"Well climb yourself in here, then."

The two went down the road leaving a plume of white smoke like a Florida mosquito fogging truck.

"What the' hell ya been up to, boy?" Mark asked.

"Just walking mostly."

"Walking? Walking where? Why ya just walking?"

"Something to do, I guess."

Mark had no idea about Lisa's death. He never read the papers or had any real friends that would know it either.

"Man, you look like hell!" Mark said as he laughed.

"Thanks, man. You look sharp yourself."

"Well you are welcome," Mark said, continuing his evil sounding laugh. "What are friends for anyway?"

"So, we are friends now?"

"What the' hell you talkin' bout, man? You know it, man!"

"Cool," Kenny said half-heartedly.

"I'm thinkin' bout goin' back up north. If it wasn't for your old lady, you could go with me. You'd love it. I got some cool friends there," Mark said, in a hyped up, peppy way.

Kenny had noticed that during the entire conversation, Mark had been hyped up for some reason.

"What are you on dude?" Kenny asked.

"On?"

"Yeah, last time I was with you, you were all laid back. Now you're running like a rabbit."

"You're messing with me, man! I ain't on nothing!"

"If you say so."

"Hell yeah, I say so! What the hell is wrong with you, man? You the one all quiet."

"I just ain't got much to say."

"Something is up with you. What?"

"I don't wanna talk about it now."

"I knew there was sum-thin' eatin' you!"

"Man, you don't even know me, how can you know that anything's eating on me?"

"I know you, man! Hell, I know you like a damn brother!"

"You don't know nothing!"

"Hell, the first time I gave you a ride I knew who you were, man. You're just like me. You ain't got no place to live, and nobody cares about you, dude, 'cept maybe your ol' lady. Yeah, I know you, man!"

"The ol' lady, as you called her, got killed, man! So back off!"

"What? the' hell, you say!"

"She got killed in a wreck a couple weeks ago. So can ya just quit running your mouth?"

"You're freakin' me out! Damn! Sorry, man."

They were almost to Bo and JoBeth's place by this time. Mark pulled over at a cattle road not far from the trailer.

"What ya doin'?" Kenny asked.

"Hey, sorry bout my mouth, man. I had no damn clue, man."

"It's okay. Let's just go. I wanna go lay down."

"Hey, I got it!"

"You got what?"

"Like I was sayin', you got nobody here now, I am sorry bout your woman, but man, that's why you need to get away from here! Let's get the hell out of here and leave these damn bad memories here!"

For the first time since he had gotten into the car, Mark was saying something that made sense. But Kenny really didn't want to go with this guy. He figured he was half crazy and probably would get them killed in a wreck while he was hyped up. But he wondered where else did he have to go anyway?

"When you talkin' about goin'?"

"Right this damn minute! If you wanna go then let's just get the' hell outta here!"

Although Kenny hadn't worked a real job in a while, he had about fifty dollars from odd jobs. He had ninety-five more that Lisa had given him. It was in a tin box under his bed in his room.

He hadn't touched that money because he and Lisa were saving to get their own place. Now, he had no need to save, but he wasn't going to tell Mark about the money. He thought he might need it if things didn't work out between the two of them.

"You got money to go with?" Kenny asked.

"Got some, will get more when I see my uncle. You?"

"A little. What's some?"

"I dunno, dude, maybe like sixty bucks. But my uncle has more. He always has some cash lying around. He'll never miss it. We can make it," Mark insisted.

"I got fifty."

"Cool, then let's go!"

"I don't know. I guess I could. When?"

"Now! I will run to the camper and get some stuff, then by my uncle's, and be back here in less than an hour. I got one stop to make first."

"Okay, I'll be here."

"Don't you try to back out, man! I am countin' on ya!"

"I ain't gonna back out. Just get back here. I'll be ready."

Kenny got out of the car after Mark pulled up to the trailer. Mark tried to speed out of the drive but only caused another plume of white smoke to cover the entire front of the property. Kenny went into the house and told JoBeth what he was about to do. Bo wasn't there, but JoBeth said she would tell him. Kenny went into his room to get his things and the cash.

After collecting his things he went into the living room to wait on Mark. After about five minutes, JoBeth came out of her room in just a t-shirt and white socks. Kenny squinted his eyes to see if what he thought he was seeing was real.

"What are you doing!?" Kenny asked her.

"Bo won't find out, he went with his cousin to Plant City and won't be back until late."

Kenny's heart was pounding. For a brief moment, he thought about it, then he had a flashback of his last time with Lisa, and suddenly all those thoughts and desires vanished. He still missed Lisa and was heartsick.

"No way!"

"Why not?"

"Cause Bo is my friend, even if I don't like him most of the time. I couldn't do that to him or anybody!"

JoBeth was thin and built very well. Kenny had a hard time looking away, but he managed to turn and walk toward the kitchen.

"It's not fair to Bo, and it's not fair to Lisa!" He said, as he reached into a cabinet for a glass and filled it with water.

"Lisa?"

"Yeah, Lisa. She is still my girl in my heart and ain't no way I could do anything with any other woman until she ain't there no more."

After Kenny brought up Lisa JoBeth had a sudden attack of guilt. She picked up a blanket and held it in front of her.

"I am sorry Kenny. I wasn't thinking about you still loving Lisa. I just always liked you, but you were always talkin' bout Lisa, and I knew you would never give me the time of day."

"Don't you love Bo?" Kenny asked.

"Yeah, well, I like him. But sometimes he is a jerk and besides he gets to drinking and leaves me cold! Sometimes he is a real moron."

"I sure didn't see that coming."

"I know. Let me get dressed. I will be out in a minute. I wanna hug before you leave."

"Okay," Kenny said with relief, as he emptied the still full glass of water into the sink.

JoBeth got dressed in less than a minute while Kenny stood in the main room of the trailer. She walked over to Kenny and gave him a tight hug. When he started to say something she grabbed his head and pulled his face down to hers and kissed him on the mouth. He began to pull back but then gave in and kissed her goodbye.

"Dang, that was good!" JoBeth said while staring at Kenny.

"Yeah, not bad."

They stood there looking a little awkward for a few seconds until Kenny heard a car pull into the yard so quickly that it kicked up gravel from the road. At first, he thought it may be Bo and even though nothing happened except for a kiss the whole thing was a little unnerving to him. When he heard the horn blowing as soon as it pulled in, he knew it was Mark.

"Bye, JoBeth. Thanks for everything and letting me hang here."

"Come back, Kenny. You can come back if you wanna."

"Sure," Kenny replied, knowing he would never stay with Bo and JoBeth again. He may be over Lisa at some point, and he may not be able to refuse her again. It was best to leave things as they were. He turned to leave, and JoBeth grabbed him and pulled him to her and kissed him again. The panic he had with the car pulling in caused Kenny to pull back quickly. He tried to kiss her on her forehead, but she moved, so he kissed her nose instead. They both laughed and said goodbye.

"Let's go, man!" Mark said.

"Ready," Kenny replied as he opened the rear door on his side and threw his things in the back.

"Oh! Wait! Be right back."

"Hey! Where ya goin'? Hurry! Let's get out of here."

Kenny grabbed a few of his tools and threw them in a box and grabbed his fishing tackle box and his fishing rod. He noticed that the pole was broken. He got mad and just threw it down, but he took his tackle box and some tools just in case they were needed. He didn't want to leave them there.

"Ready!" Kenny said as he jumped back into the running car.

"Good, what is that stuff?"

"Tools and fishing stuff."

"Fishing stuff? Ya mean like bait and hooks and stuff like that?"

"Yeah, but not live bait."

"We ain't gonna do no fishin', man! That's funny! My man brings fish bait," Mark said laughing.

They left the driveway and headed north. The gas tank was on empty, so about ten miles up the road they stopped for gas. Kenny gave Mark twenty dollars. Mark took the twenty and put fifteen more with it, and it almost filled up the tank. While Mark was in the store paying for gas, Kenny went to the restroom. Mark quickly stole several items of food and put them down his pants and into his underwear. He waved at the store clerk and walked out. Kenny was coming out at the same time.

"Let's go, you drive," Mark said.

"Me?"

"You can drive, right?"

"Yeah, but I lost my license."

"Lost them?"

"I have them, but they are no good! They got suspended for not paying a fine."

"So, we will switch seats if we get stopped. And don't speed, man, but hurry and let's get out of here. I took some stuff from the store. No one saw me, but let's get out of here in case!"

"Great! And you want me to drive?"

"Just go!"

Kenny shook his head but jumped in the driver's seat and took off, leaving another trail of white fog.

It wasn't long until it was dark. They soon hit I-75 and headed north to Ohio. Mark wanted out of the state of Florida as fast as possible.

CHAPTER TEN

DeSoto County

Early afternoon - Saturday, June 19th

A Desoto County deputy sheriff received a call to do a welfare check on a farmer in a remote area of the county. The mail carrier was attempting to deliver a package at the small farm. When he went to the door to knock, he thought he saw a figure of a man laying on the floor. After not getting an answer, the carrier went to the house closest to the farm and called the sheriff's office.

After the deputy arrived, he found an older man laying lifeless on the floor. A quick check of the body by the deputy revealed that the man was dead and might have been shot. Desoto County investigators were called to the scene and found that Shelton had been shot two times in the mid-chest and two times in the lower back area.

There was no real way to tell the exact time of death, but he was in the late stage of rigor mortis. The body was very stiff.

The body was lying with the face down but more on the right side. The investigators found three spent rounds from a .25 caliber handgun on the front porch just outside the front door. Just to the left side of the storm door, in the door frame, was a freshly made small hole, probably a bullet hole. That meant the shooter fired at least five rounds. But they only found three spent shells. The investigators wondered about the other two spent rounds.

It took most of the day to collect all the evidence and check the rest of the property for further clues. A deputy questioned the closest neighbors about possibly seeing anyone on the farm in the last two days but no one had seen anything notable.

Ned Tilly was a farmer a few miles away. Tilly and Shelton were old drinking buddies, although they hadn't had a drink together for more than ten years. When Tilly heard about his friend, he drove to Shelton's place. Tilly had been to see Shelton the morning before. Tilly had fixed a log splitter for Shelton and brought it back. He told investigators that they talked for about twenty minutes and he left about eight-fifteen that morning. He said that Shelton told him he was going to the bank and then was coming back to work on a tractor. Since Shelton's only family was a couple of nieces and a nephew from Ohio, Tilly was the closest person around Shelton. Tilly advised the investigators that Shelton was careful to never have more than a hundred dollars or so around the house. He wasn't known to carry money or have a lot of wealth. He was a simple farmer and lived a simple life alone on his farm.

Tilly asked the investigators if they had talked with Mark, Shelton's great-nephew. Tilly told them the location of the camper. A couple of DeSoto County deputies went to find the camper and speak with the nephew. When they found the camper, they discovered the front door was open. They went inside the camper to see if there were any signs of a break-in or foul play. What they found inside the camper were strange paintings on poster boards. Some were various hexagrams, and hexagrams drawn into other symbols and images. There were upside down crosses in some of the paintings. Others had strange looking goat heads with other symbols and signs drawn around them. The deputies counted about 40 different drawings and paintings around the walls in the camper. There were paintings tacked to the ceiling. Paintings in the windows blocked the outside light.

Just inside the front door, they saw an empty box of .25 caliber shells on the floor. Some clothes were on the floor, and most of the cabinets and drawers in the camper were open. There were about a dozen half-burnt candles around the camper. Four of the candles were on a small coffee table beside one of the paintings. They decided to back out of the camper, advise the investigators of their findings, and see if a search warrant was in order. One of the deputies remained on the property in his patrol car.

Back at the farm, Detective Sergeant John Gates was heading up the investigation. Deputy Phil Jacobs left the camper and drove back to see Sergeant Gates. By this time, Mitchell Delvecchio, an investigator from the State Attorney's Office, was on the scene. Delvecchio had previously worked for NYPD before moving to Florida.

Sometimes a transplanted investigator from New York City to a smaller southern area can have a difficult time adjusting and gaining the respect of the local cops. Such was not the case with Delvecchio. He had a strong New York accent but had the manners of an old southern gentleman. Instead of always giving his opinion, he asked others for their opinion first. While Delvecchio had a laid-back personal style, his attention to detail and ability to read a crime scene made him invaluable to a lead detective. When on a case he was solicitous about finding the truth. He had been instrumental in several major investigations in his district but always gave credit to his co-workers. He viewed his job as helping to get the right evidence to prosecute the bad guys successfully. He was respected by most investigators in his district and was a welcomed sight to Sergeant Gates.

Deputy Jacobs let Sergeant Gates know by radio that he needed to speak with him but did not enter the crime scene area. Gates and Delvecchio both met Deputy Jacobs at the road. Jacobs advised the two men of his findings at the camper. Delvecchio became very interested in what the deputies had seen. He told Gates that he would help Jacobs secure a search warrant for the camper.

Hearing about the box of empty shells apparently caught Delvecchio's attention, but he was also very interested in the open drawers and cabinets and the occult artwork. Delvecchio followed Jacobs back to the camper to get a better physical description and exact location of the property. He took some photos of the camper from the outside to attach to the affidavit for the search warrant. Both Jacob and Delvecchio went to Delvecchio's office and then to find a judge. The other patrol deputy remained on the property. He pulled his patrol unit across the drive but away from the camper. He wasn't afraid of the occult, but the things they had seen in the camper gave him the creeps. He was satisfied to stay in his patrol car until the others returned.

About three hours later, Delvecchio and Jacob returned and executed the search warrant. They found 38 occult type paintings and drawings. Most of the drawings or paintings contained a snake head in some form. Red and black were the only colors used in the majority of the art pieces. Each one had been signed, "MM" at the bottom. They also found two empty boxes of .25 automatic shells. Each box held fifty rounds. Photographs were taken of the camper, showing all the drawers and cabinet doors left open and a few clothes scattered on the floor. There was nothing in the camper that had Mark's full name, address, or any personal information. They were still going through Tom Shelton's place to see if they could find any family contact information.

Mark Manning was certainly a person of interest now in the murder of Tom Shelton, but at this point, they didn't even know Mark's last name. Other than the few things they found in the camper, Gates and Delvecchio didn't have much to go on at this point. They talked for a few moments about what they had so far.

Gates started by saying, "Well, the way I see it, this is what we have right now. Sometime in the last two days, Shelton was shot four times. There are three .25 shell casings outside Shelton's front door. A subject named Mark, who may have been a nephew of the victim, had been staying in a camper on Shelton's property. What else?"

Delvecchio added, "two boxes of the same type of shells found on Shelton's porch were in the camper. Someone at the camper had stored paintings that looked like signs and symbols of the occult. The inside of the camper looked as if someone left in a hurry, and Mark was not at the camper or his uncle's home."

"I guess that sums it up for now. Lots of work ahead on this one," Gates concluded.

Gates and his investigators completed the work at both the farmhouse and the camper, packed up all the evidence, and had Shelton's body taken to the morgue. An autopsy was conducted on the body of Shelton the next morning.

Gates and Delvecchio both attended the autopsy to take notes and photographs and learn any possible new clues. The forensic pathologist, Doctor Gene Phillips, did the autopsy. Doctor Phillips recovered four lead bullet fragments from Shelton's body and would send them to the Florida Department of Law-Enforcement Criminal Laboratory for examination.

Doctor Phillips' autopsy report showed that the cause of death was a penetrating gunshot wound to the chest. He listed one of the bullets as the exact cause of death and the other three as probably survivable. He wrote that the entrance of the fatal shot was on the left chest and was from an intermediate range. The path of the projectile was through the skin, right, anterior 4th intercostal space, pericardial sac, left ventricle of the heart.

The direction of the fatal bullet was directly front to back. There was no exit wound noted. He listed the manner of death as a homicide at the hands of another. They also attempted to identify any rifling on the bullet fragments left by the barrel as it exited the weapon. However, to the trained eyes of Gates and Delvecchio, they were nearly positive that the bullets were from a .25 automatic pistol. Also, the contents of Shelton's stomach were almost empty, but there was enough to indicate that he had probably eaten something between eight, and twelve hours before death. That could help the investigators narrow the time of mortality to sometime the previous evening.

CHAPTER ELEVEN

Keri

Early hours - Saturday morning – June 19th

Mark and Kenny were getting sleepy after almost four hours of driving and decided to pull into a rest area. The two were restless for a little while after stopping and almost drove on. They finally fell asleep sometime after one in the morning, and slept for nearly six hours.

Once us, they drove a short while and then got off the interstate in the small city of Alachua. Mark still felt an urgency to get out of Florida, but having more than 200 miles between him and DeSota, County seemed to allow the stress to subside somewhat.

After grabbing something to eat at a McDonald's they moved on. They stayed off the interstate for a while and drove north on US Highway 441. They weren't sure how to get back to the interstate, so they stopped at a store to get directions. They bought some cigarettes, got directions, and got back on the road. Mark was driving.

About ten miles up the road, they saw three people hitch hiking. They couldn't tell much about them until they got close. There were two teenage girls and a guy in his early twenties.

Mark pulled up beside them, and Kenny rolled down his window.

"Hey, where ya going?" Mark yelled out Kenny's window.

The guy spoke up, "Atlanta, how far Y'all going?"

"Going through there. Jump in." Mark ordered.

There wasn't much room in the back seat for all three of them. They each carried a small bag carrying their clothes. Mark hopped out of the car and opened the trunk and threw his and Kenny's stuff in the trunk. That gave the trio more room to sit.

"Hey, cops looking for you guys?" Mark asked as he sent another flume of smoke.

"No," both girls said, giggling at saying it at the same time.

"How old are you guys?" Mark continued the interrogation.

The blonde who looked like she might be fourteen spoke up, "I'm eighteen."

"Bull!" Mark fired back.

The girl laughed. "No bull, man, I'm eighteen. Ain't I, Jimmy?" she said as she looked at their male companion.

"That's what you tell people," Jimmy replied.

"That's because I am!"

"Bull! Tell me the truth, or I'm gonna put your butt out right here!" Mark told her.

The other girl spoke up. "She's fifteen."

"Keri!" The blonde yelled at the other girl.

"Well, it's true, Tiff. You are the same age as me. We are fifteen!" The girl called, Keri said.

"Jail-bait!" Kenny laughingly said while looking straight ahead.

"Fifteen huh?" Mark said.

"Yup," Keri replied.

"Hell, I know you are as old as me, dude," Mark said, talking to Jimmy.

"Probably," he answered back.

"I'm twenty-two."

The car was quiet for a while except the constant rattling of the muffler as it vibrated against the bottom of the car. It wasn't long until they were back on I-75 heading north. Soon, they were out of Florida and into Georgia.

Tiff Todd, Keri Mendez, and Jimmy Singleton were all from Ocala, Florida. They had run away from home the day before. Jimmy had a brother in the Atlanta area, so they were headed to see him. Tiff's mom found out that Tiff and Jimmy were having sex and she called the police. Before the police got to their house, Tiff left and went to her friend, Keri's house. Keri lived with her grandmother and had done so since she was eight. Keri's mother had been in and out of rehab for the last several years. Her mother had started using drugs when she was fourteen, got pregnant with Keri's brother when she was fifteen, and pregnant with Keri when she was seventeen. The heavy drug use had taken its toll on her.

By the time Keri was six her mother couldn't take care of herself let alone her kids. They were in and out of foster care until her older brother ran away from one of the foster homes. No one ever heard from him again. Keri thought that maybe he had died somehow. She figured if he was still alive that he would have come back for her at some point. Finally, Keri's grandmother stepped in and took Keri.

Her grandmother was a kind woman but had health issues and was not able to keep up with Keri when she got to be a teenager. Keri pretty much came and went as she pleased. Her grandmother tried to say something to her to correct her, but Keri just hugged her and said, "I know grandma, I'll do better," and then go on doing the same things.

When Tiff got to Keri's house, Keri was in her bedroom. Tiff walked into the house without knocking, said hi to Keri's grandmother, and went into Keri's bedroom. Tiff told Keri what had happened. They both agreed that when the police found out about Tiff and Jimmy, it would be jail for Jimmy. They packed a few clothes in a small bag. They both wore each other's clothes, so Tiff didn't have to go back home to get any clothes. They knew they could find Jimmy at the auto repair shop where he worked a few blocks away.

Jimmy grabbed a few things, and they left town, catching a ride in the bed of a pickup with a camper shell. They were dropped off near Fort White and were walking when Mark and Kenny picked them up.

After being in the cramped car for an hour or so Tiff and Jimmy began to argue over an old boyfriend. Before long, Tiff slapped Jimmy across the face.

Jimmy was no older than Tiff and Keri mentally and emotionally. He was a big kid who had gotten mixed up with an under-aged girl. Since there were seven years between their ages, he was facing a sex-offense charge if caught.

Keri told Tiff that she should not have told Jimmy that she missed her old boyfriend and that she was stupid. Soon the two girls were arguing.

"I told you guys to shut the hell up!" Mark yelled as he slammed on the brakes sending everyone forward.

"You're crazy man!" Jimmy yelled back.

"I'll show you crazy!" Mark said as he slid the car off the side of the road and jumped out.

Everyone, including Jimmy, was stunned at him sliding off the road and just sat still for a moment. Mark went around to Jimmy's door, opened it, and grabbed Jimmy. Jimmy pushed him back with his foot.

"Get the hell off of me man!" Jimmy yelled.

Mark swung a fist and hit Jimmy just below the eye causing it to bleed. Jimmy dove out of the car and tackled Mark knocking him to the ground. Jimmy punched him a couple of times in the head and once in the chest. It was obvious that Jimmy was a better fighter than Mark.

Tiff was the only other person to get out of the car. She grabbed Jimmy by the arm and pulled him off Mark. As Tiff and Jimmy argued over her pulling him off, Mark jumped into the car and took off.

"What are you doing?!" Keri yelled.

"Leaving their asses."

"Why? Let me out!"

"No, you have nowhere to go, so you can go with us," Marked said in a normal tone.

Kenny looked at Mark and said, "Are you crazy? We don't want no jail bait with us!"

"Shut up! My car, my call!"

"You are nuts man, if they catch us with her in here, we will be locked up for a long time. Not me man!"

"We'll tell 'em she is your sister. You guys look alike," Mark said as he laughed.

Kenny continued to object, but it fell on deaf ears. Keri stopped begging and sat back in the seat.

Keri was a cute girl. She had dark brown hair, which was cut short to show her ears. She had a fair complexion, rosy cheeks, and big blue eyes. She was about five feet tall and weighed around 105 pounds. She wore loose-fitting clothes most of the time—a pair of jeans, a peasant top, and tennis shoes. While Tiff had already had a few boyfriends, Keri was still a virgin. It's not something she talked about a lot, she just never met the right guy, she once told Tiff.

Keri had a gentle spirit about her most of the time. She smiled a lot and laugh often. When Keri smiled, it would make her entire face seem to light up. She was quiet around people unless she knew them well. She did okay in school but never had the help at home to stand out educationally.

They drove another few hours and decided to get off the interstate between Macon and Atlanta and stop at a state park. They all took a long walk in the park and went down some nature trails. Mark purposely held back and walked with Keri while Kenny just wanted to keep his distance from her and Mark.

Kenny had gotten several hundred yards ahead of Mark and Keri. Mark stopped and sat down on a fallen tree that was laying five or six feet off the path. He told Keri to come sit with him. She just stood on the trail for a few moments and looked up toward where she thought Kenny might be.

"Come on, sit down. I ain't gonna bite ya," Mark said to Keri.

Keri turned and looked at Mark but didn't move. "Let's just catch up with him."

"No, he will be okay. We'll catch up later, or he will come back. Just come sit down."

"I don't wanna sit; we've been sittin' in the car."

"Dang girl, come sit down and let's talk."

Finally, Keri gave in and stepped off the dirt path into the wooded area where the fallen tree was supporting Mark. She stood about three feet from him. Keri didn't really like Mark and didn't feel comfortable with him. She liked Kenny better, even though he didn't seem to want her around. After a little while, Keri finally sat down about four feet from Mark on the fallen tree.

"Why don't you like me?" Mark said while looking right at Keri.

"I like you okay."

"Then why are you sitting so far away?"

"I like you, okay, but I don't want to sit on top of you."

"I think I'd like you sittin' on top of me," Mark said laughing.

"Ha-ha!" Keri said with a smirk on her face.

"I think I would like that a lot."

"Glad you think so."

"I think you would like sitting on top of me too."

"I think you are crazy."

Mark stood up and got in front of Keri.

"What are you doing?" Keri said as she backed up on the log a little.

"I think I want you to sit on me."

"No way! Get away from me."

"No, you are gonna do me."

"Do you?! I ain't doing you! Just move!" Keri replied as she tried to get off the log, pushing Mark.

Mark grabbed her arm and pulled her off the tree and over behind the tree on a sandy clearing that was partially covered with pine nettles. He began to pull at the bottom of her jeans, trying to lift them up and off. She took her hands and held down her pants and yelled at him to stop. But he continued by grabbing at her pants with both hands, trying to unbutton them. She pushed with both hands against his chest trying to break free. He got her jeans unfastened and was about to get them unzipped when she spun around and broke free and tried to run back toward the path. Mark grabbed her from behind by the top of her pants and pulled her to the ground. He quickly jumped on top of her chest with his groin area near her throat and his knees in the sand. He looked at her and laughed as she continued to twist and turn in an attempt to get loose. He yelled at her to stop, but she kept struggling.

"If you don't stop fighting me, I'm gonna choke you down right here, I swear!" Mark said, as he slid his left hand up near her throat and pressed inward.

Keri stopped struggling and looked at Mark with a look of disbelief at what was happening. She had never had a fight with anyone, and now this grown man was sitting on top of her chest and about to choke and rape her. She just wanted to be back home with her grandmother or with Jimmy and Tiff.

"I will! I'll kill you right here, and no one will find you for days, if ever!"

Tears started to ease out of Keri's eyes. Mark eased his grip on her throat and began to slide his knees back toward her hips. Suddenly Kenny grabbed Mark's shirt collar from behind and yanked him off of Keri.

"What in the hell are you doin'?" Kenny yelled at Mark as he let go of his shirt.

Mark flipped around, still on the ground, and quickly reached into his pocket and pulled out a pistol and pointed it at Kenny.

"I'm gonna kill both of you right here!" Marked yelled, as he rotated pointing the gun between the two.

"Are you crazy!? Put the stupid gun down, Mark!" Kenny yelled back, somewhat shocked at seeing a gun in Mark's hand for the first time.

"You get out of here, or I'll kill you both right now."

Kenny looked at Keri who was sitting up but still on the ground. Her eyes were wide open and looking straight at Kenny.

"So you are gonna kill me over getting your piece of jail bait?"

"Your damn right I will!"

"Go ahead, and when they catch you, they will put you in jail for life."

"Nobody's gonna catch me unless you snitch!"

"So you just gonna kill her when you're done?"

"Don't know yet," Mark said as he glanced back at Keri.

"Well, kill me too then, Mark!"

"No problem! I will!" Mark said as he raised the gun toward

Kenny's head.

"Stop!" Keri said, "Don't kill him or me! I'll do it!"

Kenny looked at Mark with the gun in his hand and back at Keri and shook his head no but didn't say anything for fear that Mark was actually serious.

"I've killed before. Don't think for a moment I won't kill either of you."

This guy is crazy, Kenny thought.

"Nobody will be able to tell nothing on you cause it ain't rape if I agree to do it," Keri yelled, trying to stop any thoughts of killing that Mark had.

Mark stood up keeping the gun pointed at Kenny.

"Did you hear her? Now get out of here!"

Keri looked at Kenny for a brief moment, then laid down on the ground and looked at Mark. Mark started taking down his pants as Keri slowly unzipped hers. Kenny stood still for a moment, then turned and walked toward the car. He knew that both he and Keri were in trouble. He had to play this smart for both of them. He thought about just walking off and heading back south, but he couldn't just leave Keri in the hands of Mark. He wondered if Mark would kill Keri after he raped her. He decided that he could not take that chance. He knew he wasn't the best person in the world, but he could not let Mark rape this young girl. Not without a fight. He had to stop him, even if it cost him his life.

Kenny quietly moved back behind Mark. Neither Keri nor Mark saw him slip back into the area. Keri's pants were already off, and Mark's were around his ankles. Mark was pulling up her top as Kenny got closer. He grabbed Mark by the neck from behind and dragged him to the ground. Keri scrambled to get up and into the thicker woods a few feet away. She could still see Mark and Kenny fighting for control. Mark tried to reach into his pocket to get his gun, but Kenny was more powerful and kept his arms pulled back away from his body.

Kenny managed to get Mark face down on the ground and place a knee in the middle of his back while holding his head down.

"Okay, get up!" Mark yelled.

"No way, not while you have that gun," Kenny responded.

"I'm not gonna shoot you, dammit! I was not gonna kill you, I just wanted you to leave."

"I don't believe you," Kenny said while keeping Mark's head held against the ground.

"Why would I shoot you over screwing a girl? I was just mad cause you wouldn't leave. What is she to you anyway, dude?"

"She is a kid, and I ain't letting anyone mess with a kid."

"I just lost it for a little while man. Hey, I'm human. I just wasn't thinking about her being so young. You're right, man. I shouldn't have tried it. Now let me up and let's get out of here."

Kenny held him down a little longer then decided to let him up.

"You may have that gun, but if you try that again, I'll beat the hell out of you—gun or no gun. Got it?" Kenny yelled.

"Okay already, man. I said I wouldn't do it no more."

"Give me the gun," Kenny demanded.

Mark started laughing, "You sure you want to be caught with this gun? It can be traced, man. Back to my dead uncle."

Kenny thought for a moment about having the gun. He could just get rid of the gun, he thought.

"You're gonna have to kill me to get this gun, man. I'm not going around unarmed," Mark stated.

Kenny decided to let him keep it. He got the jump on him once while he had the gun, he thought. He could do it again if he had to. He let go of Mark and got off the ground. Mark got up and headed back toward the parking lot. Kenny looked around but didn't see Keri. He figured that she was long gone and he was sort of glad. That way, Mark wouldn't mess with her again, he thought.

As Kenny was walking back to the car, Keri came from behind some trees and started walking with him. Nothing was said at first. They just walked together, as if nothing had happened. Neither of them had intended to get into this situation. They didn't know what they would do about it. Keri took some comfort in knowing that Kenny would most likely try to protect her. Kenny felt good that he stood up to Mark and kept him from harming Keri. But neither knew what to do next, so they just walked.

"He won't bother you again," Kenny said in a quiet voice after a few minutes.

"Thanks!" Keri replied, briefly glancing up toward Kenny as they continued to walk.

Who is this person they are riding with? Kenny wondered. Had he been blind and not seen Mark's true colors? Now he worried about what else Mark would drag him into. What else had Mark done that he would be dragged into? He was scared, puzzled, and a little angry. It was certain that their relationship had changed. Kenny just wanted to get to where they were going and get away from Mark. Never having experienced anything as they had just experienced, neither Keri or Kenny could come to terms with it enough to just run. It was all still so surreal. So they just continued toward Mark and the ride they thought they needed.

When Kenny and Keri got to the parking lot, they saw Mark sitting on the hood of the car.

When Mark saw them, he got into the driver's seat of the car and yelled, "let's go, if you are going. Get in the front," Mark told Keri as she approached the car.

Kenny glared at Mark as he opened the back door to the car.

"Go ahead and get in the back. It's okay," Kenny said to Keri while keeping his eyes on Mark.

No one said a word for the first thirty minutes after they left. Kenny looked out the side window the whole time while Keri stared at her feet. Mark sipped on a warm coke that he had left in the car seat and drove without even glancing at Kenny.

"How much money do you have left?" Mark finally said as he turned briefly and looked at Kenny.

Kenny turned his head from looking at the trees and guardrail they were passing and looked at Mark. "I dunno."

"Well check dammit! I'm getting low, and we will need some gas soon."

"Eighteen."

"Eighteen? Just eighteen damn dollars?"

"Plus some change."

"Do you have any money?" Mark glanced back and addressed the question to Keri.

"A little," Keri answered.

"How much is a little?"

"I don't know, maybe twenty or so."

"That's great! We're already out of money!" No one but Mark was thinking of food, but he wanted to eat, so he pulled into a small country grocery store.

"Give me your money," he told Keri.

She reached into her jeans pocket, pulled out a twenty dollar bill, and laid it in his opened hand. He took the money and put it in his shirt pocket, got out of the car, and went into the store. Keri and Kenny just sat there.

"It won't happen again, I promise," Kenny said as he turned around toward Keri.

"Really? So you are gonna take the gun away from him next time?"

"If I have to. I'll do something, you can believe that."

"Thanks, but I hope not. He is crazy. We just need to get away from him."

"We will, but we have to pick the right time. Neither of us has any money or a car. Plus, he still has that gun. I should have made him give it to me back there. Sometimes I just don't think. Why I trusted him and let him up, I don't know! But, maybe he won't try anything again."

CHAPTER TWELVE
Lazy Sleeper Motel

After the details of Fisher and his car were put on the NCIC, Rivers hoped that a break would come sooner rather than later. It wasn't long before he got his wish. Early the following morning, the on-call detective, who happened to be Jesse Hawkins, called Rivers at home. Rivers had been awake since four-thirty that morning. He lay in bed and let all the wheels turn in his head.

"Hey Chief, this is Jesse, sorry to bother you, but I think we got a break in the Fisher case."

"That's okay Jesse, I've been awake about an hour. What's up?"

"Some people at a place in Kentucky may have seen our car," Jesse said.

"What kind of a place?"

"It was a motel. From what I understand, some maids saw a couple of guys back up to a dumpster and take the tag off the car. Then they apparently threw it in the dumpster," Hawkins replied.

"Where did you get this Jesse?"

"I was called by communications a little before one this morning. Mike Johnson, the night supervisor at 911, decided to run a tracer on the info you gave communications earlier. It came back that a Whitley County deputy in Kentucky ran Fisher's tag, but that was before we had the information on Fisher," Hawkins continued.

"So, Johnson got a hit back on the tag and gave it to you?"

"Not at first, he called Whitley County to see who had run the tag and what the circumstances were. Their 911 pulled up the CAD report and saw that the tag was recovered from a dumpster by the deputy."

"Did Johnson get the deputy's name?"

"Oh yeah, Mike is good."

"Yeah, that sounds like him."

"Anyway, Mike called me, and I went to the 911 Center and talked with him and got copies of everything."

"What day did this happen at the motel, Jesse?'

"From what he says, they were there Sunday night, the night of the shooting, or actually the early morning hours of Monday. I called Whitley County, and they connected me with their on-call detective. First thing this morning he is going to go to the motel and see if he can talk with the maids and motel clerk. Just check things out for us."

"Okay, yeah, sounds good. I'm going to go ahead and shower and come on in. Are you going to hang around since you have been up all night?"

"Yeah, I'll be here for a few more hours anyway. I would like to see what comes of this if anything."

"Oh, something will come of it, just what, I don't know. I'll see ya in a few."

"Okay Chief."

⭐

Tuesday, June 22nd 8:00 A.M.

MEANWHILE, A little further up north in Whitley County Kentucky, Detective John Decker finished his short nap after being awakened by the call from Tennessee. He headed to the office in Williamsburg, collected some notes, a pocket recorder, and the report from the deputy who recovered the tag. He drove to the Lazy Sleeper Motel.

Along the way he stopped for breakfast at Mother Bess' Kitchen. He knew he could get a good meal there in case his day got to be a long one. Decker had been in Special Forces in the Army, but since then he hadn't focused on his fitness. He was thirty-seven years old, ran two miles, three times a week, and ate what he wanted. He was about thirty pounds over his ideal weight but couldn't care less. He could still handle himself when the going got tough, and to him, that was good enough. He no longer enjoyed the two hours of daily fitness training that it took to stay in top shape.

Before Decker was promoted to a detective, he was known as a tough street cop. Even in the hills of Kentucky, he had faced some tough people and scary situations. He had to shoot a man once as the man came at him with a double-barrel shotgun after beating his girlfriend. The man got off one of the barrels before Decker shot him three times "center mass" and stopped him. The pellets from the shotgun struck Decker in his bullet-resistant vest and in his left arm. The perpetrator died on the way to the hospital. The girlfriend suffered a broken neck and was in a wheelchair the rest of her life. Decker suffered a broken rib and damage to the muscle in his bicep, which was later repaired in surgery.

"Good morning, John!" Pam Lawton, who was cleaning the table closest to the door, yelled as he walked through the door.

"Good morning, Pam. Where are you working today?"

responded Detective Decker.

"Just sit anywhere. I will get ya."

"Okay, I'll just sit here." Decker picked the last seat closest to the back wall.

Pam brought Decker a cup of coffee. There was no need to ask him if he wanted cream; she never knew a cop who drank coffee any way but black. She pulled up the chair beside him, laid her order pad on the table, and took a seat.

"So how have ya been? I haven't seen ya in over a week. Don't ya love me no more?" She looked him in the eyes and smiled.

"I'll always love you, Pam. You know that. I've been out of town mostly. Went to pick up a prisoner in Kansas City last week. Took me four days, by the time I got there and had to wait for the judge to let him go. Thought we had it cleared to pick him up until some loser of a lawyer decided at the last minute to file some dang writ."

"A writ?"

"Yeah, something lawyers write up to give to a judge to cause us cops trouble."

"What kind of trouble?"

"Not really trouble, but it's usually just some sort of a delay tactic to make it look like they are earning their money. Usually, they ain't worth the paper they're written on."

"Oh. Alright then, what do you want with your eggs today, Hun?"

"Just scramble me three with some sausage and biscuits and gravy."

"Grits?"

Decker looked up at her and frowned. "Like you have to ask!"

"Just checkin', smarty."

"Hey, you got today's paper laying around here anywhere?"

"I'll check, bring it when I come back with more coffee."

Detective John Decker and Pam Lawton had known each other back before she worked at Bess' and before he was a cop. Not long after Decker got out of the Army, they had both worked at Cumberland College in Williamsburg. He had been employed in maintenance, and she had worked in housekeeping. They met and dated about a year. Later, he got a job at the sheriff's office and went to the Kentucky Police Academy for eight weeks. When he returned to Williamsburg, she was with another guy. Looking back, he thought something might have been up a few weeks into the academy when he stopped getting her letters. During the weekends the academy allowed phone calls, but she didn't answer or return his calls. By the time he got home, he was prepared for the news and moved on with his life quickly. She married the guy about six months later. That was eleven years earlier. She was divorced now, and John had never married. He thought about asking her out a time or two, but each time he remembered the academy and never asked her.

Pam brought his breakfast, then walked past him and slightly messed up his hair with her fingers. He turned his head in her direction and raised his eyebrows. She chuckled and kept walking.

Decker finished breakfast, left a nickel on the table as a tip, and stuck a five-dollar bill under the plate where she couldn't see it.

"See ya Pam, and by the way your service today wasn't worth a plug nickel," Decker said with a big grin as he walked to the door after paying the check.

"Get out of here!" Pam replied with both hands on her hips and cracking a smile.

Decker headed to the motel. He was hoping to make contact with someone about the tag and find out what they had seen. He had spoken with Detective Hawkins, from Tennessee, in the early hours of the morning. He knew the importance of his mission. As he arrived at the motel, his mind flashed back to the year before when he had worked a homicide in one of the rooms. The victim was a woman who had been strangled with a necktie. He never forgot witnessing the blue and gold tie pulled so tightly around her neck that it broke the skin in several places. The woman was a beautiful twenty-eight-year-old real estate agent from Lexington. She had vanished one day after showing a home in an exclusive neighborhood in Lexington. The people to whom she had shown the house were cleared, but no one had a clue where she went after that appointment or how she ended up in Williamsburg. She had been divorced for over a year. There were some ongoing property disputes from the divorce, but the ex-husband had been out of town that week with his girlfriend. The case remained a mystery for both Whitley County Sheriff's Office and Lexington PD. Decker briefly read through the notes again that he had taken from his conversation with Johnson and re-read the report from his own department.

Ekani Nehru was the manager of the motel. Nehru was of Indian decent and spoke English but with a thick accent. He remembered Decker from the previous year and all the trips back since that time. He was used to Decker coming by.

Decker turned on his pocket recorder as he walked into the office. Nehru looked up from his desk but didn't stand up.

"Any news?" Nehru asked.

"No, but I'm here on something different today. Do you remember a deputy coming here yesterday and talking to someone about a tag that was taken off of a car and put in the dumpster?" Decker asked.

"Oh yeah, I was here," Nehru said.

"Did you see who took the tag off the car or anyone that was in the car?" Decker continued.

"Oh no, housekeeping saw them, but I saw one of them when

he came in to get a room."

"They came in here to get a room?" Decker asked wondering if it could be that easy.

"Oh yes, oh yes, I saw the one. He gave me his name and his license. It was late, so I said 'okay you stay but pay now.'"

"Did you write down his name for your records. Did he sign in?"

"Oh yes, I always write the name. Here on a card. I always write the name."

Nehru showed Decker a motel registration card that was signed by someone named Kenny Saxton. He wrote down the address of 1222 Pine Level Road Arcadia, FL.

"I'll need to take this with me. I'll give you a receipt for it, and you can get it back later if you need it," Decker advised Nehru.

"Oh, no, I no need it, you can keep that."

"Who saw them take the tag off and put it in the dumpster?"

"Housekeeping, Debbie, and Doris, they told me they both saw."

"Where are they now?"

"They are both here. Working now."

"May I speak with them?"

"Yes, I'll go get them."

"Uh, just one at a time, please. Is there somewhere I can talk with them?"

"Yes, use my office. You may use my office."

Decker waited in the lobby for Nehru to get one of the witnesses. Nehru's office was full of boxes and was a little cramped, so he decided to just talk with them outside to get the information. He could get a full statement after he knew what they had to say.

The two women walked behind Nehru as they all returned to the office to see Decker. Doris McBride was older than her co-worker by more than 30 years, but in watching the two of them walk with Nehru, it was evident which one had the most energy and worked the hardest; McBride. The younger of the two, Debbie Snider, was in her early thirties and looked like she had lived a somewhat rough life during those thirty-plus years. She put her cigarette in an outside ashtray just before she arrived at the front office. She took a piece of gum out of the pocket of her smock and put it in her mouth. She walked slowly and looked around while she was walking. She was about ten yards behind Doris and Nehru.

"Here they are," Nehru said as he walked through the door with Doris right behind him. "You can use my office."

"Thank you, Nehru, but I think we will just step out front for a few. I may need your office in a little while, Decker replied.

"Okay, you can use it whenever you need it."

"Thanks." Decker stepped to the front door and opened it for Doris before he ever said a word to her.

Decker looked at Debbie and held up one finger indicating that he will be right back with her. She understood the signal. She put her gum in the trash can and lit another cigarette. she took a seat on a bench in front of one of the nearby rooms.

"Thank you," Doris said as she walked through the opened door.

"Hello, I'm Detective Decker with Whitley County Sheriff's Department. I have just a few questions about something you may have seen yesterday. I appreciate your being willing to talk with me."

"Hello. That's fine, but if you are talkin' bout the car tag, I already told that other guy about everything I know."

"Yes, ma'am that is one thing. I just need to get a little more detail. What can you tell me about it? What did you see happen?" Decker asked her as he smiled and folded his arms over his chest.

"Like I told the other guy, Debbie and I were waiting to clean this one room so we could be done for the day. It was around eleven o'clock and check out time was eleven. We went to the laundry room for a few minutes while we waited. She went outside to smoke and noticed the two guys coming out from the room. She said they were about to leave, so I walked over to see for myself.

They walked over to their car. The taller one got something out of the back seat of the car. The other guy backed the car up near the dumpster. Then they both went to the back of the car, and the shorter of the two bent down, and I guess, was taking off the tag. He wasn't down there long. He stood up and had the tag in his hand. I could see it was the tag, but it wasn't like ours around here. Maybe it was a Georgia or Tennessee tag, I don't know. Then he walked over to the dumpster and threw it in. The taller guy bent down while the other guy was at the dumpster. I don't know what he was doing, but he wasn't there long. Then they both got in the car and left. That's it. That's all I saw. Is it a big deal? Was the car stolen?" Doris asked as she put both hands on her hips.

"Do you think you could identify these guys if you ever saw them again?" Decker asked.

"Well, that depends on when I saw them again. Today, yes, next month, I don't know."

"Fair enough," Decker said back.

Decker took out a small notepad from his shirt pocket and wrote down a description of the two from Doris. He thanked her and then walked over to where Debbie was sitting. She saw him coming, reached into her pocket, and pulled out another cigarette. Decker spoke with her and got about the same story. Their descriptions were a little different, but not enough to matter.

Decker told both women that he would be back at some point to have them review their statements after they had been typed to be sure the statements were accurate. Decker went back to his office and pulled his notes together and gave the tape to an office assistant to be transcribed.

After he had written a statement about his finding, he called Detective Hawkins at the HCSO Detective Office and gave him the details. He told Hawkins that he would fax his notes and statement to him and that the transcript was being typed.

Now Rivers and his team had a name—Kenny Saxton, and a direction of travel—north, still on I-75. Rivers figured that the best place to start checking on Kenny Saxton was in Florida, where the Toyota tag was registered.

Tuesday, June 22nd 1:00 P.M.

Rivers called for the detectives who were working the case to meet him at his office. They met for about two hours going over every lead and every piece of evidence until each investigator was on the same page with every detail.

Rivers told Hawkins to go home because he had been up most of the night. He assigned Don Blackman to work the car lead and find as much as he could about a Kenny Saxton and a yellow Toyota. Dek Bates and Carl Howe were assigned to run down all of Fisher's friends, co-workers, and others, that may have known him in the past few months.

Lieutenant Dek Bates was in charge of the division, while Rivers flew to Whitley County, Kentucky to follow up the motel lead there. The other detectives would continue to work on the local leads and be on hand in case other leads came in. The meeting was over in just twenty minutes. Rivers hated meetings as a rule. Most of the meetings he held were stand up meetings— no one sat down during the meeting. This seemed to cut down on the chatter and nonessential information.

After everyone had left his office, Rivers closed his door and sat behind his desk. He never lost sight of the fact that his primary job was chief-pie-plate-spinner. A lot was going on. Not just on the Fisher case but also on several cases they were already working. Rivers always was amused at how TV detectives had the luxury of working one case at a time. At any given time, each detective at HCSO was working fifteen to twenty cases, but part of Rivers' job was to set the priorities. He set those priorities based on several factors. A homicide case took top priority. The most recent murder took the highest priority. Time was always a factor.

Rivers leaned back in his chair and closed his eyes for a few moments. He wasn't sleepy but closing his eyes seemed to block out the constant flow of information. He sat there for just a moment, then jumped out of his chair as if he had received an electrical shock. He walked out his door and straight to the war room.

Rivers always set up a "war room" at the beginning of a who-done-it homicide. It was usually in one of the empty offices or one of the conference rooms. There were photos and maps plastered to the walls. There was always a chalkboard or white-board nearby. A list of known facts was placed on the walls. It was a place where everyone on the case could keep pace with the latest information.

When he got to the war room he looked at each poster along the wall. He went to the coffee pot, but it was cold and nearly empty. He sat down at the conference table and moved the stack of photos sitting on the table so he could go through them. He went through each picture and studied every detail. After he was finished, he moved that stack back and put the stack of photos of the yellow Toyota in their place. Once again he looked through each photograph, carefully looking at each detail. He moved from one end of the table to the other end where written statements had been placed. He stood at the end of the table and looked down at the stack of fifty papers or more. He looked back at the coffee pot, then once again at the stack of papers. He decided that he needed a little coffee before he started rereading all the statements. He made a fresh pot.

He sat down with a cup of coffee sitting on the table next to him. He carefully went through each page. About thirty minutes later, he read the last page and set the papers down. He reached for the cup of coffee. The coffee had grown cold without his taking the first sip. He took a tiny sip and sat the cold brew down. He walked around the room again, carefully inspecting each poster. He paid close attention to the time-line that Detective Dalton had made.

After a few moments, he went back and sat in his office. Once again he leaned back in his chair and closed his eyes. He felt comfortable that all the bases were being covered. He just needed to be sure that he hadn't missed anything. He was never really comfortable until the case was solved and the bad guys were sentenced.

☆

Tuesday, June 22nd 2:30 PM

Chris Nicholas walked into the sheriff's office and asked for the detective working the rest-stop-murder case. Nicholas had read the account of the killing in the Chattanooga Beacon, a local independently owned evening newspaper. He had wrestled with his conscience about coming in, and for a good reason, he stood to lose a lot.

Lieutenant Dek Bates was getting some coffee and heard Nicholas speaking to an office assistant, Kathy Meadows, as he walked by her desk.

"Can I help you?" Bates asked.

"I need to talk to someone about the rest stop case. I may have seen something" Nicholas said.

"You saw something at the rest stop Sunday night?"

"Maybe, I was there that night, and I saw some people with a guy that matches the description of the individual killed."

"Okay, well let's get out of the lobby, follow me."

Bates led Nicholas through a maze of hallways then into a conference room that still had a pot of cold coffee sitting in the middle of the table.

"Excuse the mess, have a seat. Would you like some coffee or something else to drink?" Bates asked.

"No, I'm okay… well, maybe some water. This may take a while. I don't know."

"Sure thing, I'll be right back."

Bates stepped out of the room and went down the hallway to Rivers' office. He was not in, but his door was open. That meant he was in the building somewhere. Bates walked back through the hallway maze to the detective's reception desk and asked the receptionist if she knew the whereabouts of Rivers. She told him that he was in the office with the sheriff. Bates decided not to disturb them and asked the receptionist to let Rivers know he was talking to someone fascinating in the detective conference room.

Nicholas didn't fit the image of someone hanging out in a public area to gain and give sexual favors. He was well dressed and well groomed. He was tall and somewhat handsome. His clothes looked tailored and expensive. His manners were evident, and he was very articulate.

Bates returned with a paper cup nearly full of water. He didn't bring a notepad and decided to just listen to what Nicholas had to say before trying to get an official statement. Nicholas had an excellent memory and gave a lot of details about that evening. He said he remembered that it was on that same night he was in a minor accident not far from the rest area. He told Lieutenant Bates that he remembered a guy matching the description in the newspaper, talking with another guy that night. He stated that the other guy got out of an older, small yellow car and sat on the hood.

Nicholas said there was someone else in the car, but he didn't get out until later. According to Nicholas, the man he thought could be the victim was sitting in his car, not too far from where the guy was seated on the hood. He said that the victim if he was the victim, got out of his car and walked up to the man on the hood. They talked for a little while then they both got into the victim's car and left. The third guy just stayed in the older car. Nicholas stated that in about a half an hour the possible victim's car came back and pulled right beside the yellow car. The driver got out and ran up to the yellow car and opened the back door. The other guy then jumped out of the yellow car and they both quickly loaded some stuff in the victim's car. They opened the trunk of both cars and got some things out of the yellow car to put into the other car. He stated that he never saw the man who was possibly the victim again but assumed that he was in the car's back seat. He said he thought it was odd that they left the trunk and one of the doors of the yellow car open but figured they would be back.

Rivers came into the room about halfway through Nicholas' statement. Bates introduced Rivers, and he just nodded and told him he was sorry he interrupted and to please continue. When he was finished, Bates thanked him and looked over at Rivers who was leaning against the wall near the door. Rivers nodded once again and thanked Nicholas for stepping forward. Then Rivers asked Bates to step outside for a moment.

"This is good stuff," Rivers told Bates.

"Sounds like he definitely saw something," Bates responded.

"While it may not help us catch the guys, it certainly could play a role at trial," Rivers suggested.

"Yep, plus it gives us some details of what may have happened if they are the ones. We can check their stories with what this guy says," Bates said.

"Oh yeah, you are right about that. Lock the guy down to as many details as he can remember. Go ahead and tape it too, Dek. We will get it typed up," Rivers instructed.

"It's hard to believe this guy was out there that night, but hey, I just take them as I find them," Bates said.

CHAPTER THIRTEEN

Nice Strawberries

It was mid-afternoon and Rivers had just gotten off the phone with Lieutenant Nick Taylor, who was head of the air support unit for Hamilton County. Taylor had been Rivers' training officer. Rivers had requested a fixed wing flight for early the next morning. They were leaving the Chattanooga airport at 6:00 A.M.

Lieutenant Taylor and Rivers had never struck up much of a friendship. In fact, Taylor didn't like Rivers but no one knew why. After the call, Rivers made some notes about Nicholson's statement on a pad on his desk. It was his "hot sheet" list of things to remember and things to do. They stayed on his desk until the task was completed or the information was processed.

With things lined up for the trip to Whitley County, Rivers thought would be a good time to take a much-needed break from the office. Everyone was working their assignments, and if anyone discovered any new details, they could call him at home. Like many times while working a major case, Rivers had forgotten to eat. He didn't know what he wanted to eat, but he knew he didn't want to drive through or even eat out. He hadn't been to the grocery store in days. He decided to stop by the grocery store on the way home. He would fix a healthy salad or a sandwich; it depended upon his mood once he got it home. It turned out to be a critical stop.

Rivers was pondering over the new display of strawberries that had just been put on sale. As he picked up one of the containers, he sensed someone's presence in his personal space. At first, he didn't see anything but a hand reach in front of him toward one of the containers, the hand was enough to get his attention. The nails had a flawless French manicure. There was a beautiful tri-tone gold herringbone bracelet hanging loosely on the wrist. On the right ring finger, she modeled a cabochon-red ruby ring with a diamond on each side, which sat perfectly on her finger.

Before he looked up he caught a glimpse of the shoes — a pair of red patent Stuart Weitzman flats that seemed to make the dark tan on her legs look more bronzed. He dares not stare down too long. He raised his head promptly to attempt to make eye contact and to see if the rest of this being was as stunning as what he had seen so far.

Just as his head was eye level, she turned and walked away. He was only able to see a woman wearing a beautiful black dress that hung just above the knees. The back of this woman had indeed matched the other parts of her body. He was thinking about going around to the other side of the display to see her. He needed to be coy, but he just might catch a glimpse of her face. Suddenly, as if on cue, she stopped briefly, turned and faced Rivers.

"Do you think these are ripe enough to use tonight?" she asked as if she had no doubt that he could answer her question. "I hate hard strawberries!" she exclaimed.

She was indeed stunning, he thought. He desperately wanted to respond to her question but he didn't have a clue how to tell if a strawberry was ripe other than just opening the package and eating one. There was no way that he was going to tell her no and let her walk away.

"May I see them?" he asked.

She handed them to him for examination. He opened the container, took out one big red strawberry, briefly looked it over then took a bite.

"Ah, yes, those are perfect."

She looked at him with a little disbelief at what she had just seen him do. Then she laughed out loud.

"Why didn't I think of that?"

He closed the lid but had difficulty clicking the plastic fasteners back. The lady smiled and said, "it's okay."

"I have to close this thing, or my pride will be bruised!"

"Really, it's okay, they are hard to close sometimes." She grinned while reaching for the container.

Rivers decided it was better to surrender the box than continue with his failed attempts at closing it.

"You are so funny," she said, chuckling once again at his antics.

"I hate to admit defeat; especially to a strawberry container, but it happens," he responded.

He also decided to quickly change the subject. They were both carrying a shopping basket instead of pushing a cart. Kent decided to walk with her, at least until he got the rub off.

"Mind if I escort you through the produce? Kent asked, while already walking beside her.

"Looks like you already are," she said while glancing his way with a little smile. "No, I don't mind."

"Are you entertaining a lot of people tonight?"

"Just a few girlfriends. We will eat dinner and maybe watch a movie or talk about the men in our lives, or those not there anymore. You know, girls night out. Only we are in," she responded with a smile.

"I guess I'm lucky then."

"How so?"

"I'll not be part of the conversation. But wait—I might be, depends on who your girlfriends are," Kent said with a laugh and a wink.

"Maybe you should stop by and find out for yourself."

She continued shopping while Kent walked along with her. He had lost all interest in shopping at this point. Kent didn't normally fall all over himself over a woman. But he was coming really close to doing just that with this lady.

"No, thank you. I think I'll just take my strawberries and go home. I'll probably sleep better by not knowing," Kent said with a charming look on his face.

Once again, she smiled and snickered briefly as they approached the checkout. She looked at Kent's basket and saw that he only had a container of strawberries.

"Is that all you are getting?" She asked.

Kent was so caught up in walking with her that he had forgotten all about being hungry or shopping. Now he was embarrassed to admit that he was just tagging along with her and forgot why he came to the store.

"Uh, yeah, I think so. I believe it is going to be a strawberry kind of night at my place this evening."

"Doesn't sound like much of a dinner."

"Well, I'm sure I can find something to go with it."

She put her basket on the checkout counter, and the clerk started to ring up the items.

"Are Y'all together?" the clerk asked as he was ringing up the last item in her basket.

"Oh, no, no we are not together," Kent responded before she could.

"He just came for strawberries," she said, looking at Kent and smiling.

At that point, he realized she knew that she had distracted him. Now what? He thought. He resolved that he would jump in with both feet now that she was onto him anyway.

"Yeah, just strawberries for me tonight. But what can I say? I like strawberries," Kent added as the clerk rang up his single item.

He quickly laid a five-dollar bill on the counter, not really caring if the cashier kept the change. If he could just get checked out before she walked away. She was looking through her bag of items as if checking to make sure she hadn't forgotten anything.

"That's five forty-four," the clerk advised Kent.

"Oh, sorry. Let me see if I have some change," Kent replied, hoping he found a couple of quarters in his pocket to speed up this untimely delay. "Nope. Dang!"

He pulled out a twenty and took back the five. Holly collected her bags, turned to Kent, to tell him bye when the clerk put the change into Kent's outreached hand.

"Hey, let me walk you out," Kent said, as he did a quick two-step to catch up.

She paused for a moment to wait on Kent. His mind was working overtime as he tried to come up with relevant conversation while walking with her, and at the same time find just the right investigatory verbiage to quench his keen desire for the truth about this woman.

"I noticed a gun under your jacket when you were checking out. I'm hoping that means you are a cop or something and not in the Mafia," she said with a serious look on her face but quickly cracked a smile.

"Sorry, I hope that didn't alarm you," Kent said. "I work at the sheriff's office."

"So you wear plain clothes or are you off duty?"

"Just left the office. I am a detective. So, I guess both," Kent said smiling.

"What kind of detective?"

"A good one I hope," Kent answered as he laughed.

"No, I mean what do you detect?" "Oh, well, actually I'm the chief of investigations, so I'm into about everything."

"Wow, the chief, huh? I'm honored," she said, with just a slight smile.

They arrived at her black BMW convertible. She opened her trunk to put in her groceries.

"Well, the honor is mine, but I don't even know your name."

"Holly."

"Just Holly?"

She smiled and said, "No, not just Holly. Holly Packe."

"Hi, Holly Packe. I'm Kent, Kent Rivers."

"Hello, Kent. Kent Rivers."

"Well, Holly Packe, I hope you have fun at your 'girls-in' party tonight."

"It's not really a party, but thanks the same.

"Hmm, well I'm sure you will enjoy talking about either your man or your ex." Kent swallowed hard, not believing he actually said that.

"No. Neither."

Neither was what he was looking for. It didn't tell him what he yearned to know. Was she single or was there someone? He had a good idea that she wasn't married because there was no wedding ring, and the girl's night at her house also indicated that she probably wasn't married. Either that or the husband was having a boy's night out. What now, he thought? He decided that the direct approach was the best at this point, but before he could pose his next question, she spoke up.

"If you are wondering if I'm married or seeing someone, the answer to that is neither as well," Holly said without even a hint of a smile.

"I guess I was wondering," Kent chuckled. "So thank you. I was also wondering if you would allow me to buy you dinner one night. Sort of a boy's and girl's night out."

"A boy's and girl's night out?"

"Really, I was hoping more for a boy-girl night out."

"Oh, boy-girl," Holly said finally breaking out with a smile. "How do I know I can trust you, Chief Detective Kent Rivers? I mean, you have a gun, and I don't. Is that really fair?"

"I tell you what, I could pick you up on a Saturday, bring my other gun, and take you out to the range. Would that make you feel better?"

"I don't know, I've never shot a gun in my life. Not sure I want to start now. Maybe I could just trust you to behave."

"You can trust me, but not sure you can trust me to behave. I certainly could try if that made a difference in your going or not." Kent had been smiling the entire conversation, but now he stopped smiling and raised his eyebrow a little as he was waiting for her final answer.

"I tell you what, you give me your card and I'll let you know if I decide to trust you or not."

"Okay, I was hoping to get your number, but I'll settle for your having mine."

Kent pulled out a card from inside his jacket pocket. He took his pen and wrote his direct office line and home phone number on the card.

"Here ya go. Now don't lose that. I would hate for those numbers to fall into the wrong hands."

"I think they will stay in the right hands, Chief," Holly said as she walked to the driver's door and placed her hand on the handle.

Kent smiled, "That's good. I'll sleep better at night knowing that."

"Goodbye, Kent. Thanks for helping with the strawberries," she said as she climbed into the driver's seat.

"You are welcome, Holly Packe. Have a splendid evening."

"Plan to," Holly said as she glanced back at Kent.

She smiled then winked as she closed her door. Kent stood there a moment as she cranked the black Beamer and drove away. He casually looked around the parking lot for his car and noticed it was two parking spaces away.

"Oh, there you were all along," he said out loud. He put his strawberries in the passenger's seat and drove away.

His mind kept flashing back on his first glimpse of Holly. She was one of the most beautiful women he had ever seen. "And she is witty and has a great smile," he said out loud as if someone had been listening. He decided to drive through a nearby Hibachi Grill and take home a chicken and shrimp plate. He could eat the strawberries later, he decided.

For a few minutes, while driving home, Kent forgot about the ongoing cases and the role he played in each. He was listening to his favorite CD, and his mind was on his personal life— something that Kent seldom thought about or allowed himself to do. As he pulled into the driveway of his house, he paused before hitting the garage button. Kent looked at his home and briefly took inventory of his life. Had he done his best? He was forty-one, alone, no kids, an empty house—but had a great job that he loved. He had the respect of his co-workers and many in the community. He was proud of what he had accomplished in his career. But still, he was forth-one, alone, no kids, and an empty house.

Kent Rivers could have gone out every night of the week. No shortage of females desired his attention and company. Many of them were not shy about letting him know. He seemed to have it all—financial security included. He had put his money to work for him and had been both lucky and wise. He went out sometimes but had a difficult time letting someone into his world. He saw Diane on occasion, but they both understood that their relationship was more friendship than anything else. When either needed companionship, they made themselves available, but both knew it was not anything more. They dated other people and talked about it openly with the other. But Holly had his head spinning. She seemed to have it all, he thought.

CHAPTER FORTEEN

Trooper Glascott

After he finished his meal he ate a few strawberries and poured himself a short glass of California red wine. He turned on the TV with the sound muted and settled into his comfortable chair that he hadn't seen much of in the last few days. He made a couple of phone calls to the other detectives to check their status and findings. He was content that he had covered the bases and knew that he could let his mind relax for the evening.

In place of the sound from the TV was his favorite Dwight Yoakum CD. Kent Rivers enjoyed Dwight Yoakum and his Bakersfield sound. "Now that's talent," he said as the first few notes rang through the room. He loved talent in any form. Sometimes he closed his eyes and listened to Bach or Rachmaninoff. He loved classic piano and guitar music. Then other times he put on some Tom Petty and the Heartbreakers or Whitesnake and rock out.

But at this moment he was listening to one of his favorite Dwight Yoakum songs, "A Thousand Miles From Nowhere." As he sat in his chair with his wine glass in his hand, he reflected on how at times he felt a thousand miles from nowhere. He thought how much he loved that old chair. It was a place he could go and have some peace, even in the middle of a sometimes-raging life.

Kent couldn't get his mind off of Holly. He didn't know if it was all about Holly, or if she had gotten him to thinking about his life and relationships. Either way, he was positively affected by his encounter with the lovely Holly Packe.

It wasn't long until he got up and set the empty wine glass on the table. He changed the music to a collection of soft rock hits and poured himself another short glass of wine. He sat back down and closed his eyes as he sipped the wine and listened to the music.

Soon Roberta Flack's, "I Feel Like Makin' Love," began to play. His mind and his heart started to alternate thoughts until they both came to Adelicia. She was the only woman to have completely captured his heart, and that was one of her favorite songs. He reflected on their first date. Kent met Adelicia, met her Dad, and went on their first date all in the same evening. He remembered who he had to wait three dates before he got his first kiss.

It was the one kiss that he never forgot. He remembered it like it was last week. They both loved music. They had just returned from a musical production in Nashville. They were driving back to Chattanooga and decided to stop at an all-night diner. They didn't even know they were hungry until they looked at the menu. It was eleven at night, but they both ordered breakfast with the works.

"Oh my gosh, this is so good! I didn't realize I was so hungry until now," Adelicia said as she swallowed her second bite of the hot waffle, closed her eyes and savored the moment.

"I know, me either, but you didn't order any grits. I thought you were a Southern girl."

"I'm a Southern girl except when it comes to those things. They have no taste!"

"Oh, but they make everything else taste good. Well, except a waffle," Kent said with a big grin.

"I'm proud of you Kent, but I'll never eat grits. I tried them when I was a kid and never put them back in my mouth again."

Kent laughed out loud, "Okay, I'll never force you to eat grits, but you have to promise never to force me to eat Brussels sprouts!"

"Deal!" Adelicia quickly replied.

Kent remembered that night well. It was the night that he knew he was in love. As they left the diner, he grabbed her hand and held it tight all the way to the car. The parking lot was half full. It was a cloudy night, but some stars had managed to poke through the black sky. As Kent reached to open the car door for Adelicia, he stopped and turned his face toward hers. He placed his left hand on the small of her back, and gently pulled her into his body. He took his right hand and put it behind her head and slowly pulled her face toward his and leaned into her. He stopped as their faces were just inches apart. He locked his green eyes on her deep blue eyes. The sounds from the nearby road vanished, so all they could hear was the sound of their own breathing.

They gazed into each other's eyes, then again he pressed the small of her back and pulled her in as tightly as he could into his body. They both moved their heads slowing toward the other, never blinking or taking their eyes away from their intense gaze. Their lips slowly pressed together. He felt the warmth and smooth wetness of her mouth. Her arms were wrapped around his waist, holding on tightly as if his body was about to launch toward the sky. They each closed their eyes at the exact same moment.

Adelicia let a slight moan rise from within and travel

throughout her body until it reached her throat. She let it gently escape as she opened her eyes briefly to make sure she wasn't dreaming. After the kiss, they just held onto each other for several moments. Kent pulled back just a little, still looking into her deep blue eyes.

"I could fall for you," gently slid off his tongue.

The sound of his words tenderly rolled passed his lips and into the night air. She pulled him in tight and squeezed him as securely as her arms allowed.

She paused for a few seconds then lifted her head to look into his green eyes and said, "I feel it, Kent."

Their lips touched firmly one more time.

Kent came out of his reminiscing daze and sat up in his chair. He leaned forward and placed the wine glass on the end table. He laid his head back again. His thoughts dashed through his mind, much like a video on fast-forward. His life with Adelicia flashed before his eyes through their wedding day, the honeymoon in the Florida Keys, and their first home. He recalled the trips, the dancing, the movies, the parties, and the wonderful nights together in their bedroom.

Four years after they were married, Kent received his appointment as the chief of the investigative division. It was a big title and more significantly, responsibility. The promotion was the beginning of great things for him. Adelicia had a huge party in his honor. She even managed to have the governor stop by briefly. After all, she wondered, what good was her Dad's money if she couldn't call in a favor once in a while? Kent recalled that after the party they made the sweetest love. They were both passionate and romantic, so there were many such nights, but that night stood out as one of the best in his mind.

He shook his head slowly side to side as he mentally went through each frame of their life together. He still believed that if he had only done more, she'd be sitting there now beside him. He couldn't forget the big scare the week before he lost her.

Adelicia had been to Nashville to visit her Dad for the weekend. Kent couldn't go because he was preparing for a court case that Monday and spent most of the weekend at his office. They were not apart often, but when they were, they were like two sixteen-year-old kids missing each other moments after they had parted. They talked before bedtime, and the conversations lasted for a couple of hours. They told each other how much they loved the other and how they couldn't wait to be back together. Such was the case on that Sunday night before she went to bed. They talked about forty-five minutes. They kept it short because Kent had to get up early and be in court.

On her drive home the following morning, she started feeling weak and dizzy. She pulled over at a gas station at the Manchester exit, which was about half way home. She got a bottled water and some peanuts. She thought maybe the feeling was from not eating breakfast. Adelicia was always concerned about her figure, so sometimes she went a little overboard trying to stay slim. Kent fussed at her for not eating. He told her that she was beautiful with or without a few pounds more. She got back into her SUV and decided that she felt better and continued the drive home. She made it to the Monteagle Mountain.

A little over a quarter of a mile down the steep curvy slope, she became dizzy again. This time was worse than the last. She was on the left lane of the three downhill lanes. She tried to pull over to the shoulder of the road but only made it one lane before she passed out.

The SUV swerved immediately to her right and struck the rear trailer wheels of a semi-tractor trailer rig. The glancing contact caused her SUV to dart back across the two left lanes. No other vehicles were coming down the mountain in her vicinity, so she continued down the mountain on the left shoulder. She traveled another 500 feet when the SUV struck the base of the sandy runaway truck ramp causing her to come to a stop.

There was a Tennessee Highway Patrol weigh station a short distance up the mountain on the eastbound side, so it wasn't long until help had arrived. When the trooper got to her, she had come to but was shaken and disoriented. She had a small cut on her forehead where she struck the visor when the SUV came to the sudden stop.

The state trooper communications office had already notified a local EMT unit, and it was on its way. Soon another trooper, Trooper Dana Glascott, arrived on the scene. She was not assigned to the weigh station but had been close when she heard the radio call about the accident.

Trooper Glascott knew Adelicia and Kent because three years earlier she had worked at the Hamilton County Sheriff's Office. Glascott got to know Adelicia because a group of the wives had joined forces to feed the deputies two times a year at roll call. Adelicia was always a leader, and she started the group to honor the working deputies and the deputies and officers killed in the line of duty. She did the same thing at the Chattanooga Police Department. Trooper Glascott and her husband, Jim, had been to the Rivers' home to watch football on several occasions. Jim Glascott was a football coach at UTC. He was younger than Kent but had heard of the DD and was impressed by what the two had accomplished.

Once Glascott realized it was Adelicia, she asked her if she wanted her to contact Kent. Adelicia thought it was better if Dana called Kent because she was still somewhat discombobulated. The EMT crew had just pulled onto the scene, so Trooper Glascott decided to wait until they checked Adelicia out before calling Kent. She felt that she might have more information about her condition then. The EMT crew felt it was best if she were checked out at the hospital. It was not so much the injuries received from the accident that caused them concern, but more the reason for the crash. Her forehead needed stitches, but other than a few bumps and bruises, she was okay.

Kent Rivers was helping one of the detectives with the interview of a witness to a robbery when he received a call from Trooper Glascott. Zona Cash, the detective division office manager, tapped lightly on the meeting room door. The atmosphere in the department was always relaxed, but if a knock on the door came during an interview, everyone knew that it must be somewhat important.

"Excuse me, Chief, but you have an urgent call on line three. It's a state trooper," Zona informed him in a soft voice, as Kent closed the interview room door behind him.

Zona Cash was a well-dressed, attractive, but no-nonsense woman in her late fifties. She had been a widow since her husband died of complications from wounds he received during the Vietnam War. He had lived several years after receiving his injuries, but never fully recovered. He spent the last few years of his life in and out of hospitals, and she never left his side. She had never even considered another man or dating since his death. Rivers always believed that there was a real love story buried somewhere under her tough exterior. She smiled when he ask her about it, but she never gave a hint that she would ever reveal the secrets of her heart. While Zona was direct, she could not be called a harsh woman. She was, however, occasionally guilty of responding to what she considered a stupid question with an acrimonious answer. She had the respect from all that knew her, and the love of those who had known her well. No one doubted who ran the day-to-day administrative operations. Even Kent Rivers gave way to Zona when it came to running the office.

Rivers counted on her, and she always delivered.

"A trooper?" Rivers asked as he walked toward his office to take the call.

"That's what she said. Trooper Glascott."

"Oh, she's a friend. I wonder what she is calling me about that couldn't wait? Did she say?"

"No, just told me she needed to speak with you and that it was important. I asked her if it was important enough to interrupt an interview and she said it was."

"Hey Dana, what's going on?" Kent said as he picked up the receiver.

"Hey, Kent. Listen, everything is okay, but Adelicia was in an accident."

"Where is she now?"

"She is on her way to get checked out. She had a cut on her forehead that probably needs stitches, but otherwise, I think she is okay."

"By Ambulance, I presume?"

"Yeah. They took her to South Pittsburg Hospital. It's the closest one."

"How long ago did it happen?"

"Not long, they just now left with her."

"Okay, well I'll call the hospital and tell them that I'm heading that way."

"No need to call, I'm about to leave and go there myself. I'll tell her you are on your way. She knew that I was calling you."

"Did she seem okay other than the cut on the head?"

"Yeah, she was disoriented, but that's to be expected."

"Was anyone else hurt?"

"No, she hit the rear wheels on the trailer of a semi, but it didn't do any damage to the trailer. The driver was the one that stopped and called it in. For some reason, she must have crossed the line, hit the trailer, then bounced across the highway to the runaway ramp. Her SUV has some damage. I'll tow it somewhere close."

"That's wild; I'm glad she was not hurt badly. Okay, thanks, Dana, I'm leaving here now. Thanks so much for calling me."

"Sure, I'll probably see you at the hospital."

"Okay, thanks."

Adelicia received eight stitches on her forehead, but the doctor told her that it would heal without much of a scar. The doctor told her that she needed to do a follow up with her doctor in one week to get the stitches out and to find out why she became dizzy.

During the next week, Kent took three days off from work to be around the house with Adelicia. He told Adelicia that he needed a few days off to get away from work, but Adelicia knew it was to keep an eye on her. Kent was always careful not to bring his work tactics home. He didn't want to come across as the interrogator when issues came up in their relationship, but this week it was clear that he had a difficult time not playing investigator. He wanted to know all about what led up to the accident and why she thought she had been dizzy. He even asked her if she thought she could be pregnant. She assured him that she wasn't. They had always planned to have kids, but they both just figured that the time was coming when everything was right.

Adelicia was satisfied that nothing was wrong with her, and she continued to assure Kent that she must have had a light touch of a virus. She also tried to convince her doctor that she was fine, but the doctor wasn't easily averted. Her doctor completed a couple of preliminary blood tests and then scheduled her for a CT Scan of her head later that day and an EEG later in the week to check for epilepsy. Kent was with her at the doctor's office and for the CT Scan that afternoon. Between the physician's visit and the CT Scan at the hospital's outpatient center, they decided to grab lunch at the Ogletree Deli, a couple of miles from the hospital.

Ogletree's was famous for their international selections.

Kent loved the authentic Cuban sandwich, and Adelicia almost always ordered the "O'gyro" with extra tzatziki sauce and Greek fries with feta cheese. Kent usually made some crazed facial expression when she ordered the extra tzatziki sauce.

Typically, Kent enjoyed various tastes and cuisines, but he never liked the smell of goat cheese so could never bring himself to eat it. They both laughed and talked about everything but the accident and the reason they were making the medical rounds.

The two never seemed to tire of their time together. They always found something to talk about, which usually, included some laughter. Today's lunch conversation centered on the different periods they had been at Ogletree's with other people over the years.

Kent told her about the first time Bruce Rider, and he was at Ogletree's with some of their teammates. He laughed when he told her about convincing Bruce that feta cheese was made from women's breast milk. Bruce had grown up on basic Southern American dishes, such as fried chicken, meatloaf, pork chops, and pot roast. The only thing he knew about cheese was that it came from cows and that it was yellow. Most of his cheese experience had been American cheese on a sandwich.

Bruce had tasted the feta cheese on a salad on one of the guy's plates and decided he liked it so well that he had a side order of feta cheese and crackers brought to him. The server was in on the prank, and they all had a big laugh. The owner had learned what all the commotion was about and joined in on the laugh. Once Bruce realized he was the object of a joke, he turned almost as red as his hair but then thought it was funny himself. The owner gave Bruce his meal on the house and an order of feta cheese to go.

CHAPTER FIFTEEN

You are my Hero

It was a bright, spring Saturday morning on the weekend before Adelicia was to find out the results of her tests. Both Kent and Adelicia woke up early. Usually, on a Saturday morning, one of them got up before the other. The early riser made the coffee, then weather permitting, step out quietly onto the back deck to enjoy the morning.

On this Saturday, they both woke up before 7:00. Adelicia went out to the deck while Kent made the coffee. They both sat quietly at first. The sun was just coming up over the nearby hills. Adelicia reached over to Kent, who was seated in the chair just to her right and placed her hand on top of his. He turned his head, smiled, and began stroking her fingers gently with his thumb.

"I'm going to be okay you know," she said as she smiled back and winked.

"I know you are. I'm sorry about my failed attempts at being subtle this week about my concerns. I hope I didn't bother you with it."

"Bother me? You were the cutest that I've seen you in a while."

161

"Gee, thanks. A guy could take that two ways," Kent said with a straight face.

Adelicia's smile gave way to a laugh as she said, "I mean, you're cute all the time, well, most of the time, but this week you were a particular kind of cute. Made me feel good Baby. Feels good to know you care so much for me."

"Adelicia, I would be lost without you."

"Nah, you'd do just fine. Just don't be fine for a little while, miss me just a little," she said as she smiled and winked once more while squeezing his hand.

"Stop it. I'm serious. I've never been happier in my life. We have a good life, Doll."

"Yes we do, and Monday we will find out that I have some deficiencies in some chemical my body needs. I'll take a pill until it gets healthy, and I'll be as good as new. I still think I could have had a virus."

"That's right! Why am I concerned about? You are too beautiful and too sexy for anything to be wrong with you!" Kent said while standing up to collect their empty cups.

He stood beside but a little behind Adelicia and leaned over to kiss her tenderly as she turned her lips to meet his.

"I love you, Kent. You are my hero. You make it easy to love you."

Adelicia wanted to ensure Kent understood what she was saying, so she stood up, took the two cups out of Kent's hands, and set them on the table. She reached up and put her right hand behind Kent's neck and pulled his head down just a little. She stood on her tiptoes, and looked him right in the eye.

"Kent Rivers, you have made my life more enjoyable than I could ever have imagined. I feel so safe, so full, and so alive, with you. When I say that you are my hero, I mean that! I so admire you. I so love you!"

Kent put his arms around her to pull her close, then kissed her on her lips. It was a long and passionate kiss. Kent wanted the kiss to do his talking for him. Adelicia moved in just a little, to make their embrace even tighter. She let out just a little moan as she completely relaxed in his arms and listened to each unspoken word of his kiss. She took him by the hand and led him to their bedroom, where they made sweet, slow, hot, morning love.

Adelicia got out of the shower and found Kent in bed sound asleep. His head was almost face down and half covered with her pillow. He was holding onto the other half. He was still naked but had the dark red sheets pulled up to his waist.

They planned to do a few things around the house that morning and then run to one of the malls to look for some new spring clothes, but Adelicia decided to let Kent sleep while she drove to the mall. She knew that Kent only said he would go with her to make her happy. She quickly dried and brushed out her hair, put on some light makeup, and was ready to go. She wrote Kent a note telling him where she went and kissed it to leave a little lipstick on the paper.

The Santana CD that was playing earlier had looped and was still playing. She left it on as she tiptoed out of the room. She grabbed a bottle of water out of the refrigerator and turned on the dishwasher on her way to the garage. She always opened the garage door before she got into her car. This was something that Kent had asked her to do for safety reasons. She also knew it was to keep her from forgetting the door was down and backing out. She readily admitted that she could get something on her mind and be oblivious to the rest of the world. So backing into the closed garage door was not something that was outside the realm of possibilities if the conditions were right.

The cold, dark garage was instantly transformed as the sunlight and warm morning air rushed in the opening door. Adelicia stood for just a moment after the door was completely up and briefly took in the fresh air and bright sunlight. She had always loved being in the sun. She never used a tanning bed, but during the summer always keep a deep, dark tan that made her blue eyes seem to glow.

The Rivers lived on six acres of land off of Hwy 58, not far from Harrison Bay. Adelicia loved to shop even when she didn't buy anything. She enjoyed the malls and the people at the malls, but today she wanted to just get a few things and get back home to Kent. She headed to the closest mall to her house. It wasn't as big as the one she frequently went to, but it would save time and be less crowded. She was feeling good and looking forward to a lovely weekend they had planned.

Back at the house, Kent finally woke up. He sat on the edge of the bed, rubbed his eyes, then his head, and looked around the room for Adelicia. He didn't see her, so he turned his head and glanced on the other side of the bed. He stood up and realized that he was still in the raw and pulled up the sheet as if someone may walk into the room. He looked on the floor beside the bed where he thought he had left his boxers. Then he saw Adelicia's note. He read the short note and smiled at the lip prints as he gently rubbed his thumb across them. He dropped the sheet onto the bed and walked across the room to the shower.

Adelicia was listening to the local talk radio station as she was driving on the bridge over the Tennessee River. She enjoyed a Saturday morning gardening program. She didn't have time to work in the yard a lot, so she loved the ideas she heard on the radio program.

She was about halfway across the bridge when suddenly and without warning she blacked out for a second then came right out of it. She tried to remain focused. She was still feeling hazy and unsure of what was happening to her. She could hear the radio playing but no longer could understand what they were saying. It was just noise now. In her confused state of mind, she felt she had to make it to the end of the bridge to get out of traffic.

In another split second she was dizzy, and everything turned a faint yellow and was spinning. She no longer could see clearly enough to keep the SUV straight. She could feel herself starting to fade. This time she had a little warning. However, she wasn't able to think clearly enough to process the data that was bombarding her brain. She did know one thing-she had to stop the vehicle quickly. The problem was, her brain just wasn't able to get the right messages to her body in order to affect the needed reactions. This was not the place to black out again and run off the bridge. She finally hit the brakes and stopped in the middle of the bridge.

CHAPTER SIXTEEN

Fire, Ambulance, and Police

Jeff Haggerty, Ben Jackson, and Seth Davis were all high school football players on their way to the school to complete a Saturday morning workout. Spring practice started the upcoming Monday, and this was their last chance for a good workout, before starting practice. They had spent the night at Seth's house the previous night. They took Jeff's old pickup to get to practice. It was a little crowded but the all fit.

Ben and Seth had been teasing Jeff about his old truck with the cracked windshield, broken glove box door, and faded out dash. He had jokingly told them that he would kick them out and make them walk if they didn't show a little more respect for his truck.

As they started across the bridge, Seth told Jeff that they would layoff about his old nasty truck until they got across the bridge. Seth wasn't crazy about the way Jeff drove so he didn't want him distracted while crossing the tall bridge.

As they got to the top of the bridge, Jeff brought the subject up again and told them that he should just stop right there and let them walk. They began to joust back and forth and were laughing and having fun. Suddenly, Ben looked up and yelled, "Jeff!" just before the truck slammed into the rear of Adelicia Rivers'stopped SUV at full speed. The impact sent Adelicia, and her SUV, over the guardrail and down onto the large boulders about forty feet below. They were past the deep water part of the bridge, but were still high above the ground.

The pickup continued a short distance, crossed into the left lane and was struck by a furniture delivery truck, which knocked it back into the right lane. A speeding motorcycle was trying to go around the delivery truck on the right side when the truck hit Jeff's pickup. The driver of the bike was not able to stop in time and struck the side of the pickup after it bounced off the front of the delivery truck. The fuel line to the motorcycle broke off after hitting the truck, causing gasoline to spill onto the pavement and under the pickup. A spark resulted from all the metal twisting and wires coming loose and the pickup truck burst into flames. An instant plume of gray smoke quickly lifted high into the clear blue sky.

The southbound lanes were divided by the Tennessee River and the traffic in the northbound lanes was blocked by the wrecked vehicles. The delivery truck driver, Chase (Bubba) Hastings, was just slightly injured and was quickly out of the cab of his truck with a fire extinguisher in his hand. Bubba had been a volunteer firefighter a few years back. He knew how to lay the foam to try to stop the fire before it spread or caused a massive explosion.

Ben, sitting in the middle of the pickup, was not wearing a seat belt. They had joked about him being, odd man out after they got into the truck because the middle seat belt fastener was broken. The junior takes the risk, they told him jokingly. When the pickup hit Adelicia's SUV, Ben was immediately launched into the dash of the pickup. His neck broke, and he died almost instantly.

After striking the SUV, the pickup's momentum shifted to the left and spun the pickup into the left lane. The impact of the delivery truck smashed the bed of the truck and crushed the back portion of Seth's door. Seth was wearing his seat belt, but the blow from the delivery truck caused his head to bang hard into the metal framework around the door. He was knocked unconscious before the motorcycle hit his door. The cyclist hit the front part of the pickup's passenger door. The cyclist was killed instantly. Parts of the cycle flew into the passenger's side window, which had been broken by the force of the delivery truck. A piece of the chromed mirrors off the cycle hit Seth in the right cheek causing severe bleeding.

Jeff was also wearing his seat belt. The initial impact of hitting Adelicia's SUV had knocked Jeff unconscious, but after the pickup had come to a stop, he regained consciousness. His door was jammed, but the door glass was mostly out, so he managed to smash the remaining glass out. He crawled out of the truck just when the flames began to engulf his pickup.

Since all northbound lanes were blocked, rescue, fire, ambulance, and police, all came to the scene by coming south in the northbound lanes. It was quicker than trying to work their way through the traffic jam behind the vehicular carnage.

Officer Brad Thomas of the Chattanooga Police Department was the first to arrive on the scene. Officer Thomas had been on the force about three years. He had never seen a traffic accident with this much destruction in such a small and confined space. Soon, fire and rescue personnel were on the scene, as well as emergency medical technicians.

At first, no one noticed the collapsed guardrail, or the SUV resting on the large rocks below. Bubba Hastings had extinguished the fire before the firefighters arrived on the scene, but the fire crew laid extra foam on the pavement to prevent a re-occurrence of fire. The rescue members were busy trying to extract Seth and Ben from the pickup truck. The doors were jammed, and they had to cut into the vehicle to get the boys out. At the time they did not realize that Ben had already perished. It was evident by his wounds that the cyclist was dead. He was covered with a sheet until his body could be removed.

Officer Thomas decided that fire and rescue and EMTs were handling the medical needs at the accident and turned his attention to the vehicles and damage on the bridge. His limited yet valuable experience and training allowed him to take a quick assessment of the scene. He noticed the damaged guardrail did not match the position of any of the vehicles on the bridge. He walked to the edge of the bridge at the end of the damaged railing and notice Adelicia's SUV laying bout forty feet below. He immediately notified the fire and rescue captain on the scene, Josh Stafford, of his findings. He knew that it would take extra men and equipment to get to the vehicle. He could not tell how many people were in the SUV, but he was aware that time was not on their side.

Captain Stafford quickly assessed the situation and called for another unit to bring the necessary repelling equipment to the scene. Rescue member, Bob Rich, who had been assisting the extraction of Seth and Ben from the pickup, heard the call and remembered that his vehicle had two sets of repelling gear. He left the two boys in the hands of other rescue members and told Captain Stafford about the gear.

Stafford and Rich donned the repelling gear. By this time other Chattanooga police officers had arrived on the scene. Together with Officer Thomas, they helped Stafford and Rich repel to Adelicia and the SUV. Once they landed on the rocky terrain, they discovered that Adelicia was the only occupant of the vehicle. Other rescuers arrived on the scene with repelling gear and quickly repelled to the SUV with a backboard and other gear to lift Adelicia from her damaged car.

Getting Adelicia to the top of the bridge would take a team effort and some time. Captain Stafford knew that Adelicia did not have time. He called for an airlift to be waiting for her once they were able to get her to the top. The collision by the pickup into the rear of the SUV caused Adelicia's seat back to collapse.

By the time the SUV came to a final rest on the rocks, Adelicia had experience trauma to her neck, face, back, and head. She was also bleeding internally from the force placed upon her body by the loosened seat belt

Captain Stafford was able to find a faint pulse and could see Adelicia's shallow breaths. Her cuts were bad, but the bleeding was minimal, so his concern was to lift her off the rocks and get her to the trauma center fast. She opened her eyes a couple of times, but there were no responses to Captain Stafford's questions about her ability to understand or communicate with him. Rich found Adelicia's purse and strapped it to his body as he was lifted back to the bridge. By this time Adelicia was being transported by airlift to the Trauma Center at Erlanger Hospital.

CHAPTER SEVENTEEN

Two Nights in Gatlinburg

Kent was out of the shower and had fixed some cheese toast and retrieved the newspaper from the front yard as he waited for Adelicia to return. He knew that Adelicia was a quick shopper when she wanted to be, and he was anxious to leave town for their special weekend.

He had always started in the sports section since he was a teen playing football. He finished the sports page, then went to the front page and followed it in order until he reached the classified ads. He stopped at the classified ads and placed the folded paper on the kitchen counter as he put away the dish from his cheese toast. He was thinking that Adelicia must have lost track of time because it was going on 1:00 in the afternoon, and they planned to be gone by three-thirty.

He saw the reflection of the sun off of a vehicle pulling into the driveway and was relieved that Adelicia was finally home. The fact that she had blacked out the previous week was still heavy on his mind. He had intended to go with Adelicia that morning instead of falling asleep. He wished Adelicia had gotten him up.

He was going to tell her he was sorry when she came through the garage door.

The ringing of the doorbell seemed odd to Kent. Adelicia should be coming through the garage, he thought. He surmised that she probably wanted him to run out to her car and go with her someplace. She had apparently left her car running and had to ring the doorbell, he figured. He was not expecting anyone and never had unexpected visitors on a Saturday afternoon.

When he opened the door, he saw Deputy Angie Fuller. Kent had known Angie since she started at the sheriff's office. Deputy Fuller was thirty-eight years old and was one of those deputies who enjoyed her job as a patrol deputy and didn't want a transfer or promotion. She was a seasoned deputy that Kent could always count on for good information from the community.

"Hey, Angie! What in the world are you doing here?" Kent said with a smile, while he opened the door wide for her to enter his home.

"I don't want to be here Chief, but I need to take you to Erlanger. Adelicia's been in a serious accident," Angie said with a grim face.

"What? Adelicia? When?" Kent said as he stepped back into the doorway.

"She just arrived at the hospital about thirty minutes ago. I got the call to come get you and take you to the hospital. That's all I know, Kent."

"Come in while I grab my shoes. I can't believe this."

Kent's mind went straight to the phone call he received a little over a week ago from his friend, Trooper Dana Glascott. He was already blaming himself for letting Adelicia go alone. Angie Fuller knew more than what she was telling Kent, but she saw no need to get into that conversation at the door. She needed Kent to get in the car and go with her. She stepped into the door of the house but kept the door open. Fuller insisted that Kent rode with her. She assured him that she would get him back home.

During the trip to the hospital, Fuller turned on the blue lights and bumped the siren when they came upon a red light. She drove fast on the interstate, but her voice remained calm and steady as she spoke with Kent. Fuller wasn't sure that Adelicia would still be alive when they got to the hospital, but she didn't want her voice or actions to add to Kent's anxiety.

Kent and Adelicia had planned to leave around three-thirty that afternoon to spend the next two nights in Gatlinburg. They were going to come back Monday in time for Adelicia's doctor appointment. But by three-thirty that afternoon, Kent was sitting alone with his tears, inside the chapel at Erlanger Hospital. The bleeding and swelling in Adelicia's head from the trauma could not be stopped. By three o'clock she was on life support, but there was no brain activity. Her body was alive, but Adelicia was gone.

Being a cop is like belonging to a small community. It wasn't long before everyone connected to Kent knew about the accident. Dek Bates, Don Blackman, and Chief Deputy Sal Dillard were all waiting outside the Chapel trying to decide the right time and the right person to go in to see Kent. They decided the time was then and the person was Dek, Rivers' second in command and long-time friend. Dek slowly opened the chapel door and quietly walked over to where Kent was sitting. He didn't say a word or touch Kent. He quietly sat down in the seat next to him. Both men were looking straight ahead at a light flickering on a gold cross sitting on a table in the front of the chapel. Someone had lit a candle near the cross a few minutes before Kent came into the room. The only words finally spoken between the two came from Kent.

"I should have gone with her. I had planned to go with her," he said in a quiet whisper.

Dek didn't respond verbally, but put his hand briefly on Kent's knee and shook his head very slightly in disbelief at what had happened. Adelicia was a donor, and Kent knew that she would want him to follow through with her wishes, but Kent could not believe that Adelicia was gone. He had gone over and over in his head the words from the neurologist that told him Adelicia was gone. He finally asked Dek to walk with him to where they were keeping Adelicia so he could sign the papers.

By this time Detectives, Pete Sanchez and Jesse Hawkins had arrived, as well as the sheriff, Neil Self. They were waiting outside the chapel along with a couple of their wives who were friends of Adelicia's. Kent and Dek exited the chapel slowly. Dek held the door open for Kent. Chief Sal Dillard, grabbed the door handle and held it open from the outside. The chief and Jesse Hawkins were standing closest to the door at the time. The sheriff was the first to walk over to Kent. He put his right hand on Kent's forearm and spoke softly to him.

"This breaks my heart, Kent. I can't imagine what it is doing to you. Needless to say, but please take off as long as you need, and know that you can call me anytime. You know I mean that, too."

"Thanks, Sheriff. I'm in a fog right now, but thank you."

As the sheriff was speaking to Kent, Dek took the opportunity to step a few feet away and quietly clarify that he was going with Kent to sign the donor papers and to stop the life support. He asked them to wait in the chapel for them to return.

By the time they came back down, Pastor Dale Simms of The New Hope Baptist Church was in the chapel. He was sitting quietly in a rear pew. No one knew who he was or why he was there. Kent and Adelicia did not attend church on a regular basis, but they both believed in Jesus and the Christian doctrine. Kent had grown up attending a Pentecostal church, and Adelicia had grown up in a Methodist church. They went to church about once a month, and sometimes twice a month at the small Baptist church about a mile from their house. They were well known and liked by the regular members of the church and many occasional attendees as well. The pastor, Dale Simms, had been the pastor of larger churches during his ministry but had retired. He was a widower who lost his wife just before retiring. He was called back into service to fill in after the former pastor left. That was five years prior, and he was still the pastor by unanimous consent. Kent and Adelicia both loved Pastor Simms, and he loved them. He never worried them about coming to church more often. The pastor knew their hearts and their busy lives, and was happy to have them there when they came. Pastor Simms was a gentle man who cared for people and everyone he met knew his heart within a short time. He would handle the funeral for Kent.

When Kent and Dek returned to the chapel, Dale Simms was the first person that Kent saw. Pastor Simms stood up. He was as tall as Kent and Kent immediately grabbed him in a bear hug and began crying nearly uncontrollably. At the sight of this, there wasn't a dry eye in the chapel.

A week after Adelicia's funeral, Kent went to see Seth Davis, who was still in the hospital recovering from his injuries. Jeff Haggerty had been released from the hospital the day after the accident. He had a broken ankle, a broken nose, and a nasty cut on his forehead. Ben Jackson was dead on arrival at the hospital and had been buried two days after Adelicia. The cyclist, age 22, was from Costa Rica and had been visiting family. He had borrowed his cousin's motorcycle just ten minutes before the accident. It was only the second time that he had ever been on a bike.

The officer investigating the accident told Kent that Adelicia had apparently come to a quick stop on the bridge for some unknown reason. Kent knew then that she had once again experienced the blackouts. For that reason, he not only felt responsible for Adelicia, but he felt responsible for the boys in the pickup and the cyclist. Kent felt that if he had only been with Adelicia, none of it would have happened. Kent wrote a letter to Jeff and his family and to Ben's parents, and to Jose's family. But he never personally met with them. For some reason he felt the need to reach out to Seth. He wished Seth a full recovery and wished him well in his football career.

Kent had heard of Seth, the star quarterback since he played at the high school near where Kent and Adelicia had lived. Later that year he watched Seth play in several game. He spoke to Seth and his family after the games. While they never became good friends, the family had a lot of respect for Kent and his actions after the loss of Adelicia.

During the last game of the season, they had a special moment before the game, honoring Ben Jackson. The entire team was collected at mid-field. On the field beside Seth and his parents, was Kent Rivers. To Kent's surprise, the team had gotten together, along with the parents of Seth, Jeff, and Ben, to include Adelicia Rivers and Jose' in their pre-game memorial.

CHAPTER EIGHTEEN

They need to Pay

Kent fell asleep in his chair after a long evening of reflecting and flashbacks. He woke up around two in the morning. He got up and undressed as he walked to the bedroom, threw his clothes on a chair at the end of his bed, set the clock for 4:30, and crawled between the cool sheets. He was back asleep in seconds. Kent seldom set his alarm clock. Even on those occasions when he did, he woke up fifteen minutes before it sounded. But this morning it rang out like Big Ben was in his room. It startled Kent, and he jumped out of bed and landed on his feet before he got his eyes opened wide enough to see.

As he gained his composure, he reached over and turned off the annoying old fashion bell alarm. Kent stumbled to the shower trying only to use one eye, letting the other eye rest a little longer. As the warm water began to wake his body and mind, he began to reflect on his flashback from the night before. Perhaps it was because he had met Holly a few hours earlier, but after last night he felt a loosening in the grip of guilt about the accident. The awful thoughts about Adelicia that had haunted him for the past several years took on a new, distant feel. While reflecting in the shower about the previous night, he tapped into a river of peaceful emotions. The flow of the new emotions began to wash away the regret and anger that he had hidden away so neatly and so completely. Like warm water over sugar, the self-inflicted misery started to melt and found its way running down his cheeks and down the drain.

As he got out of the shower, he felt a sense of hope and renewal. For a moment, he wondered why he hadn't faced his anger and guilt before. He wasn't going to worry long about that, though. He liked his new panorama, and he wasn't going to rationalize it. He wasn't sure he wanted to admit it, but Holly Packe may have been the conduit to his epiphany. He left for the airport wondering if she would call.

Rivers called the communication center on his radio and learned that Nick Taylor was standing by at the airport. He wanted to hear what Blackman had found out about the yellow Toyota and the Florida connection, but it was five-thirty-five and Blackman would most likely still be in bed. He would have to call him after they landed in Williamsburg.

Rivers had a list of things that he wanted the other investigators to get done that morning, but Dek was as updated as he was, and he could lead the charge for the day. He would check with him after landing. Rivers' mind went to the upcoming flight with Nick Taylor. He and Nick had not said fifty words to each other since he was his training officer, other than the occasional departmental business that caused them to cross paths.

Rivers wasn't looking forward to a long flight in a small aircraft with a man rubbing his cold shoulder against him all the way. But in a homicide case, it was a well-known and proven fact that time was crucial. By flying he could save precious hours. He thought that maybe he could break the ice somehow. While he had his share of haters, he usually knew why. That was not the case with Taylor. Taylor had shown his dislike for Rivers since the day they met. Rivers knew very little about Nick Taylor other than the fact he was from Florida and had been his training officer.

Taylor had never brought up the loss of his wife and his business in Florida to anyone at the department. The hurt had been almost more than he could bear. It changed his life's plans, his outlook, and to a great extent, his personality. He realized that he was still bitter about it all, but the bitterness had become useful to him. The fact that Rivers could almost have passed for his former partner's twin brother was what Nick could not get past. It was not just Kent's looks. His confidence and type-A personality was a match, as well. As long as he carried his bitterness, he would dislike the physical reminder named Kent Rivers.

Rivers arrived at the airport at five-forty-five. Nick Taylor was looking at his watch as Rivers came through the county's hanger door.

"We leave in fifteen minutes you know," Taylor barked at Rivers.

"Yeah, I know. I have five-forty-five. What do you have?" Kent replied as humbly as he could.

"You ready?" Taylor spoke back, ignoring Rivers' question about the time.

"Yeah, I'm ready. Just taking my briefcase."

"Give it here, and I'll put it in the back," Taylor said as he took Rivers' leather briefcase and placed it on the passenger's seat.

They were taking the department's twin-engine Piper Seneca III plane. Taylor took his job seriously and was a professional. Rivers was in good hands. The ride might be a quiet one, as far as the conversation went, but Rivers knew he could relax with Taylor as the pilot. Nick Taylor had already fueled the plane and completed all of the pre-flight checks. They were in the air and headed to

Williamsburg by six-twelve A.M.

During the flight, Rivers attempted to talk with Taylor a few times. He received three yeah answers, two nope answers, and four, I don't know answers. Rivers decided to read a magazine he had brought with him for just this occasion.

Taylor asked one question just before they landed, "Is this the case from the interstate a few days ago?"

Rivers smiled as he got to respond just, "Yeah."

Detective John Decker picked them up at the airport hanger. At first, Taylor was just going to hang out at the airport and read, but Decker talked him into coming along. Taylor liked Decker. He didn't remind him of anyone.

Rivers and Taylor went with Decker to the Whitley County Sheriff's Office. Decker went over what he had learned since he received the call for assistance from Hamilton County. The Whitley County deputy that answered the call at the motel had placed Fisher's tag in one of their evidence bags. Rivers had brought some evidence bags and forms, so he put it in his evidence bag. They sent it to the crime lab for possible finger or palm prints.

"You want to go to the motel?" asked Decker.

"That would be great," Rivers responded.

Taylor just stood near the door, occasionally scratching his head and shifting his weight from one foot to the other. He was not comfortable working with the detectives. He had always been in uniform until he went full time to air support. But he was there, and he did like Decker so far, so he was at least act interested.

"I know we have his statement, but while we are here, is there any way to talk with the deputy who found the tag?" Rivers asked Decker.

"I'm sure you can. I think I heard him on the radio earlier this afternoon. He is probably working day shift. We will round him up. Did you want to do that before we go to the motel?" Decker inquired."

"Well, it depends on when he gets off. We don't want to hold him over on his shift," Rivers answered.

"Hang on; I'll check." Decker picked up the phone, "Hey, this is Decker. Is Bill Turner busy?"

"As far as I know, he is not signed out," the officer replied.

"Could you ask him to come to my office? I have a couple of Tennessee detectives that need to speak with him."

When Decker said he had a couple of detectives that needed to talk to him, Taylor started to speak up to say he wasn't a detective. Not because he didn't respect the job they did, but because he didn't like feeling like people thought he was something that he wasn't.

"Will do," the communications officer replied.

About ten minutes after the call, Deputy Bill Turner knocked on Decker's door.

"Hey, come on in," Decker said as Rivers stood up to greet the deputy.

"Hey, I'm Kent Rivers, and this is…" Rivers was interrupted by Taylor before he could say his name.

"Hi. Nick Taylor. I'm the pilot," Taylor inserted and shook Turner's hand.

"We are from the Hamilton County Tennessee Sheriff's Office. I understand you found a tag in a dumpster," Rivers said as he shook Turner's hand.

Turner was not someone you soon forgot. He was 6' 8" and weighed about 300 pounds. He wasn't what you was call fat, but he was a very big man. His hand swallowed Rivers' and Taylor's during the handshakes.

"Yeah, I guess you read my statement." Turner responded in a soft, bass voice with a distinctly southern
accent.

"Oh, yeah, appreciate that," Rivers answered still standing— partly out of courtesy and partly out of awe of
the size of the deputy.

"I gotta call to see one of the maids out there at the motel. When I got there, two maids were waiting. They told me about these two creepy-looking guys that had stayed late that morning. They were the only one's left at the motel, and the maids were ready to go home. So they were just sittin' and waitin' for them to leave," the deputy reported.

"So your statement says they took you to the dumpster where they had thrown the tag?" Rivers asked.

"Yeah, they did. It was lying on top of some trash. I used a stick and sorta fished it out. The maids gave me a garbage bag to put it in. I didn't know if we would need prints or what kind of shit may be on the thing. Anyway, I slid it into the trash bag, but first I flipped it over to see if there was anything on the other side. There wasn't, so I wrote down the number and then bagged it up. When I got back to my unit, I called it in. Nothing came back on it, so I took it to the office and put it in the evidence box," the deputy finished.

"The housekeepers gave you a description of the two, and you put that in your statement. Was there anything else you can remember about your conversation with them or the manager?" Rivers asked.

"No, other than one of the dumb-asses gave the motel owner his driver's license. They can't be too smart," the deputy surmised. "Oh, there is one thing. Not sure if it's important or not, but I figured since you came all the way here, might as well give you everything and let you decide."

"Yeah, what's that?" Taylor asked.

Rivers gave Taylor a quick glance, then turned back to Turner. He was a little surprised Taylor finally spoke up and asked a question.

"I didn't know if I should put it in my statement because I Don't know how long it had been there; it might not connect to this. But, I asked the owner, at the motel, if I could see the room they were in. The maids had cleaned it by then—took out the trash and all. No way to know what trash in the dumpster came from that room, but, I went to the room anyway. I just happened to see the motel bible on the lamp stand. Like you always find in places. But this one had some of the pages all dented in, you know like it had been abused."

"The Holy Bible?" Decker asked.

"Yeah, you know, like you take to church. One of those that group of guys put in rooms."

"Gideons?" Taylor asked.

"Yeah, I guess," Turner said, although he wasn't sure what Taylor was saying. "Anyway, I opened it up, you know, to try to fix the pages. I'm funny, I guess. Just didn't want to see the Bible messed up. I don't go to church much, but my wife and mom do. Anyway, there was like red and black marks in it. Not all over it, but on some pages. Just marks, nothing you could tell what it was, just marks—like some language. But on the back page, the one that's left blank, it had a drawing of a snake head and some other weird stuff. Looked evil to me. Dunno if any of that has anything to do with these guys, but the maids said they looked creepy, so thought I'd tell ya."

"I don't know, interesting. What do you think Nick?" Rivers asked Taylor but looked at Decker also.

Taylor looked at Rivers for a second without responding, sat on a nearby desktop, then faced Decker.

"Where's it at now? Did you leave it in the room?" Decker asked.

"I don't know where it is. I left it in the room but asked if the maids could find another one to put in there. They didn't know and didn't seem to care, so I guessed it's still in the room."

"Yeah, it's interesting enough that if we can find it, I think we should keep it—just in case. Is that okay with you?" Rivers asked as he looked at Decker.

"Oh yeah. Whatever you guys need is fine with me. Better to have it and not need it than need it and not have it. We'll see if it's still there or if the housekeepers may know where it is," Decker replied.

"Okay, thanks, Turner. We appreciate it," Rivers said.

Taylor nodded toward Turner in agreement with Rivers.

"No problem guys. I hope it helps put these guys away. If they did it; they need to pay," Turner answered.

Decker and the two Tennessee deputies went to the motel. Decker drove, and they rode with him. It was a little after nine when they arrived at the motel. If the housekeepers were not there by then, maybe they could find that Bible while they were waiting.

When they arrived, only Debbie Snider, the younger of the two housekeepers was working. Doris McBride was off that day. They spoke with Debbie, and she remembered the Bible. Debbie said that they had left it in the room, but it wasn't check-out time and the room occupied. Rivers went over Debbie's statement with her in an attempt to see if she remembered anything new since Decker had talked with her. She had not remembered anything new but was with Deputy Turner when he tried to fix the pages in the bible. She said she was interested in what Turner had seen, so when he sat the Bible back down, she picked it up and flipped through the pages. She had the same impression as Turner of what was in the book and used the words, evil looking and weird, to describe it. She said that the reason she left it in the room was she didn't want anything to do with it. She said it gave her the willies.

Decker went to talk with the day-shift clerk that was working. Ekani Nehru, the manager, had traveled to Nashville the night before but was expected back anytime. The clerk was Ekani's wife. Decker asked if she knew where Doris McBride lived. She knew where she lived because she had to pick her up for work a few times when her car was broken down. She gave Decker the address. The phone number Mrs. Nehru had belonged to Doris' neighbor. Once Rivers finished talking with Debbie, they got with Decker and decided to drive to Doris' apartment to redeem the time. There was time for the room with the Bible to be vacant now. For some reason, they all thought the Bible seemed important now, but none of them could explain why they felt that way. When they arrived at Doris' place, no one was at home.

Decker left his card on her door with a note requesting that she call him. It had started raining, and they decided that a cup of coffee and maybe a doughnut was in order. Kent loved donuts, but he only ate them at home. He didn't like the stereotype about cops and donuts. They stopped at Mother Bess' Kitchen, which was Decker's

favorite stop. Partly because of the good food but mostly he enjoyed seeing Pam Lawton—although he did not confess that to her or even to himself. Rivers made a call to the office and talked briefly with Zona and Blackman. Blackman gave him an update on the DeSota County, Florida case.

It started raining harder, so the three investigators were in no big hurry to get back to work. Since Doris apparently had not tried to call there was time to relax with coffee and tell a few war stories while it rained.

☆

Blackman was one of life's characters. Someone that was just different than everyone else. He was a very smart man and an excellent detective, but if you saw him on the street, you would think he was a taxi driver or perhaps a plumber. He was clean but seldom saw a reason to dress up. He wore a tie when he had to, but even the tie knew that it looked out of place around his neck. His office was no different. It wasn't dirty, but it was thought of as, The Cave. Blackman couldn't understand why no one wanted to have meetings in his office.

"Anything new from Florida?" Zona asked. "Kent left a message on the phone for me with a list of expectations. He said he would call back this morning. First thing on the list was to ask you about Florida." "Not yet on the car, but I did speak with a detective from DeSota County. They are working a recent homicide case involving a twenty-five caliber. They don't have a suspect yet, but they are missing the victim's nephew. He may be about the same age as our guy from the motel in Kentucky. He is gonna call me back this morning as soon as he talks with the lead detective on the case," Blackman responded.

"Kent will find that interesting," Zona said as she moved some files to sit down in a chair.

"Yeah, the Florida detective was interested in the fact that our shooter used a twenty-five caliber and we have a car from Florida that may be involved. I think I'll get a call soon," Blackman continued.

After a few minutes of talking about the case and a few other cases, Detective John Gates from DeSota County, Florida called Blackman. They talked for nearly a half hour, exchanging information and asking questions.

Blackman had just finished writing down all of his notes from the phone call when Rivers called.

"Hey! What's up?" Rivers asked when Blackman picked up the phone.

"Dang, do you have the place bugged? I just got off the phone with Florida not ten minutes ago," Blackman replied.

"Yeah, you didn't know it was bugged? So is your car and your house. I've meant to speak to you about a few things, but that can wait. What did you find out from Florida?"

"You are a funny man, Chief. I'm here working my ass off, and you are off flying around the country with your best friend. Yeah, I got some info from down south, but I'll save the county some money. I'll hang up and talk to the walls so you can get it from your wire," Blackman said with a big laugh.

"Okay, that's fine, I'll remember that the next time I need someone to go to a malodorous autopsy," Rivers said laughing back.

Blackman hated to attend autopsies and the ones that had been dead for a while really got to him. On more than one occasion Blackman had to leave the room after gagging and almost throwing up. One time he had to leave four times during the autopsy because the smell was so bad. Later the forensic examiner talked to Rivers about giving Blackman a break from having to attend them. Rivers just smiled at the medical examiner, and they both started laughing at him.

"Alright, you win. The detective in DeSota County, Florida believes that his suspect is the nephew of the victim," Blackman said as he looked at a note he had in his hand for the nephew's name. "His name is Mark Manning, he's in his mid-twenties, and guess what kind of car he drives?"

"A pink Caddy?" "No, funny man, an old yellow Toyota, or at

least that's what a few neighbors had seen him drive. No word yet on whether he owns it or not. He didn't know what year. Didn't have the license number, and from what they have been able to find out, he may never have registered it in Florida. Oh, and he confirmed that his victim was shot with a twenty-five caliber. Good work-huh?" Blackman asked.

"Never doubted you, my man, never for one minute. Sounds like things are getting interesting for the driver of the Toyota. Anything else?" River questioned.

"He had some questions about our case and what we knew about our shooter or shooters. I told him that we were hoping to get more info on that today. He is trying to track down some of his victim's relatives in hopes of learning more about the nephew and where he may be headed."

"Did you ask that DeSota detective if he had ever heard of the name we got from Kentucky, what was it, Saxton?"

"Yeah, Kenny Saxton. I asked him, they are going to do some checking. He had never heard of him, neither had another detective in the room, but they will run it down. It's to their advantage also, so I think they will jump right on it. Sounds like the same perps right now."

"Good. I would like to find out who these guys are and start rocking their world. If we can find them," Rivers said.

"Yeah, me too."

"Okay, I think I'm going to get off the phone and see what we can find out here. We have been delayed a little. Only one of the housekeepers was working today, and the motel manager won't be back until after lunch. You got plans?" Rivers asked.

"Right now I'm gonna write up everything I got from Florida and run down a lead on another case I've been working. You know, the missing girl, the nineteen-year-old girl from Hixson," Bates stated.

"Oh, yeah, anything new there?" Rivers asked.

"Not a whole lot, but I'm leaning toward no foul play right now."

"Yeah, from what I could tell when we talked to the mother, it looked more like someone who was tired of living at home but didn't want to face mom. But don't let me influence you."

"I won't. But do you blame her? I dread facing the mom myself. But, I think I may have found a friend that will at least let us know that she is safe. Then it will be between her and her mom."

"Okay, let me know what you find out. I would like to get her off my mind if she is just getting away from mom." "Will do, boss." "I'll call back and let you know what I find out. That way you can call Florida back. I don't want to let too much time lapse before we call them again."

"Gotcha!"

CHAPTER NINETEEN

Snakes and Triangles

The three investigators went back to the Lazy Sleeper. It was past checkout time, and the room was vacant. They retrieved the key from the desk clerk and entered the room. Taylor found the Bible on the nightstand. He handed it to Rivers. Rivers took it and he sat down in a chair at a small desk. Taylor and Decker made themselves comfortable on corners of the unmade bed.

The crinkles in the book didn't look accidental. They looked like someone had held it in one hand and hit the pages with something narrow, but dull.

When Rivers opened the book to the first page, he saw a red and black mark. It looked a little like Greek lettering. He thumbed through the book and saw several similar markings, all red and black and all took the shape of some unknown language. On the back cover page, there was the snake figure that Turner had mentioned.

The snake had what looked like hind legs, a horn, and huge eyes. Whoever had made the drawing was a talented artist, Rivers thought. The snake was on top of a circle that contained a triangle.

Inside the triangle was a single large eye. The pupil of the eye was colored red. The drawing was almost entirely done in black and had a dark, red background.

Rivers took some pictures of the drawing and some of the markings in the book. They still didn't know what they had, or why they wanted to keep it. It was weird and found in the room where some possible murder suspects had stayed a few days earlier. To Rivers, that was reason enough. Rivers gave the motel clerk a receipt for the Bible and put it in his briefcase. Once again, they headed to Doris McBride's place.

Doris had just returned from shopping with her daughter. She let them know that she was glad to help them but didn't know what more she could do. Rivers told her that they were only there to review her previous statement and maybe ask a few new questions, based on what they had learned since they last talked.

Doris was cooperative and answered their questions to the best of her memory. There was little doubt that if a witness from the motel were needed, Doris McBride would be the one to put on the stand.

As they were finishing with their interview, Doris volunteered some new information. She had never said anything about it during the two prior interviews, because she wasn't a hundred percent sure about it and thought she should only give them entirely accurate information.

"There is something that has been bothering me. I've thought about it several times over the past two days. I didn't say anything about it earlier because it didn't have anything to do with seeing them throw away the tag and it is probably nothing," Doris stated.

Decker had zoned out a little, thinking about some of his own case workload. When he heard her say something about new information, he perked up.

"Let me assure you, Ms. McBride, that no piece of information is too small or insignificant. I learned that crucial lesson the hard way early on in my career. Please, tell us what you are talking about," Rivers responded.

"Well, when I first got to work that morning, about seven o'clock, I was walking through the parking lot near the laundry room. I noticed what looked like a young girl walking in front of the rooms. I thought to myself that she was too young to be staying alone, so I watched to see what room she was headed for. About then, the supply delivery truck pulled in and Jack, the driver, yelled at me. I waved at him and looked away for just a moment. I mean, just a quick moment. That's what bothers me. When I looked back, the young girl was gone. What bothers me is, the last place I saw her was right in front of those guy's room. I can't swear to it, but I don't think she could have made it to the next room, no longer than I looked away," Doris told the detectives.

"How old would you say she was?" asked Rivers.

"It was still just a little dark, cloudy, but I think she couldn't have been over 14 or 15, at the most. She was a small girl."

"What else can your remember about her. Do you remember what she was wearing?" Rivers continued.

"She was wearing what nurses wear. You know, those uniforms type shirts, and a pair of jeans. She was a cute girl. Hair down to about her shoulders—dark."

"Did you see her again that morning?" Taylor asked.

"No, that's why I dismissed it. I thought, well, if she was in that room with those guys, I never saw her get into the car, or saw her again anywhere that morning."

"Is it possible that she could have already gotten into the car before you and Debbie came out?" Asked Decker.

"Sure, it's possible. We didn't just watch the room the entire time. Yeah, it was possible, I guess. I just don't know. I never saw her again after that morning. That's for sure. So, if she was with someone else, I didn't see her leave. I was busy, so I didn't see everyone leave that morning, but I do try to keep an eye out for when people are leaving so I'll know when to clean the rooms. My gut just tell me that she was with them. That's all. Maybe just a gut feeling more than anything."

"Do you think you would recognize her if you saw her again?" Rivers asked.

"Like I told him," she said as she glanced at Decker, "the last time he talked with me, I don't know if I could recognize anyone a month from now. But today, if I saw her, yeah."

"Did Debbie see her?" Decker asked.

"I don't think so. If Debbie did, she didn't say anything if she did. Of course, I didn't say anything to her about seeing the girl. At the time I didn't think it was anything. I just started thinking that maybe I should say something and let Y'all decide if it was significant."

"Well, we appreciate that, Ms. McBride. Thank you. And I appreciate you taking the time on your day off. I'm sorry we had to track you down, but we would like to get finished here and get back to Chattanooga," Rivers told her.

They left Doris' apartment and went back to Decker's office and talked about the girl and the Bible. They decided that it was more than a good chance that the girl was with them. But if she was with them, where did she come from, and when did she get with them?

It was about 1:30 in the afternoon by the time they had everything straight in their minds and made their notes. Rivers thanked Decker for all of his help and assured him that they would be back in touch. Taylor told Decker that he was glad he came, if for no other reason to meet him.

Decker drove them back to the airfield. Taylor went through his pre-flight checks while Decker and Rivers chatted a little longer. It wasn't long before Rivers and Taylor were back in the air, Chattanooga bound. There was a different feel to the trip back. Neither man said a word for the first 15 minutes. Then Rivers tried once again to break the ice.

"Thanks for your help. I appreciate it," Rivers said.

"It wasn't anything. I felt like a third wheel. I probably should have just hung out at the airport." Taylor responded, keeping his eyes looking straight ahead.

"No, I appreciate your coming, and you had some insightful questions. I was glad you were there."

"I didn't ask anything that you wasn't have asked if I hadn't been there. I just did it to keep from feeling like an idiot in front of the others. It wasn't intended to help or interfere, either one. I made no real contribution. It just helped me feel better being there."

"Well, good. Glad it helped."

It was another 10 minutes before anyone spoke. Rivers took the opportunity to find out why Taylor didn't like him.

"I'm just going to ask you—what is your problem with me? Or do you treat everyone like a cold piece of meat?" Rivers said half smiling.

"I don't have a problem with you. I just think you are a know-it-all, ego-maniac, self-serving, self-promoter, that's all."

"Now, that is funny," Rivers responded laughing out loud.

"It figures that you would think so," Taylor replied.

"You started treating me this way from the first time you laid eyes on me, so yeah, I do find it funny that you thank I am all those things. You didn't even know me when you started this crap," Rivers said, this time without a smile.

"That's not true. I was just a training officer and didn't want to mix friendship with training. It was a job to me—a job that I took seriously, that's all."

"Other than the training time, and a few times here and there since, we haven't even been together that much. So give me some examples of my being a know-it-all or self-serving."

"I'm not gonna get into all of that right now."

"You can't think of any, can you?"

"Okay, this is an example right here of your being an egomaniac. You can't stand it that someone may not like you."

"I don't care if you don't like me. I don't even care if you think I'm all of those things. That's your business. But I'm me, so I act like me. You can like it, love it, be indifferent, or hate it, but it doesn't change my shoe size or the way I walk. I'm not you, and that is something we can both be proud of."

"Oh wow, that was a mouthful!" Taylor said as he started laughing. "Have you been saving that line or is it your standard response when people think you're a jerk?"

Rivers just shook his head and picked up the magazine that he was reading on the trip up. He had already read everything he was interested in, but it was better than continuing his argument for peace.

"You are something, Nick. You don't even know me," Rivers said as he settled on a page to re-read.

"I've known people like you all my life," Nick replied, while Rivers just kept his face in the magazine.

They were both quiet for another 15 minutes after that exchange. Taylor began to reflect on their visit to Williamsburg and that while there he hadn't seen any of the attributes he called Rivers. In fact, other than feeling that he looked like Jake Long, he found him to be a pretty nice guy. But now was not the time to think about Jake Long or that whole situation, he thought. If he changed how he felt about Rivers, he might have to face the past. Rivers had become the object of his bitterness. He was the only person around that reminded him of his past and his pain. How could he forgive Rivers for being that symbol? From the first time he met Rivers he had been the face of his pain. Rivers may not be all I said, he thought, but I still don't have to like him, not right now.

About 10 minutes before landing in Chattanooga, Taylor relented just a little.

"You may not be all of those things. You are right; I don't really know you. But you remind me of so many people that are those things. Maybe we could just agree to disagree and not be hostile."

"That's a good start. Thanks!" Rivers replied.

Taylor mumbled something back, but Rivers couldn't understand him and decided he probably wouldn't want to hear it anyway.

Once back in Chattanooga, Rivers gathered those at the office working on the Fisher case. He went over what he and Taylor had learned in Williamsburg, and Blackman went over what he had learned in Florida. Rivers had asked Zona to attend that meeting. She came in a little late and took notes. Rivers let everyone go home early that afternoon so that they would get a fresh start at seven-thirty the next morning.

Thursday, June 24th 5:00 A.M.

Rivers was out the door by five-thirty the next morning. He reviewed the notes from the night before and made a few of his own. He went into the war room to consider new facts along with some older points. Once again he reviewed all the photographs, the reports and statements, and the entire case to date. By seven-thirty his game plan was ready for the players when they got to work.

Blackman arrived at the office about seven and noticed Rivers was in the War room. He chose to not bother him. Rivers came out of the room about Seven-fifteen and chatted with Blackman about the local missing girl case that Blackman was working. Blackman had been able to track down the missing teen and made sure she was safe.

Rivers waited until seven-thirty to talk about the Fisher case. He didn't want anyone to miss a detail and was afraid that if he started giving it out piece mill, he was forget something. He always started his meetings on time — not a moment before and not a minute later. Everyone knew to be there on time.

Detectives Lieutenant Dek Bates, Carl Howe, Jesse Hawkins, Pete Sanchez, Kevin Dalton, Jen Rogers, and Blackman were in the meeting. Rivers had invited Chief Deputy Sal Dillard and TBI agent Baker Willis, as well as Zona, to the early morning session. Everyone was in the room but TBI agent Willis. Rivers knew he would probably be running late. Willis wanted to attend to catch up on the case and compare it to some unsolved cases elsewhere in the state. Dillard was there to show his support for the division and the Fisher investigation.

Rivers believed that the new information obtained in Williamsburg could be significant. The information about the young girl the housekeeper saw at the motel was interesting to him. The marked up Bible was also of interest to him. If the young lady was a teenager 14 or 15 years old, it could mean that she was a runaway or even kidnapped.

Rivers assigned Pete Sanchez the task of running down any information on teenage girls missing anywhere from Florida through Kentucky. Since Blackman was already working with

DeSoto County

Sheriff's Office on their homicide case. Rivers had Blackman inquire about any strange drawings or paintings in their case. If there were similar drawings, Blackman would be headed to Florida.

Shortly after the meeting, Zona told Rivers that he had a call and that the caller only said that Holly was calling. Rivers didn't even ask what line. He glanced at the buttons on the phone and picked one was lit up. He put the phone against his chest to block his voice as he whispered thank you to Zona and asked her to close the door as she left. Zona smiled while doing an exaggerated tiptoe out of the office. Rivers made a face at her and raised his eyebrows. Zona had never seen Kent respond to a call like he did this one. She found it amusing.

"Hello, this is Kent Rivers," Kent said, pretending he didn't have a clue who was on the other end.

"Hello, Kent. Do you know who this is?" Holly replied.

"Of course I do. How could I forget that voice? It's Shania How are you, Shania? It's been a while," Kent responded, not being able to restrain a huge smile.

"Oh, I'm sorry, I must have called the wrong Kent. I just knew that the Kent I met would remember me. I'm sorry I bothered you," Holly shot back with a straight-face tease of her own.

"No!" Kent said, projecting his voice a little more than he had intended. "No," he repeated in a softer voice. "I know who it is. Of course, I know who it is." Kent managed a nervous laugh. "How are you, Holly? It's great to hear from you."

"I'm doing great. How about you? Holly responded.

"Good. I'm good. Just working on some cases," Kent replied, feeling a little silly for trying to make a joke.

"Great. Well, listen, I know you are busy, and I don't want to keep you."

"No, it's fine. I have time."

"I actually just called with a question. I don't know if you would call it a legal issue or not, but I wasn't sure who to ask. Then I thought about you. I was going to call yesterday, but I couldn't find your card. I finally found it between the seats in the car this morning when I dropped my phone in the same place," Holly said, knowing she was punching him again with a straight-face tease.

Disappointed that she hadn't tucked his number safely away, he replied, "I'm glad you dropped your phone then."

Holly laughed. "Me, too. I would hate to call an attorney just to ask a simple question."

"I can understand that, so what's your question? Kent asked.

"I was hoping I could get you to stop by the house and let me show you a paper that I received. There is no rush; I just need to decide what to do about it. I thought that you might be able to help."

Feeling redeemed from the lost card, Kent replied, "Sure, I will. When?"

"Oh, that is totally up to you. I'm free most of the time."

"This afternoon?" Kent had responded before he thought about how desperate he might sound.

"Today?" Holly questioned in a puzzled tone.

"If you are ready for me to stop by. If not then, just tell me when and I'll try to make it."

"Oh, that's fine with me, if you are sure it's okay with your schedule."

"I have some time this afternoon. That will work for me."

"Okay. What time should I expect you?"

"Three-thirty okay?"

"Three-thirty it is. Thank you so much! I'll try not to take up much of your time."

"Don't worry about that. I'll be done here for the day once I leave. Providing that no one decides to kill anyone while I'm gone, that is," Kent replied with a gentle laugh.

Holly gave Kent her address before they hung up. Kent leaned back in his chair and replayed the call in his mind line by line. He was a little deflated after she told him that she couldn't find his card. He had hoped that he had made a better impression on her. She had indeed had made an impression on him. Getting invited to her home made up for losing the card. He hoped that nothing would come up before he went to meet her. He felt there might be something more with Holly. He found himself hoping so anyway.

CHAPTER TWENTY

Sunday Morning In Georgia

Saturday, June 19th 7:30 P.M.

By the time Mark, Kenny, and Keri left the state park, the sun had to started to go down. They got back on the Interstate and heading toward Atlanta. Mark was laughing, making jokes, and acted as if nothing had happened. Keri and Kenny were puzzled by Mark's behavior. They had never seen anyone act so violently and then be so nonchalant about it. But without even looking at each other, they decided to play his game and act as if nothing had happened.

Without enough money, Mark knew they could not make it all the way to their destination. He had committed more crimes in the last several days than he had committed over his entire lifetime, so he reasoned a few more wouldn't matter.

Mark had disconnected from any thought about the murder of his uncle, the things he had stolen, and the attempted rape of a young girl. He was not feeling any guilt for his offenses. In reality, Mark had never felt guilty about anything.

After a few more minutes of silence, Mark told Kenny and Keri that he was coming up with a plan to get some money.

"What kind of plan?" Kenny asked, worried about what his twisted travel mate had in mind.

"Don't worry about it. I'll take care of it," Mark responded.

"Somebody better start worrying about, or you will have us spending a lifetime in jail!" Kenny spoke emphatically.

"You haven't gotten into anything," Mark countered.

"The hell I haven't!"

"What have you done?"

"I don't even know what all, but by just being with you, they could say I am as guilty as you are!"

"You keep talking about getting caught. Well, I ain't getting caught! We have to finish this trip, so act like you've got some balls!"

"Yeah, you might see a lot more balls than you want when they lock your balls up!"

"Who will catch us? No one saw me shoot my uncle. By the time they started looking for us for stealing the stuff, we were long gone. So unless you run your damn mouth, or she says something, nobody is gonna know anything about us. Are Y'all gonna run your mouths?" Mark asked as his eyes bounced from Kenny To Keri.

"I'm not saying nothing! Leave me out of this conversation." Keri quickly responded.

"Nobody has to say anything. You think the cops are stupid?" Kenny asked.

Mark looked at Kenny and grinned as he said, "yeah, pretty much."

"Well, they're not. Jail is full of smart people like us," Kenny said, almost yelling.

"Y'all just keep your mouth shut and nobody will ever know

anything. I am not gonna jail because somebody couldn't keep their damn mouth shut. Got that?" Mark yelled as he looked at Kenny then at Keri.

"I'm not talking to nobody. Who am I gonna talk to? I'm just saying what could happen to all of us. I'm not saying anything. You think I want to go to jail? Kenny responded.

"So, what's your plan Mark?" Keri asked softly, hoping to change the subject and cool things down.

"I don't know yet, but I know I've got to do something. Unless you have a bright idea," Mark responded.

"I don't have any ideas," Keri said almost whispering.

"I know one thing, we have to get off the interstate and go to some small place in the country to do whatever were gonna do," Mark told the two.

"Whatever it is, don't use the gun. That can only mean trouble for everybody," Kenny insisted.

"I'm not going anywhere without my gun, so just get used to that," Mark fired back.

"I'm not saying don't have it with you; I'm saying don't pull it out. It's just more trouble," Kenny continued.

"What? You think I'm just gonna shoot somebody for no reason?" Mark asked.

"You said you killed your uncle. I have no clue why you shot him. How am I to know what your reasons are? You sure he's dead?" Kenny inquired.

"Yes, he's dead, take my word for that. And I've got my reasons. Now shut up about the gun!" Mark countered.

Everyone in the car got quiet again. About fifteen minutes later, Mark got off the interstate and headed towards Griffin, Georgia. After a few miles, Mark turned onto a secondary road and ended up on a small, country road. Mark was looking for a store but after a few miles and a few more turns, he never found one.

Mark turned onto an old logging road. He traveled down the dirt trail several hundred feet deep into a wooded area. It was almost dark by then but a bright moon was shining. Many of the trees had been cut down around them, and the moon gave them plenty of light. Mark opened his door and got out, lit a cigarette, and set on the hood of the car. After a few moments, Kenny decided to get out and see what was on Mark's mind. Keri laid down in the backseat. She picked up some clothing from the floor to make a pillow and intended to go to sleep.

Kenny took out a pack of cigarettes from his pants pocket, lit it, and leaned against the car a few feet away from where Mark was sitting on the hood. Neither of the two said anything for several minutes.

Finally, Kenny spoke up and asked Mark what he was doing.

"I'm just thinking."

"Thinking about what?" Kenny asked.

"How I'm gonna get some more money?"

"So how are you?"

"I don't know yet, so quit bugging me till I decide."

"I'm not bugging you; I was just trying to figure out what we're doing out here in the middle of nowhere."

"I told you, I'm thinking."

"Let's just get back on the interstate and go on. We should have enough money for gas to get to Ohio."

"Yeah, maybe so. So we get to Ohio broke, is that your plan?"

"I just don't like hanging around. And if we get into something else, that is just gonna bring heat on us. So let's just get the hell outta here, and when we get to Ohio, we can figure out what to do then."

"You just don't get it, do you? We try to get some money there, and the chances of getting caught are a lot higher than here. We get money here, and we'll be long gone before they figure out what happened. So let me think so that I can figure something out."

Keri had fallen asleep in the backseat. Mark and Kenny got back into the car. When Mark tried to start the vehicle, it didn't start. The engine was turning over, but he could not get it started.

"That's just great," Kenny said.

"See what's wrong with it!" Mark demanded.

"Sounds like it's not getting gas. Try to start it when I tell you to," Kenny said.

"Okay, I hope you know what you're doing," Mark replied, as he climbed back into the driver's seat.

Kenny had worked on cars off and on since he was a kid. He went back and got a few tools that he had in his tackle box. After a few minutes, he had Mark try to start the car. They tried several times to get the car started, but it didn't start. Keri was sound asleep in the backseat and hadn't moved. Kenny stepped to the back of the car and sat on the trunk. Mark got out of the car and walked over to Kenny.

"What you doing?" Mark asked Kenny.

"I'm thinking."

"Can't you fix it?"

"I'm not sure if it's in the fuel line or something is stopping it up. It could be trash in the line and the vacuum's messing up. I don't know."

"Well, we can't just sit here. Are you not gonna try to fix it?"

"I can't see to fix it! Kenny yelled at Mark. "And I don't know if I even have the tools to fix it when I can see it!"

"What kind of tools do you need?"

"Depends on what's wrong. If it's in the fuel lines, I can probably just blow them out. It shouldn't be too hard to get to the fuel lines. At least at daylight, I can see. But if it's in the carburetor, we're screwed."

"How ya gonna find out?"

Kenny lit another cigarette, looked at Mark, and shrugged his shoulders. Mark spit on the ground and went to the front of the car and looked under the hood. Mark did not know anything about car engines. He stepped away from under the hood, walked over to the driver's side of the car, leaned up against the door with his backside, and lit cigarette. After a few moments, when Kenny had finished about half of his cigarette, he put it out and placed the remaining half back into his pack. He told Mark to get

back in the car and try to start it again on his cue. The engine turned over a few times but sounded like the battery was dying. They decided they would sleep there until morning.

They didn't have a lot of food left in the car, but they ate what they had. They sat on the trunk of the car for a while making small talk and smoking cigarettes. Finally, they decided to try to sleep. It was a warm night, but a gentle breeze was blowing. Mark rolled up a couple of shirts to make a pillow. He crawled onto the hood of the car and leaned his head against the windshield. Kenny grabbed a few clothes from the car and made a bed in a clearing about twenty-five feet from the car.

Keri only got out of the car one time. For a long time, she just stared out at the bright moon and thought about her life and the trip she was now taking. The life she had with her grandmother seemed like a different life. Everything took on a different feel and an entirely unexpected look now. She found herself caught up in an ordeal filled with apprehension and agony. She had always thought of herself as a good girl and certainly never intended to go down the road her mother had traveled. She decided that she must not lose hope. She would come out of this a better person, she thought. She climbed back into the back seat of the car. As she faded off to sleep again, she thought of how good it would be to awake from this horrible dream. Soon she was sound asleep. Except for a few Georgia mosquitoes, it had been an uneventful night for her, and she was thankful, even for just a few moments of peace.

The sun came up Sunday morning, but the three stayed asleep like they were lying in their beds at home with nothing to do. Finally, the morning sun got warm on the hood of the car, and Mark woke up. They all woke up within a few minutes of each other. They decided to try to start the car again. When Mark turned the key, the car started immediately. Kenny jumped back into the car and told Mark, "Let's go!"

"What did you do?" Mark asked.

"Nothing, something must have been clogging the fuel line. We must have sat here long enough for it to settle. That don't mean it ain't gonna do it again."

"Do it again?!" Mark asked in a loud, angry voice.

"That's what I said. It can happen again. Just never know."

"So it could just strand us in the middle of nowhere?"

Kenny looked around at the woods around them and laughed at Mark's comment and said, "In the middle of nowhere? What do you call this?"

"Damn! That's just what I need," Mark yelled.

"Well, it's running now, so let's get outta here," Keri said boldly.

Both Mark and Kenny were surprised to hear Keri speak in such a tone. But they both agreed, so neither of them said anything back.

Mark had trouble turning the car around on the small narrow logging road but finally got it headed back toward the main road. He was driving slowly, and when he went about half a mile, he turned into a driveway. Kenny asked him what he was doing, but Mark just looked at him and smiled and got out of the car.

There was a woman in her mid-sixties working in her flower bed as Mark approached the house. The woman, Loretta Beasley, didn't hear the car pull up and was startled when she saw Mark just a few feet away from her. Normally she would have been in church on a Sunday, but her husband had to work, and she didn't like to go to church without him. Mark smiled at her then asked her for directions to the interstate.

There was one car sitting in the carport at the house. It was an older Buick but looked like it was in running condition. Mrs. Beasley attempted to give Mark directions to the interstate, but Mark acted like he could not understand her directions, and asked if she could draw him a map. He wanted her to go into the house so he could follow her. He was trying to decide if she was home alone or if someone else was in the house. Keri and Kenny remained in the car and wondered what Mark was saying to the woman. They decided that whatever he was up to, they did not want to take part and would stay in the car. They were both concerned about what Mark might do, but neither one of them felt like they were in a position to do anything about it. They had already experienced Mark's capacity for violence. They had already talked about leaving Mark at the first opportunity but was have to do it when they could make a clean getaway.

Mrs. Beasley was reluctant to go into the house, but at the same time, she didn't feel comfortable outside talking with Mark. He was smiling and polite, but she could feel there was something that wasn't right about him.

There were no neighbors within sight of her home, and all of them were in church anyway. She wasn't expecting her husband back for more than three hours. Mrs. Beasley told Mark that she was not good at drawing maps, but her brother lived directly up the road so she could call him and let Mark talk to him on the phone. She paused, then she changed her mind and asked him if he would just go up the road to where her brother lived. She assured him it was just a short distance. She didn't know if her brother was home or not, but it would give her a chance to get away from Mark.

Mark smiled and told her that he didn't mind talking to him on the phone. Mrs. Beasley did not want Mark to go into the house and realized she made a mistake by saying that she could call her brother. She now faced the choice of telling Mark to leave and being unfriendly or taking a chance and going into the house to make a phone call. She had seen another guy and girl in the car and thought that maybe indeed they were lost.

Mrs. Beasley went to the side door of her house, and Mark followed her while smiling and making small talk about her Buick. Once they were inside, Mark closed the door behind him and pulled out his gun. At first, she was not looking at Mark and kept walking towards the phone. When she turned around and saw the gun, she screamed and backed into a stool which caused her to fall. Mark instructed her to be quiet and asked her where she kept the cash. At the time, she was scared and couldn't remember whether or not she had any cash in the house.

Mark grabbed her by the arm and made her stand up. He put the gun to her head and told her that he had already killed two people and did not mind making her the third. After just a few moments she recalled some cash that her husband had put in his dresser drawer. He had sold a riding lawn more a few days before and had not taken the money to the bank. She told Mark about the money and that it was inside the dresser and told him to get it. She did not want to go into her bedroom with him. Mark insisted that she get the money.

She reluctantly walked into the bedroom towards the dresser. She opened the top drawer, lifted a T-shirt, and pulled out $425 cash. She handed the money to Mark and immediately started to leave the bedroom, but Mark grabbed her.

Keri and Kenny were getting nervous about what was taking Mark so long. They had gotten out of the car and smoked two cigarettes each. Mark returned to the car smiling and told them that she was a really nice lady and had given them some food. He didn't tell them about the money, or what he had done in the house. They all got back in the car and Mark backed out of the driveway and headed back towards the interstate.

They had only been gone from the house 25 minutes, when Mrs. Beasley's daughter, Amy, and granddaughter, Megan pulled into Beasley's driveway. Amy was late for Sunday School as she was about to pass her parent's house. She decided to Sunday School and stop to see what her mom was doing for lunch before heading to church services. Amy told her daughter to stay in the car and that she would be right back.

The storm door was closed, but the house door was open. Amy didn't think anything about it because her mom was always going in and out of the house when working in the yard. She called for her mother but didn't get an answer. She walked into her mom's room and saw her mother's naked, lifeless body on the bed. Because a bloody nightgown was over her mother's face, she knew she was hurt badly, but she did not know that her mother was shot. She ran to pull the nightgown off her mother's face hoping that she was still alive. When she saw her mother's wound, she almost fainted. She ran to the bathroom to throw up.

When she came back into the bedroom, she shook her mother to see if she could get a response at all, even though she already knew the answer. She panicked when she realized her daughter was still in the car outside and she had no clue where the person was who shot her mother. She ran to the front door and opened it so she could see her daughter. No one was around the car, and her daughter waved at her. She ran to the phone and called 911. After making the call, she ran to her car, got inside, and locked the doors.

CHAPTER TWENTY-ONE
'87 Monte Carlo

It took the first Spalding County, Georgia deputy sheriff only four minutes to arrive. He found Amy and her daughter sitting in her locked car with the engine running. When Amy saw the deputy,

she rolled down her window and told the deputy that her mother was in the back bedroom. She was careful not to say much in front of her daughter.

The deputy instructed her to stay in the car while he checked the residence. About three minutes later a second deputy arrived at the house. The two deputies checked the property to be sure that the perpetrator was not still inside the house. Not long after the second deputy arrived, the emergency medical team was on the scene. The medics were in the house no more than ten minutes. As they were leaving each one simply did a quick head nod to Amy. It was their way of showing respect for her deceased mother without saying anything.

The deputies came outside and closed the doors behind them. Two Spalding County detectives, Brian Gunter and Leo Chapman,

heard the call and was already in route to the home. After
conferring with the two deputies at the scene on an alternate
radio channel, Spalding County Chief Deputy Rick Delaney
advised communications to have the mobile crime scene vehicle
and personnel respond to the Beasley's as soon as possible. The
chief responded to the crime scene to assist the investigation
team.

Once at the scene, Detective Lieutenant Brian Gunter took
charge of the scene. He had been the lead homicide detective for
Spalding County the last twelve years. The investigative team
examined the house with a fine-toothed comb. Chief Delaney
learned from Amy where her father was working and went to
speak with the victim's husband personally before he came home
and found the carnage. He didn't want Mr. Beasley to come home
and discover that his peaceful home had turned into a crime
scene.

Amy did not want to leave the house or her mother and
struggled between staying or taking her daughter home. Chief
Delaney talked her into going home. Before Amy left, Chief
Delaney had a deputy follow her home and remain with her until
Amy's husband was located.

When Mr. Beasley arrived at the house, Chief Delaney was
there to meet him. The chief asked the
husband, James Beasley if he would mind waiting outside with
him until the crime scene personnel could complete their task. Mr.
Beasley desperately wanted to go into the house, but the chief
persuaded him it would be best to wait. It wasn't long after Mr.
Beasley arrived that a volunteer chaplain for the Spalding County
Sheriff's Office pulled into the driveway. The chaplain, Bill Baltz,
was a pastor at a local Methodist church and knew the Beasley
family.

It was after dark before the crime scene personnel finished their task. Mrs. Beasley's body had been removed about two hours before dark. By this time, family members and friends of the family arrived at the Beasley residence. Mr. Beasley's two brothers and both of his sons, as well as two of his best friends, came to the house. The pastor of his church arrived a short time later.

Mr. Beasley's two best friends handled the task of cleaning up the bedroom after the crime scene techs had left. Mr. Beasley's son, Troy, called his dad's doctor and the Doctor called in a prescription for a sedative, so he would be able to sleep later. His son, Tony, took Mr. Beasley to his home to stay with him for a few days.

The crime scene techs roped off the entire yard including the driveway. They found four cigarette butts in the dirt next to the driveway. They found no evidence that anyone in the Beasley home had smoked, other than an old pipe discovered in the den. The cigarettes were two different brands. One brand was smoked to the very end while the other brand had teeth marks in the filter and were not smoked to the end. The detectives felt if the person or persons responsible for the murder had smoked the cigarettes, there were two of them and they would have been in the driveway for at least twenty minutes. Detective Killian suggested that there could have been three or four people involved. He thought that two might have stood watch while one or two others went into the house. They were in hopes that someone might have driven by the house and seen a car and/or individuals in the driveway.

Detective Lieutenant Gunter and Detective Chapman remained at the scene after the crime scene techs had left. They spoke to each of the family members alone and briefly with Mr. Beasley. While the crime scene techs and the detectives were at the scene; Chief Delaney had patrol units deputies go house to house in both directions to see if anyone had noticed anything earlier that day that might help them in their investigation.

Deputy Zach Miller talked to some guys in a logging crew that was working about a mile from the Beasley House. They were on break when he walked up. There were six guys sitting on a recently cut log and one man leaning against a pickup truck.

"Hey guys, there was a lady killed up the road from here and we are trying to see if anyone saw anything in the last few hours down here," Miller asked the crew.

The guys on the log looked at each other in surprise then shook their heads no. Jimmy Stevens was leaning against his pickup. He owned the equipment and the trucks that were harvesting the trees. He looked at Miller for a moment then walked toward him. He had a big chew of tobacco in his cheek and he spit tobacco juice on a stump as he walked toward the deputy.

"Ya say there's a woman killed on this road this mornin'?" Jimmy Stevens asked with a strong Georgia accent.

"Yes sir, not too far east of here."

"When did this happen?" Stevens asked.

"Not sure exactly, but sometime this morning."

"Well, I dunno know if'n it had anythin' to do with it, but there was this car parked not too awful far from here all night last night. Had a couple of guys and a girl in it," Stevens stated.

"When was this?" Miller asked.

"Well, I first saw it last night as I wuss leaving here. We gotta get this area done by the end of the week, so we been workin' late and on the weekends. Anyways, everyone else had already gone, and I was a workin' on the Feller Buncher. It has some leaks. After I had left here, I noticed a car goin' down a loggin' road about a quarter- to a half-mile from here. It was 'bout dark, so I mainly just saw its lights as it was goin' back in there. I just figured there was jus' some kids parkin', so I paid no 'tension to it," Stevens said as he spit a long stream of juice several feet onto some broken branches.

"This was last night?" Miller asked.

"Yeah, that was last night. Yeah, and after we'd been workin' here for a while this mornin,' I headed back to the shop to get a couple more chains. As I passed the place where the car had pulled off, I saw a yeller car, a small one, like a Toyota or Honda or sum-pin'. Anyways, it was 'bout two hundred feet from the road when I passed it. I slowed down a mite as I was comin' up to it. I could see three people in the car. There were a couple of guys in the front and what 'peered like a girl in the backseat. She leanin' 'gainst the window. I went on passed 'em and watched 'em pull out from my rear view," Stevens stated.

"About what time was this?" Miller asked.

"Not for sure', but I'd say 'bout ten or eleven this mornin'.

"Did you say they went east after they got back on the paved road?" Miller asked.

"Yep, back that a ways," Stevens said as he spat the juice again and pointed east. "Didn't see it no more after that. I went on up th' road. It was still way back behind me when I last saw it."

Deputy Miller got all of the guys' names and addresses of the crew and that of the owner, Jimmy Stevens.

After speaking with Chief Delaney, the deputy put out a lookout for a small, older model yellow car with two males and one female. The surrounding counties and cities including those close to Atlanta, in addition to the Georgia Highway Patrol, received the information.

Although Mark had committed his crime less than half an hour before the victim's daughter arrived, he and the others were already out of Spalding County. Georgia law enforcement never saw the vehicle.

Mark, Keri, and Kenny made it through Atlanta without any

delays or problems other than the Toyota experiencing some jerks and sputters. By the time they made it to the Tennessee line, they were hungry. They got off the interstate at the first Tennessee exit. They found a restaurant that served country cooking. Now that they had money, they were ready to eat something other than crackers and cheese and a fast-food hamburger.

Mark did not tell Keri or Kenny exactly what happened at the house in Georgia. They never asked him. They both assumed that somehow Mark managed to steal the money without her seeing him. Since neither one of them heard a shot fired, they did not know that he killed the woman.

They placed their order and ate their food as if the events of the last two days had never occurred. Mark talked with Keri and Kenny like they were old school buddies, and they responded in kind. For a few moments, everything in their world seemed ordinary.

After eating, they walked across the restaurant parking lot to a small, food market. Mark bought each of them two packs of cigarettes and a couple of candy bars and drinks. They walked back to their car, each of them lighting a cigarette along the way. When they got to the car, Keri climbed into the back seat to lie down. Mark told Kenny it was his time to drive. Kenny tried but failed, to start the car. Kenny surmised there was something in the fuel line causing the problem.

After working on the car for about half an hour, it finally started. Once again, Kenny wasn't sure that he did anything to cause the vehicle to start. Once again, they were on their way on I-75 northbound toward Ohio.

It didn't take long for Keri to fall asleep and Mark was not far behind her. They made it about nine miles into Tennessee before the car started sputtering badly, so Kenny pulled into a rest area. Mark woke up as soon as he pulled off the interstate, but Keri remained asleep. After several attempts of trying to restart the car, Kenny decided to wait to see if the vehicle started on its own later.

"How far did we go?" Mark asked Kenny.

"Not far, still in Chattanooga," Kenny responded.

"Damn! We ain't ever gonna get to Ohio. I'm tired of this cheap car!" Mark blasted out while throwing a half bottle of Coke across the parking lot. "It's just getting worse!"

"Maybe when it gets daylight, I could borrow some tools from somebody around here and try to clean the lines out," Kenny suggested.

"No way am I spending the night here!" Barked Mark.

"I don't think I can fix it in the dark, even with a flashlight and we don't have the tools or a flashlight, so we are stuck Dude," Kenny barked back.

"I'm just not staying here all night, that's for damn sure. I'll think of something," Mark said.

The rest area they were in was just a parking lot and mostly used by truckers. It did not have any lights or facilities. There were a few cars in the parking lot and several trucks. The only lights in the area were the occasional lights from the cars and trucks as they pulled in and out of the parking area.

Eventually, more trucks and cars pulled into the rest area. After waiting more than an hour, and trying several more attempts at starting the car, Mark grew more frustrated. It was a warm, humid night and that didn't help Mark's temper. Kenny had approached a couple of trucks in hopes of talking to someone about borrowing some tools. The truckers had pulled into the parking area to sleep, and they were not about to open their doors for anyone.

"I hate being stuck. I hate it! I don't like nothing or nobody holding me back." Mark grumbled.

"Well I don't know what else to do but wait until morning and see if someone will loan me their tools," Kenny said quietly.

Mark stood quiet for a few moments. He walked up to the far north end of the parking area and just stood there. After about fifteen minutes he started walking rapidly back toward his car.

"I know what I'm gonna do; I'm gonna pick me up a fag," Mark said, as he took off his shirt and threw it inside the car.

"What?" Kenny questioned.

"Look man, fags everywhere out here. There are two in the car over by those trees. One guy sitting over there by himself has been there since we got here with this car running, so, I'm gonna get one to talk to me then I'm gonna steal his car," Mark said sitting shirtless on his hood.

"They are not gonna just come up here and talk to you just because you took your shirt off. You're crazy," Kenny responded laughing out loud.

"I bet one does!" Mark said, making a mocking laugh toward Kenny.

"You've done it before? Picked up gays?" Kenny asked.

"Don't make a big deal out of it. Just get your ass in the car or walk off somewhere and let me do this," Mark insisted.

"You're nuts," Kenny said, still laughing, as he climbed into the front seat of the car and laid the seat back.

Keri had been asleep in the backseat this whole time, but when Kenny put the seat back, it bumped her, and she woke up.

"What's going on?" Keri asked without raising her head up.

"The car messed up and it won't start again," Kenny responded while closing his eyes.

"Where's Mark?"

"He's sitting on the car with his shirt off, thinking he's gonna get a gay guy to talk to him so he can steal his car."

"What?"

"You heard me right. He's gonna try to pick a gay guy and steal his car."

"That guy is crazy."

"Can't argue with ya there."

"I wonder how he got the money from that old lady. I don't trust him at all. I think he would do anything."

"I don't know. I try to not think about it to be honest."

"How did I get mixed up with this guy? He may take us all to hell with him."

"Yeah, I didn't know he was this way, or I would never have left Florida with him. Just have to wait for the right time for us to get away from him. There is no telling what he has done. I just keep looking for a way to get away from him without him knowing. I'm really not sure what he would do if he thought we were just going to take off. Besides, you and I are broke."

"Yeah, just think, last week the only trouble I had was with my grandma for staying out and that was nothing. Now, look at me, traveling with the crazy guy that I can't get away from. I'll never do this ever again if I ever get away from him. I still worry that he may kill me before this is over. I thought for sure that he was gonna kill you," Keri said.

"Yeah, I figured I was dead, too. It's like he just loses his mind and then the next minute he acts like nothing happened. Scary as hell to me. He's always got that damn gun. A little while ago, I thought to myself, man if he goes to sleep tonight I might smash his brains in. But my luck he would wake up and shoot me," Kenny said with a slight chuckle.

"Yeah, he does seem to be lucky so far. And there's no telling what he's done before he was with us. Was he your friend in Florida?"

"No, I'd only met him a time or two before we left. I regret leaving now, but at the time it seemed like the right thing to do," Kenny said as he turned his head to look at Keri.

"Why?" Keri inquired.

"I guess that I had felt I needed to get away. My girlfriend was killed in a car wreck a few weeks before we left. I was so bummed out that I about went crazy. But this is insane!" Kenny said closing his eyes when he finished.

"Oh my god, your girlfriend was killed?"

"Yes, in a terrible car wreck," Kenny replied, with his eyes still closed. "Two of her friends were killed, too. I got there not long after it happened. I saw the car; it was so smashed that I couldn't tell that it was her girlfriend's car. The state trooper said it was her. After that, I went into a fog and don't remember much that happened after that. I guess Mark caught me at just the right time."

"Oh man, I'm so sorry. It's a wonder that you're not going crazy here. Had Y'all been seeing each other long?"

"Yeah, and we were gonna get married as soon as I found a job. Let's change the subject, okay? Laying here in this car with that prick outside and thinking about her is freaking me out."

"That's cool. We'll get away from him as soon as we can," Keri agreed.

"Hey, don't look, but there's some dude out there talking to him," Kenny whispered.

"Are you serious?" Keri whispered back.

"Yeah, let's listen and see if we can hear them talking."

"Okay, I'll shut up," Keri said as she smiled at Kenny.

Kenny winked and smiled back at her. Outside, Mark was talking to a guy who was only wearing a pair of red shorts and tennis shoes. Kenny could barely see him if he raised his head off of the seat. He could hear them talking but couldn't tell what they were saying. Once in a while, he could hear one or both of them laughing. After about ten minutes, Mark and the other guy walked away from the car.

"Hey, they're both walking away," Kenny said at a whisper. "Can I look now?"

"Yeah, but just enough to see. They're headed back over that way," Kenny said as he pointed toward his left.

"Oh, I see them. Where do you think they are going?"

"I don't have a clue, but there's nothing over there but woods that I can see."

"Oh wow! Do you think they're gonna do anything?"

"Hell, I don't know. There's no telling what he's gonna do."

"That's just gross."

"To each his own."

"I guess."

Keri and Kenny continued to watch in the direction that the two had gone, but they faded into the darkness. After about fifteen minutes, Mark returned to the car. He got his shirt off of the hood, then leaned in through the car window and told Kenny and Keri that they were going to get something to eat. He told them to be ready when he got back because he was going to steal the guy's car and dump him off. The guy pulled his car around toward Mark's car to pick him up. It was a 1987 Monte Carlo.

"Nice car. What year is it?" Mark asked while looking over the car as he climbed in.

"Thanks, it's a '87 Monte Carlo."

"Wow, man, you have really taken care of it."

"Actually it was in pretty good shape when I got it."

"Cool, where we going?" Mark asked.

"There's a good place at the next exit. I thought we'd go there."

"Sounds good to me."

"So, you from here?" the driver asked.

"Originally I'm from Ohio but mostly from all over. My dad died when I was young, and my mom died a few years ago. There's just me now, no aunts, no uncles, no brothers, no sisters, just me," Mark said.

He didn't know why he lied about his mother being dead, but it just seemed to fit at the moment. The only thing that was true about the statement was that his dad died when he was young. Of course, now he was short one uncle. Right now, Mark's mindset was that he was all alone in the world. He didn't need anybody, and he didn't want anyone. Whatever part of him that was controlling his mind didn't want anything to do with any ties to any other person. He wasn't going to deal with any guilt, compassion, or restraints. This part of him had always been there, but the more he gave into it, the more it claimed control. He had let go of the steering wheel of his soul and was only pressing the gas pedal, sitting back and enjoying the ride.

"How about you? Have you always lived around here?"

"Yeah, pretty much. There is just my mom and me. My dad was killed in a truck accident when I was younger. I do have some uncles and one aunt."

"Do you get high?" Mark asked.

"Sometimes."

"You have any smoke on you?" Mark asked.

"No," he said laughing. "I never have any on me, but I do have some friends that keep it. I smoke when I'm with them. I don't really do enough to buy any for myself."

They picked up their food and got back on the interstate. They had to go southbound to the next exit to turn around and get back to the rest area. It was a couple of miles to the next exit and then about a mile after that to the rest area. The exit areas were all well lit on this part of the interstate. Except for the passing cars, the areas between the exits were dark. But halfway between the exit and the rest area, Mark decided it was time to take the car.

"Hey man, I need you to pull over real quick. I gotta piss," Mark said suddenly.

The driver pulled off onto the shoulder, but Mark just sat there.

"What's wrong?" The driver asked.

Mark slowly looked out each window to observe where they were and if anyone was around before he spoke.

"It's like this man; I need your car. Mine's broke down and I have to keep moving, so I gotta take yours," He said smiling.

"You're kidding me! Don't mess with me like that man. You're scaring me."

"I ain't kidding you man, so open the damn door, and get out."

"Please don't do this man."

"Just get out of the damn car. Now!" Mark yelled without the smile.

"I'm begging you man please don't do this."

"I'm not telling you again, get out!" Mark said to him again with a soft, calm voice.

"Please, please man, please don't do this. I have to have my car." He put his hands together in a praying position in front of his face.

"I tried to tell you, but you didn't listen. It was your choice," Mark said as he pulled his gun from his front pants pocket. He cocked the hammer and pointed it about a foot from the driver's head.

"Oh my god! Don't shoot me! I'm getting out! Just please don't shoot me! Please! Oh God! Please! Please don't shoot me!" He begged while trying to find the door handle and keeping his eyes on Mark.

"Too late, asshole!" Mark yelled as he fired the gun repeatedly into the driver's face. The body immediately slumped into the seat belt. The body shook uncontrollably for a few moments.

Mark looked at the now bloody driver and seemed amazed that he was still taking quick shallow breaths and quivering.

The driver's eyes were partly open and fixed. His seat belt kept him from slumping completely forward. Mark got out of the car and walked around to the driver's side door, released the seat belt, and dragged the body onto the pavement.

CHAPTER TWENTY-TWO

Where is Wauchula?

Friday, June 25th 6:00 A.M.

Don Blackman boarded a flight early Friday morning in
Chattanooga and headed to Tampa, Florida. He arrived at Tampa
International at 9:45 AM. He rented a car and headed for Arcadia.
Once in Arcadia, he found the hotel where the CID office had
made his reservations. It was an older hotel but well maintained.
He went to his room to put up his things and freshen up before
his 2:00 meeting with Detective Sergeant John Gates. DeSoto
County is a small rural county in Southwest Florida. Arcadia is
the county seat, with a population of a little under seven
thousand. Mark's uncle, Tom Shelton, lived in the southwest part
of the county. It is mostly made up of small and medium-sized
farms. Shelton's estate was average size in that part of the county.
  Mark Manning had lived in a camper on the part of his uncle,
Tom Shelton's land. Years earlier, Before Tom owned it, that
section of Shelton's 139 acres, had been used by area residents to
hunt. But after Shelton bought it, he had it fenced in and used it to

keep occasional livestock. Shelton had put the old camper there a few years earlier when he was taking care of some cattle that were getting out of his fence at night.

On the drive from the motel to the sheriff's office, Blackman stopped for a pack of cigarettes, a Coke, and a bag of peanuts. He never liked to eat a meal before a meeting or before a court appearance. Blackman arrived at the DeSoto County Sheriff's Office around 1:45 that afternoon. Since he was fifteen minutes early, he stayed in the car and snacked on a few peanuts. After a few minutes he got out of the rental car to smoke a cigarette and ready his mind for the upcoming meeting. A little before 2:00, he grabbed his briefcase and headed to meet Gates.

Delvecchio had not arrived but John Gates was there. Gates had the conference room set up for their meeting. It was a small room with an oval table for six, several chairs, and a table for the coffee pot and a small cup with a dollar sign designated for donations to the coffee fund. There were four large, framed photos of former sheriff's of DeSoto County, hung on the wall.

Gates had already moved some of the items from the case, some photos, crime scene drawings, and a few other items from the case, and placed them on the conference table. Laying on one of the chairs were eighteen black-and-red drawings found in the camper where Mark had been staying.

Blackman announced himself at the front desk. He walked to a conference room escorted by one of the office clerks. Gates was already in the conference room so he greeted Blackman at the door. Gates asked about his trip, and made some initial small talk about where he was staying, and if he needed anything.

After just a few minutes Delvecchio came in and apologized for being late. Soon, they were into the cases and exchanging case information.

"So your victim was shot five times in the face with a .25 caliber pistol. Did you find any shell casings?" Gates asked Blackman.

"Yes, a .25 caliber pistol; the lab reports says," Blackman answered.

"Like I said, our victim was also shot with a .25 caliber pistol. We also found out that our victim is missing a .25 automatic pistol. We found an open desk drawer with an empty gun box. The top of the box was sitting on top of the bureau," Gates advised.

"We've also discovered that our victim's nephew had been staying in a camper on the farm, and from what we have been told, he drives a yellow Toyota. So it looks like we might have a connection," Said Delvecchio.

"And you have no clue where the nephew is at this time?" Blackman asked.

"No, no one had seen him since his uncle was killed," Gates replied.

"The yellow Toyota we have in Chattanooga was last registered in Ohio. The tag that was on it was a Florida tag that came back to someone in Sarasota County. They reported it stolen a day after our victim was killed," Blackman stated.

"Yeah, we have talked to the person who reported it stolen. It took them a while to notice that it was missing. Seems legit," Delvecchio said.

"How about the name Kenny Saxton, were you ever able to find anything out about him?" Blackman inquired.

"Just a little so far. But if you have time and want to, we think we have located where he had been living. If you like, we can go there after we finish here," Gates advised.

"That would be great. So far, we don't know if Saxton has any connection to the Toyota or your victim's nephew, right?"

"That's right. We haven't even found anyone that really knows Saxton. But we were able to run down a lead. It came from a state trooper. I ran into him in court yesterday. He was asking me about this case. He lives about three miles from the Shelton farm, so he was interested. When I told him about the nephew and possibly someone named Kenny Saxton, he said that he believed that was the name of a boyfriend of one of the girls killed in a wreck a couple of weeks ago. He wasn't a hundred percent sure, and we weren't able to do a lot with it yet," Delvecchio said.

"Sounds like the place to start," Blackman said.

"I've got a copy of the accident report. We can run down information from there," Delvecchio answered.

"That's great. I've got a Bible that I brought with me that I was like for you guys to see. I understand there are drawings you guys found," Blackman said.

"Yeah, they're over here on the chair. Where's your Bible?" Gates asked.

"It's right here, in my briefcase," Blackman said.

They compared the marks and drawings in the Bible with the artwork that found inside the camper on Shelton property. The drawing that was in the back of the Bible looked almost identical to some of the drawings that had come out of the camper. There was little doubt in their minds that the Bible drawings were by the same person that drew those in the camper. Delvecchio took some pictures of the drawings and the markings in the Bible. Blackman took photos of the poster drawings that came from the Shelton camper.

After comparing more notes, looking at more photographs, and having a couple more cups of coffee, the three decided to follow up on the information from the accident report. They started with the car the girls were riding in when they died. The report listed it as a 1988 Honda Civic; registered to a John Booth in Wauchula, FL. Gates and Blackman inquired simultaneously about the name. Delvecchio assured them that it was what the report showed.

"Where is Wauchula?" Asked Blackman.

"It's not far from here. It's in the next county up, Hardee County," Gates said.

"We can take my car if you guys don't mind," Delvecchio said.

"Okay with me, but I'm gonna step out to my car just a minute. I've gotta burn one. I have a feeling it may be a while before I have another chance," Blackman responded.

"Hang on for just a minute, and I'll go with you. I'm going to get the key to lock the stuff up in this room," Gates requested.

"I'll pass. I'm going to see if the nice lady up front will let me make some copies of this accident report to give you guys. I quit smoking nine years ago, and you guys are a bad influence on me," Delvecchio stated.

After a smoke break and a restroom break, the three investigators headed for Wauchula in hopes of finding John Booth. Delvecchio wanted to run out to the Shelton farm to show Blackman that crime scene, but Gates talked him into doing that later since it was in the opposite direction from Wauchula. In less than a half an hour, they arrived at the address on S. Florida Avenue, in Wauchula.

It was a small, frame house that looked like it needed paint job a few summers back. There was a small garage with double doors in the backyard. The doors were open, and an old Ford Mustang with the hood up was backed into the garage. There was an old, white Buick Park Avenue left in the dirt driveway. The house had a small, screened-in front porch where a large Rottweiler stood guard. It didn't take the Rottweiler long to sound the alarm that the three investigators were approaching. There was nothing between the three men and the large, barking dog but transparent, mesh screen. The Rottweiler let the trio know that they were not coming through the door. But he didn't seemed to have a desire to break through the thin screen. The three investigators were grateful for his lack of desire or his good training. Either way, they were glad.

Soon, a short man came around from the right of the house. He was wearing a white, oil-stained T-shirt, a Florida Gator cap, cut-off blue-jean shorts, white socks, and black tennis shoes. He was carrying a large wrench in one hand, and had a screwdriver in the other hand. He had a two-inch, unlit remnant of a well worn cigar stuck in his mouth. As he came around the corner of the house he seemed surprised to see the three men. He paused for a moment and glared at the men like he was sizing them up for a possible fight.

Delvecchio smiled at the man and tried to tell him why they were there, but the Rottweiler's barking was too loud to overcome.

"Leroy! Lay down!" The man yelled at the dog. The dog stopped barking instantly and went to the rear of the porch without making another sound. All three investigators looked at the dog then back towards the man with facial expressions showing they were impressed.

"What do Y'all want?" The short man asked.

"We wanted to see if we can talk to John Booth," Gates stated.

"I'm John, what do Y'all want with me? Who are Y'all?" Booth asked.

"I'm Detective Gates, with the DeSoto County Sheriff's Office. Over here is Mitchell Delvecchio from the State's Attorney's Office. And this is Detective Blackman, with the sheriff's office in Chattanooga, Tennessee. We hate to bother you, but we are looking for some information and hope you can help us."

"What kind of information? I haven't done anything, and I don't even know anyone from Tennessee. What's this about?"

"It's about the people that were in the red Honda that was in an accident a couple of weeks ago. We are trying to locate the boyfriend of one of the girls," Delvecchio stated.

"All three girls were killed, including my daughter, Nikki."

"I'm very sorry for your loss. I'm sure that this is a very difficult time for you, but we are

hoping that someone knows something about Lisa's boyfriend. Did you know Lisa?" Delvecchio asked.

"I knew all three of the girls. They had been friends since they were kids. Before my wife and I split up, they come to the house in Arcadia all the time. They were always spending the night with Nikki. Since my wife and I split up last year, I had only seen the girls four or five times. I do know Lisa had a boyfriend. I've never seen him, but I'm sure that my wife has," Booth responded.

"Thank you, Mr. Booth. Do you mind telling us where your ex-wife lives? And, what does she go by?" Delvecchio asked.

"We're still married. We just don't live together anymore. The car was in my name. I bought it last year. It had a blown engine, but I fixed it and gave it to Nikki. My wife lives on the other side of Arcadia. You want the address?"

"That would be great!" Gates advised.

"My wife is still bad off about losing Nikki. We still talk, and I've been over there some, especially after Nikki was killed. We just are better off not living together. So, please don't upset her. It would be easy to do."

Gates assured Booth that they would use caution and do their best not to upset her. Booth gave the investigators his wife's address and phone number. The three thanked him for the information, give their condolences once again, and headed for Mrs. Booth's house.

After about thirty minutes, the three investigators found Joyce Booth's home on South Airport Road. There were no close neighbors. There was an older model, blue Chevy Camaro sitting in the driveway. The three investigators approached the house and found Ms. Booth at home. Detective Gates explained why they were there and apologized for having to be there at such a sad time for her.

At first, Joyce Booth didn't seem to know anything about Lisa's boyfriend, but after a few minutes, she told them that she knew she had a boyfriend. She told them she did not remember the boyfriend's name and did not know where he lived, but she said that Lisa's brother, David, may know where he had been staying. She did not know David's address, but she gave the investigators an approximate location of David Angel's trailer. Gates knew the area and believed he could find the trailer.

CHAPTER TWENTY-THREE

Do you have a Badge?

The three investigators traveled west out of Arcadia on Highway 72 a few miles out of town. There were several mobile homes along the highway. Gates narrowed down the area within a quarter of a mile. From there they just knocked on a few doors to see if they could get lucky and find it, or if someone may have known David Angel.

With each door came suspicious looks and reluctant responses. Finally, one lady knew where David lived. The problem was, he didn't live there any longer. According to the woman, David lived two driveways down from her and across the street. But she told them that the previous month she saw him load up a couple of pickup trucks with furniture and boxes and hasn't seen him since. For good news, they had an address. From there they may be able to get a forwarding address from the post office.

To be sure that David had moved, they went to the mobile home that the woman said had belonged to him. When they pulled into the relatively long driveway leading to the trailer, it looked like someone might be home. They decided not to overwhelm the occupant, so only Gates went to the door. He could hear music playing loudly in the trailer. He knocked three times, each time a little harder until he was banging his fist on the door. The music suddenly stopped. Everything was quiet for a few moments. He knocked once more, this time lightly. He noticed the curtain in the narrow window of the trailer door being pushed back so someone could peek out to see who was there.

The door opened about an inch and a soft female voice spoke through the small opening.

"Can I help you?" the voice inquired.

"Hi, I'm Detective Gates with the sheriff's office. I was hoping to talk with David Angel. Does he live here? Do you know David?" Gates asked the voice.

"Do you have a badge?" the voice countered.

"Oh yes, I'm sorry; I should have shown you." Gates reached into his jacket pocket and pulled out his county ID card and badge.

The door opened about another half of an inch so that the person could get a good look at the identification. Then the door closed. Gates could hear the sliding of a chain lock on the door. Then the door came completely open. Standing in the doorway was a young girl about fifteen years old. She was chewing gum and smoking a cigarette at the same time.

"Who are you looking for?" the girl asked.

"David Angel, I understand that he either lives here or used to live here. Do you know him or anything about him?" Gates asked.

By this time Delvecchio had stepped out of the car and was walking to the door.

"Is he in trouble?" She asked.

"No, he is not in trouble as far as I know. We just need to ask him about a person," Gates replied.

"Who you need to know about?" She asked while blowing out a

stream of smoke. "I may know them. I know
lots of people."

"Well, maybe you do, but first do you know where David is?"
Gates asked.

"Who are you?" She asked Delvecchio as he walked up.

"Hi, I'm Mitchell Delvecchio, and I'm an investigator, too."

"Do you have a badge?" She asked.

"Yes, I do, as a matter of fact," Delvecchio said with a big smile.

"Yours looks different than his," she responded.

"Yes, I work with the State's Attorney's Office," he answered
once again with a smile.

"Who are you?" Delvecchio asked.

"Megan Patterson," she replied, while chewing her gum in a
big way.

"Well, Megan, do you know where we can find David? It's
important," Gates asked.

"I don't know where he is right this second. But I know where
he is staying."

"You do? Do you know the address or how to get there?" Gates
asked.

"Yep, right here." Megan started laughing. "But he ain't here
right now, don't know when he will be back. So, ask me about the
person you need to know about. I bet I know them."

"He lives here? With you?" Delvecchio asked.

"Yep. Well, not with me. I don't live here. My sister does. I'm
just hanging out for a few days. You gonna tell me?"

"Tell you what?" Gates asked.

"Who you need to know about. Dang people, keep up." Megan
said, putting one hand on her hip and turning her other hand in
the air to emphasize her point, all while chewing her gum like it
was her last piece ever.

"Where is your sister?" Delvecchio said, this time laughing out loud at the girl's exhibition.

"She ain't here either. They are together, and I don't know when they will be back. I think they went to Sarasota, but ain't sure."

"Are you alone?" Gates asked.

"Yep, 'cept for Y'all," she said and smiled.

"Okay, well, have you ever heard of Kenny Saxton?" Gates asked, not thinking that she would know.

"Yep. But he ain't around here no more. He was David's sister's boyfriend. But she got killed in a car wreck, and he left. Told you I knew."

"Yes, you did. Do you know where he lived before he left?" Delvecchio asked.

"Yep, know that, too. Hey, is there like a reward for this?

Do I get any money for telling Y'all this stuff?" Megan took a last drag on her cigarette leaned out the door, and threw the butt in the yard.

"No, sorry, just the reward of doing the right thing," Gates told her.

"Yeah, like I'll get rich that way." Megan laughed out loud. "Okay, sorry, had to ask ya know. Yeah, he used to live with Bo Dixon and his girlfriend. They live up north of town. I don't know the address, but I can show ya."

"Bo Dixon?" Gates asked.

"Yep, Bo Dixon. Don't remember what his girlfriend's name is, maybe JoAnn or something like that. I only seen her once. Want me to take you there?"

"Well, could you draw a map?" Delvecchio asked.

"I ain't no good at drawing. I can't draw no map. Dang people, you want to go there or not? She said, still pumping that chewing gum.

"Where is your mom or dad?" Gates asked.

"Dad ain't been around in years. Mom is at work. Why?"

"Well, we would like to ask her if it is okay if you go with us before we just leave with you. Where does she work?" Delvecchio asked.

"Dang, she don't care. She works in Port Charlotte and ain't got no phone where she works. You the cops, right? What's she gonna say, 'Don't go with the cops?' Dang, ain't like Y'all gonna molest me or something."

Gates looked at Delvecchio and shrugged his shoulders. Delvecchio responded likewise.

"Okay, but we need to leave a note for your sister," Gates insisted.

"Cool. Let me get my cigarettes," Megan said.

"Just leave a note. You can't smoke in my car, Megan," Delvecchio said.

"Dang, I may need a cigarette by the time this trip is over."

"You will be okay; leave the note," Delvecchio said, smiling.

Megan left a note and showed it to Gates to see if it met with his approval. They got into the car and left. As she guided them she would not give them more information than just one road at a time. She was in control and was enjoying the moment. Blackman introduced himself to her, and they rode in the backseat together toward Bo Dixon's place.

"Will Y'all at least buy me a Coke?" Megan asked as they rode along a bumpy back road.

"Sure, I'll buy you a Coke and some chips, too," Blackman replied.

"Okay, turn right up here to the left. It will be a trailer up here on the right." For the first time, Megan gave more than one road at a time. "It's in a small trailer park."

They traveled less than a mile after the last turn and Megan pointed to the trailer.

"Okay, thanks, Megan." Gates passed the trailer and turned around at a wide place in the road, then passed the trailer again.

"You didn't stop!" Megan said, in a disgusted tone. "Ain't you gonna talk to Bo?"

"Yes, but first we are going to get you back to your sister's" Gates told her.

"Y'all are no fun," she pouted. "You still gonna get me a Coke and chips?" She directed her question at Blackman.

"Yes, we will stop and let you get them," Gates answered.

They stopped at an old country store on Highway 72 and Blackman gave her a ten-dollar bill. She went to the store alone and soon returned with four Cokes and a large bag of chips.

"Got you guys a Coke, too." Megan handed each of them a drink. They thanked her, and Blackman told her to keep the change. Megan laughed and showed Blackman two quarters and a penny that was left from purchase.

They dropped Megan back off at the trailer. Delvecchio walked her to the door. David and Megan's sister had not returned. Delvecchio left his card and told her to give it to David and have him call him. She gave him a hug, then ran back to the car and told Blackman thanks, then ran over to Gates' window and made him roll it down. She gave him a hug, then ran into the trailer and closed the door. She opened the door and waved, then closed the door again.

Delvecchio smiled as he walked back to the car. They all agreed that Megan Patterson was a special young lady. They waved back at Megan, even though the door had ready closed. Delvecchio pulled out of the driveway and headed east on Highway 72 toward Bo Dixon's trailer.

When they got back to Bo's place, there were two vehicles parked in the yard. This time Gates and Delvecchio went to the door, and Blackman stood outside the car and waited to see if they had any contact. Delvecchio knocked loudly on the door. It was just a second, and the door swung open. Bo Dixon was standing in the doorway, and JoBeth Davis was standing immediately behind him. There was another male in the room, but it was dark and neither Gates or Delvecchio could tell much about him. Bo and JoBeth stood silent and didn't said a word. They just looked at the two at the door and glanced out at Blackman.

"Are you Bo Dixon?" Gates asked as he showed them his badge.

"Yeah, what ya want? I haven't done anything wrong," Bo replied.

"No, we don't think you did, but we need to talk to you and your girlfriend or wife about Kenny Saxton. Do you know Kenny?" Gates inquired.

"Yeah, we know him, but he ain't here no more." JoBeth stepped into the doorway, almost edging Bo out, and answered.

"We need to talk with you about him and maybe some of his other friends. May we come in?" Delvecchio asked as he motioned for Blackman to come to the door.

"Who's that?" Bo asked about Blackman.

"He is an investigator from another town. He may have some questions, too," Gates answered.

"So this is about Kenny, and that's all? Bo asked.

"As far as we know at this moment this is just about Kenny Saxton and possibly another friend that you may or may not know," Gates replied.

Bo and JoBeth walked away from the door, leaving it open, but not saying anything about coming in. The three investigators followed them into the trailer. The third person was Ben Westmoreland, JoBeth's stepdad, who owned the trailer.

Westmoreland was a rough looking guy. Each arm had several

tattoos. He had a large scar across his cheek running onto his chin. He was 6'4" and weighed about 230 pounds. He had been to prison for auto theft and aggravated battery when he was young. After he got out of jail, he met JoBeth's mom and settled down. He worked as a welder and diesel mechanic and owned three Class C tow trucks. He wasn't rich by most people's standards, but in his circle of friends, he was doing very well.

"What's this about?" Westmoreland said while looked the three investigators over.

"Could I find out who you are sir?" Delvecchio asked Westmoreland.

"I'm Ben Westmoreland. I'm JoBeth's step dad and own this trailer."

"I'm Detective John Gates with the DeSota County Sheriff's Office, this is Mitchell Delvecchio with the State's Attorney's Office and this is Detective Blackman. We are here to ask some questions about Kenny Saxton."

"Do you know Kenny Saxton, Mr. Westmoreland?" Delvecchio asked.

"I know who he is. I have seen him. Can I ask what this has to do with these kids?"

"I don't exactly know yet, that's what we would like to find out," Delvecchio stated.

"Kenny hasn't been here for several days. He left last Friday or Saturday," Bo spoke up.

"He used to live with us, for a few months. But after his girlfriend died, he got weird and said he
needed to leave. I don't blame him I guess," JoBeth added.

"Do you know how he left?" Gates asked.

"He left with some guy. I don't know who it was, someone he met hitchhiking," JoBeth answered.

"Did you ever see the guy he left with? Do you know his

name?" Gates asked.

"She was here when he left; I wasn't. I have no clue who it was," Bo responded.

"I never met the guy, or actually even seen him close up. I only saw him drop Kenny off and then come back and get him later. He stayed in the car, so I don't really know what he looks like," JoBeth continued.

"What kind of car did the guy drive?" Blackman asked JoBeth.

"It was a yellow Toyota, I think. It could have been a Honda. No, I'm pretty sure it was a Toyota, 'cause Bo's mom used to have one like it. That's about all I know about him. I think Kenny told me that he had to see his uncle or get something from his uncle then he was coming right back. He wasn't gone but maybe forty-five minutes or an hour," JoBeth stated.

"Wait a minute. A yellow beat up Toyota, JoBeth?" Westmoreland asked.

"Yeah, it was kind of beat up," JoBeth replied.

"Was the guy's name Mark?" Westmoreland asked JoBeth.

"Do you know him?" Delvecchio asked Westmoreland.

"If his name is Mark, I do. He owes me some money. Not a lot, but he owes me for fixing a bracket on his car. He would stop by my shop sometimes. Just hang out for a little while and then leave. Sort of a weird guy. I told him I didn't have time to sit and chat. Seems like that was what he wanted to do," Westmoreland answered.

"When did you last see him?" Blackman asked.

"A few days ago. Maybe one-day last week. That's when I fixed a bracket for his battery. Just a small spot weld. I think he was some kin to a guy that owns a farm on past my place," Westmoreland replied.

"Yeah, I think I heard Kenny say that a guy named Mark was picking him up that day," JoBeth added.

"Do you know what day that was JoBeth? It could be important," Gates asked.

"I'm pretty sure it was late Friday. Bo had gone somewhere, and I was here alone when he left. The guy in the car was in a real hurry. He kept telling Kenny to hurry up. I could hear him holler from in here." JoBeth sat down at the kitchen table and lit up a cigarette.

"Y'all want some coffee? I can make some real quick; it's no problem," JoBeth asked.

"No thanks, we won't be here that long. What time on Friday was it? Do you remember, JoBeth, when they left?" Delvecchio asked her.

"I don't know exactly, but I know it was getting late. Not like dark late, but late in the day. Maybe six? I don't know, but I'm guessing maybe six." JoBeth said while exhaled her smoke into the small kitchen. "But I do know he was in a hurry. He came sliding into the yard and started blowing the horn right away."

"Do you remember what time or day the Toyota was at your shop?" Delvecchio asked Westmoreland.

"No, but after thinking 'bout it, I think it was Friday. I had planned to leave early that day, but we got a wrecker call, and I was waiting for the driver to get back. So, yeah, it was Friday. I remember that Bobby, the driver, didn't get back until after seven Friday evening. It was about two or three hours before he got back. So, maybe four or five on Friday. I can't be real sure, but I'm pretty sure," Westmoreland replied.

"Well, that's about all I have for now. You guys have anything else?" Gates asked the other investigators.

"Just one more thing. Does anyone know anything about a young girl traveling with them?" Blackman asked.

"A young girl?" JoBeth asked back.

"Yeah, maybe 15 or 16, around that age." Blackman added.

"No, there was no girl with them that I could see when they left here. I was looking out the window as they were leaving. I would have noticed a girl," JoBeth spoke up.

"Did Kenny have another girlfriend?" Blackman continued.

"No, there is no way that Kenny had another girlfriend. Not this soon after losing Lisa. No way," JoBeth stated while shaking her head back and forth signaling no.

"He could have somebody and we not know it, JoBeth," Bo inserted.

"No, he couldn't. I know!" JoBeth countered.

"How can you be so sure, you don't know what he was doing the past week? You don't know," Bo continued.

"I'm sure officer. There is no way Kenny had a new girlfriend this soon. Trust me," JoBeth declared as she looked at Blackman and turned her back toward Bo.

Bo just shook his head and walked into the kitchen. He opened the refrigerator and took out a bottle of beer. "You guys wanna beer?" he asked, as he walked back into the living room.

"No, thanks," Gates and Delvecchio said at the same time.

"Not right now," Blackman said with a smile.

Gates and the other detectives thanks them and told them that they would be back in touch with them soon for follow-up questions. When they got back to the sheriff's office they compared notes to see what they needed to do next. It appeared to all three that Kenny and Mark were traveling together. They each knew that these two were the one's they were looking for, but how to put it all together was now the question.

They knew that Mark's uncle was killed the night that Mark and Kenny left.

They knew that both victims had been shot with a .25

automatic.

They had not completed a ballistics test on the different rounds, but that would come soon.

They knew that Mark, Kenny, and an unknown girl were seen at the motel in Kentucky with the Tennessee victim's car.

They knew that Kenny used his real name to register at the motel.

They knew that the car fitting the description of the one Mark was driving was near the murder scene in

Tennessee.

They knew that the same type drawings that were at the motel in Kentucky were at the camper where

Mark had been staying.

They knew that Mark seemed to have left in a hurry.

They wanted to know if Kenny had anything to do with Shelton's murder, and they wanted to

know about the girl.

CHAPTER TWENTY-FOUR

On the Side of the Road

Mark climbed into the driver seat and headed to the rest area. For a moment he thought about leaving Keri and Kenny and going on to Ohio. But he decided that it wasn't time for them to separate. He pulled into the rest area beside his Toyota. He jumped out of the car and yelled at Kenny to get all the stuff out the car and put it into the Monte Carlo. Mark grabbed the keys out of the Toyota and opened his trunk, and then he quickly went back to the Monte Carlo grabbed the keys and opened the trunk. He hurriedly started pulling stuff from the trunk of the Toyota and throwing it into the trunk of the Monte Carlo. He was yelling at Kenny to hurry up and get everything out of the front of the Toyota and from the back seat.

"Where's Keri?" Mark yelled in a frustrated tone.

"She went to pee."

"Where? We've got to get out of here!" Marked yelled.

"She walked up that way." Kenny pointed toward the wooded area near the lane that went out of the rest area.

"You got everything out of the front?" Mark shouted.

"Yeah, I think so."

"Let's get the hell out of here."

Mark got into the driver seat and had the car cranked and in gear before Kenny ever opened the passenger door. He rolled down the passenger window and yelled once again for Kenny to come on. Kenny grabbed a few other things as Mark pressed the gas pedal and started to move away. Kenny opened the back door to the Monte Carlo and threw the rest of the stuff in, leaving the trunk and a door open on the Toyota and a few things scattered on the ground. Mark nearly floored the accelerator as Kenny jumped into the front seat. He saw Keri walking toward them near the exit to the rest area. He pulled up beside her, rolled down his window, and told her to jump in the backseat. She did, and Mark floored the accelerator.

"Where did you leave the gay dude?" Kenny asked Mark.

"On the side of the road," Mark said with a laugh.

"This his wallet?" Kenny asked as he picked it up from the console and started going through it.

"Guess it is. See if there's any money or credit cards and then throw the damn thing out the window," Mark replied.

"Yeah, he's got some money, doesn't look like much. Let's see, twenty, sixty, five, six, seven, looks like eighty-nine dollars. No credit cards," Kenny said while going through the wallet. He took out the driver's license and threw it out the window.

"What are you doing?" Mark asked in a loud voice.

"I'm gonna keep the wallet; I don't have one."

"No! Throw it all out but the money! And hurry!"

"That's stupid; it looks new. I'm gonna keep it."

"Yeah, just be caught with a dead man's wallet."

Kenny already had the window rolled down, so he didn't waste any time on the wallet and threw it out the window. Keri had been listening and watching from the backseat, but because the window was down, she couldn't hear clearly.

"Did you say he was dead?" Keri gasped, as she leaned forward between Kenny and Mark.

"Yeah, I did. And we have got to get rid of everything including the tags on the car. But

first I want to get out of Tennessee."

"So you shot him?" Kenny said as his eyes met Keri's in disbelief.

"He's dead; let's leave it at that," Mark said flatly.

No one said another word for the next two hours. Keri sat back in the seat and closed her eyes in shock and horror. Her mind went back to the old lady in Georgia. She couldn't help but wonder now what actually happened back in that house. The nightmare got worse hour by hour with Mark. Her mind became numb at the thought of it all, so she closed her eyes to erase the sight of him. She began to be sick to her stomach, so she laid down hoping that helped her feel better

Mark turned the radio from one station to another to replace the silence. First, it was country, then rock, then heavy metal, then to some guy talking about guns and politics, then back to the country station.

Kenny vacillated between staring straight ahead out the windshield and looking out the passenger window. He only looked at Mark a couple of times as he was changing radio stations. Kenny began to wonder about the lady at the house in Georgia too. But he couldn't think about all that now. Kenny thought he would go crazy if he tried to analyze everything that had taken place on this trip to hell. After about an hour and a half on the road, he glanced at the gas gauge. It was more than half-full. In a way, he had wished it was nearly empty, so he would have a chance for him and Keri to get away from this madman.

Mark dismissed everything from his mind that had taken place since he left Florida. He now only focused on getting back to Ohio. He had friends in Ohio, at least a few. He justified the things he had done as a means to an end. People looked down on him, at least in his mind. People were different from him, and it was time that they felt the difference instead of him. People thought he was defective and evil so he would be dangerous and sinister. Maybe he was one of those individuals who had more wrong in him than good. Perhaps the bad had emerged as a conqueror over the right, but he liked how it felt. Now he was in control, no questions, no doubts, and no turning back.

Mark wasn't sure what he was going to do with Keri and Kenny. He had not thought that through. But at some point, he must think about it. Right now, they may serve a purpose. He would ponder that later. Right now he was still pumped from his last killing. He felt a huge adrenaline rush to have that much control over another person. He had killed three people that week, and he might kill again.

As they crossed the Tennessee line and got in Kentucky, Mark decided it was time to rest. He started looking for a place where they could stay. As he thought about taking 15-year-old Keri, to the motel bed, he felt an evil desire to rape her. That thought now burned in his mind, and the sooner he stopped, the sooner he could satisfy his lust. But he would have to be careful. No one could see her coming or going from the room; that could draw unwelcome attention.

Mark began to see billboards advertising motels ahead. As he approached Williamsburg, Kentucky, he started looking for a good place to stop. Keri and Kenny had been asleep for the last hour. Mark spoke up and told them both to wake up. He told them that they were going to stay in a motel, but first, they needed to find a parking lot with a lot of cars so they could steal a tag. Kenny suggested that they find a car in the parking lot of a motel. He said if they found an out-of-state tag, the people may not notice that it was gone until a day or two later. Mark pulled into a motel parking lot half-full of cars.

Kenny found a screwdriver and a pair of pliers in his tackle box that was in the backseat, and Mark dropped him off in the middle of a parking lot. The plan was for Kenny to get a tag off of an out-of-state car and walk back to the road. Mark would come by and pick him up. Kenny was not a killer by any means but never felt much guilt about petty larceny. So he got a Michigan tag and met Mark and Keri along the road.

They got back on the interstate and drove about two miles and took the exit. They found three motels near the interstate. They drove to the last one, the Lazy Sleeper Motel. Mark told Kenny and Keri that they needed to be careful about letting anyone see Keri coming or going to the room with them. He told them that she could draw attention to them if they were seen going in together. Mark sent Kenny into the motel with the money to get a room.

Kenny walked in the motel office and started talking with the owner, Ekani Nehru about a room. He asked Kenny for an ID and the tag number on the car. Even though they were not valid, Kenny gave him his driver's license. Kenny told the clerk that it wasn't his car and that he didn't know the tag number. Nehru said that he didn't have to have it but wanted the state of registration and make of vehicle. Kenny thought for a moment and decided to say it was from Tennessee.

Ekani Nehru chatted with Kenny for a few minutes and asked him where he was heading and what he did for a living. Kenny knew that Mark would be waiting, and that made him nervous. Noticing his demeanor, Nehru asked him if everything was okay. He told him he had been sick and wanted to lie down. Nehru gave him a key and followed him out after he left. Mark noticed that Nehru came outside the office and asked Kenny if anything was wrong. Kenny simply said, no.

Mark and Kenny had to go into the room without Keri since Nehru was still standing outside smoking when they got out of the car. It wasn't long before Nehru went back in the office. Keri quickly collected a few things and jogged to the door of the room. Mark had been watching out the curtains and opened the door as she approached. She ran in, and Mark stuck his head out the door to see if anyone had seen her and closed the door. Both Keri and Kenny had thought about how Mark would react to staying in a motel room with Keri. Although they had not discussed it, they both knew they would respond when the need arose.

Since Nehru had been standing outside, they did not have a chance to change the tag. Mark drove the car around the block a few times, then backed the car in so the tag was not be easily seen. For the first time, Mark was feeling the significance of his recent behavior. Not a sudden attack of conscience, but thinking about the consequences should he be caught. The added tension caused Mark's desire for Keri to subside. When it came time for bed, Keri grabbed a blanket and slept on top of the covers with Kenny. Soon they were all sound asleep.

It was Monday morning. Keri woke up early and was thirsty. She had some coins in her pocket, so she walked to the drink machine outside. She had placed a clothes hangar at the bottom of the door, so it would not close.

For a moment, Keri thought about leaving. She felt she might be able to get away without Mark knowing before she was long gone. But the thought also scared her. Where was she go? How would she explain what had happened over the past few days if questioned? She didn't have any money or any way to get any.

She wondered how she would survive once she left the group? She wondered what would happen if Mark found her? She was fifteen years old in a big world for the first time, and it had been a world filled with horror, violence, and uncertainty since she met Mark. She decided that when she left, she would want Kenny to go with her. She went back to the room and went back to sleep.

They were all exhausted, so they slept well into the morning. Kenny was the first to get up. He walked over to the window and looked outside to be sure everything looked normal. He noticed that there was only one other car besides the Monte Carlo in the parking lot. He felt the stolen Monte Carlo stood out more now. He started getting nervous.

Kenny started to wake the others. He wanted to get out of the room and get going. Kenny was aware that he was culpable in some of the crimes. At this point, both he and Mark wanted to avoid law-enforcement. He assumed that Keri would be okay if they encountered cops. She was more a victim than anything.

They all slept in the clothes they had been traveling in. Keri wanted to take a shower and change clothes, but she didn't want to tempt fate with Mark. She collected her things and left the room. Mark told her to walk up the road toward the interstate, and he would pick her up.

When they got to the car, Kenny told Mark to pull over beside the dumpster where he could change the tag in a less conspicuous place. They both got in the car, and Mark drove to the dumpster. They paused for a minute to look around to be sure no one was watching. Mark got out and opened the trunk and pretended he was

looking for something while Kenny changed the tag. In the meantime, Keri walked around the back of the motel to get to the road.

Kenny changed the tag and tossed the old tag in the dumpster.

Mark calmly drove out of the parking lot, and picked up Keri about three-hundred feet from the motel. They got back on the interstate and headed north.

They went through Kentucky without any problems. When they crossed into Ohio, they went around the heavy populated areas and stuck to less traveled roads. As each mile took him a little closer to his hometown, Mark grew more confident he would make it. Once he was in Greenville, he hoped to find some old friends that might let him and the other two stay for a few days until he made a better plan. He had not considered that Kenny and Keri might leave him if the opportunity presented itself.

Mark drove into the city of Brookville doing forty-eight miles an hour in a thirty-five mile an hour zone. He was oblivious to the speed limit and the police officer sitting at a closed store running radar. It had been a long journey, and they all felt like it was almost over. Mark had let his guard down. By the time he saw the police cruiser in his rear view mirror, the officer had already turned on the blue lights.

The officer had surprised the three, and they all had different opinions about what they should do.

"Shit!" Mark said in a loud voice.

"Were you speeding, man?" Kenny asked.

"Hell, I don't know!" Mark responded.

"Pull over!" Keri yelled. She was afraid Mark would speed up and try to outrun the cop. She feared that scenario would not end well.

"No! I ain't pulling over! He will want to check the car out," Mark stated.

"Maybe he will just give you a damn ticket. He ain't nothing but a small-town cop, man. They just want your ticket money. He ain't gonna run the tag. If you run, every cop around here will be on our ass. You can't outrun the cops, man; not their radios!" Kenny said.

But Mark never thought about stopping. He was just looking for the best place to take off. Mark had been in Brookville before, but he didn't know the streets that well. He decided to act like he was going to stop and let the officer walk up to the car before taking off. He figured that might give him enough time to lose the cop. Mark turned on the right turn signal.

"You stopping?" Kenny asked. Mark didn't say a word. So Kenny asked him again.

"No!" Mark yelled back. "I'm just letting them get out so I can have a jump on them."

"Don't you pull out your damn gun, man! You will get us all killed!" Kenny yelled back.

Keri started to panic when she heard Kenny's comments to Mark.

"I want out! Let me get out now!" She yelled.

"Shut up and sit back!" Marked yelled back at her.

Officer Julie Scott pulled behind the Monte Carlo and exited her patrol unit. Keri was still in a panic and started crying. Officer Scott noticed Keri popping up from the back seat and looking at her. She noticed that her face seemed distressed.

Mark let the officer walk up to his window to get her as far away from her patrol car as he could before taking off. As he was rolling the window down Keri saw it as her best chance to get away.

"Help!" Keri screamed as she beat on the window on her side of the car.

Officer Scott was surprised by Keri's actions. She reacted by stepping back and drawing her gun. When Mark saw her pull her gun, he grabbed his pistol and fired three shots out of the window toward the officer. One shot hit the top of her vest near her left shoulder, one shot missed entirely, and one shot struck her in the neck. She immediately fell to the ground. She was hurt but still able to fire her weapon into the side of the Monte Carlo as it sped away.

One of the four shots she managed to get off came through the car and struck Keri above her right knee. The bullet did not penetrate her but cut across the top of her leg, leaving a deep gash. Keri let out a loud scream when she saw the blood on her leg. Mark kept speeding away, never saying a word. Kenny climbed into the back seat to try to assess the wound and calm Keri down.

CHAPTER TWENTY-FIVE

I Planned on Leaving Alone

Retired Army First Sergeant Dave Livingston was pumping gas at a station near the Monte Carlo stop by Officer Scott. He had been watching it, partly because it was an attractive female officer making the stop and partly because he didn't have anything to do other than watch the spinning numbers on the pump. When he saw the shooting, he put the pump handle back in the receiver and ran out to the officer lying in the road. Officer Scott was losing a lot of blood, so he took off his shirt and applied pressure to the wound on her neck. He knew that she would be in bad shape soon without proper medical attention.

A woman who was passing by didn't see the shooting but saw Officer Scott lying in the road and stopped to help her. She happened to be an emergency room nurse at a Dayton Hospital on her way home from work. She took over the first aid while the sergeant ran to Scott's patrol and called for help on her radio. Within minutes of the sergeant's call, emergency responders were on the scene.

It didn't take the on-duty 911 operator long to piece together what had happened. While Officer Scott did not run a check on the tag number before stopping the vehicle, she did call in the tag number and a brief description of the vehicle. The operator quickly put out an all-points lookout for any vehicle matching that description.

Darke County Sheriff's Office and Greenville Police Department also received the information. Every available law-enforcement officer was out in force to cover the roads in the area. The Ohio State Highway Patrol was also notified to be on the lookout.

Officer Scott could not speak due to the bleeding in the throat area, so she was not able to pass on the information about Keri and the two men in the car. She was not in any condition to write a note either. She had to get help quickly or she would be in serious trouble.

Sergeant Livingston told police on the scene that he believed that there were three or four people in the car and that one was a young girl in the back. He also told them that he thought that Officer Scott did shoot back, but he wasn't sure where the bullets struck. Officer Scott was transported by a medical helicopter to a trauma center in Dayton.

Mark drove like a madman out of Brookville. Instead of heading toward Greenville, he took a few back roads south. They didn't pass one patrol car along their way out of town. After driving about twenty minutes they passed an old small airport. It looked abandoned, so Mark did a u-turn and drove up to the gate. The gate was closed and padlocked. Mark quickly looked around to see if anyone was watching, he pulled up to the gate and pressed the gas pedal. The chain held fast, but the metal frame of the gate was rusted, so it gave way at the right-side hinges. The right side of the gate snapped open. Mark pulled the Monte Carlo through the opening. Mark stopped once inside the fence and told

Kenny to put the gate back where it was so it would not look like someone had crashed it. Kenny objected with his eyes, but got out and did as Mark said.

Mark pulled the car to the rear of what use to be the maintenance building. He got out of the car and walked to the side of the building. Once he felt comfortable that no one could see the car from the road, he sat on some neatly stacked old cinder blocks and lit a cigarette. He stared across the old runway that had become an empty field of scattered weeds.

Kenny crawled into the back seat to check on Keri. She had calmed down and was holding a piece of cloth on her wounded leg. Kenny pulled the rag back to get a look at the injury. The bleeding had slowed down and almost stopped. He helped her get out of the car and carried her to a grassy spot outside the building and helped her to lie down. He went back to the car and found a roll of duct tape that he had kept in his tool kit. He took the bloody rag off of the wound and took a piece of newspaper he had folded up and taped it to her leg. Then he walked over to where Mark was sitting.

"Well, ain't this some shit?" Kenny said in a calm voice.

"It's her fault." Mark said quietly as he blew smoke out of his mouth and looked over toward Keri.

"Her fault? You shot a cop, and it's her fault? If that cop dies, you will fry, man. Do you know that?" Kenny asked Mark. "Not her! You!" Kenny continued as he pointed toward Keri.

"If she hadn't of spooked that cop we would be long gone now. What the hell was she doing?" Mark responded.

"I guess she was afraid you were gonna get us killed. She's only fifteen man, and you almost did. Man, you are one destructive son-of-a-bitch," Kenny responded.

"Yeah, I am! Don't you forget that!" Mark countered.

"I ain't likely to forget it for the rest of my life. You have gotten us into more shit than we will ever be able to get out of. So if that is a threat, save it, jerk face! None of us will have much of a life after this. Your threats are worthless to me."

"Big man now huh?" Mark laughed loudly.

"No, I ain't nothing anymore. And I don't give a damn," Kenny told Mark as he walked back toward Keri.

Keri had been watching the two talk, but she was about forty feet away so she could not hear everything they were saying.

"What's he sayin' now?" Keri asked Kenny.

"Nothing new, just the same stuff he has been sayin' since we started this trip. The guy is crazy; I swear he is. I mean, I ain't perfect, and I've done some things in my life, but this guy doesn't care about nothing or nobody," Kenny replied.

"How are we gonna get away from him now?" Keri asked.

"I don't know. I don't even know what he is thinking. Every cop in Ohio will be covering every road everywhere by now. You're hurt, so you can't walk." "I think I could walk. If I had to," Keri responded.

"Let's see what the genius is gonna try next. That may force our next move."

Mark began to think about his chances of getting away in the car. He figured that there was no way not to be seen, even at night. Mark thought he could walk out and try to catch a ride. "

"No one would be looking for a hitchhiker," Mark said, not realizing he spoke the words out loud.

He looked over at Keri and Kenny. They didn't act like they had heard him. He realized he would need to leave alone in order for it to work. Kenny and Keri were no longer wanted or useful to him. If he killed them here, it would probably be a long time before anyone found them. If he just left them, they may get caught and tell everything they know and name him as the shooter. Mark liked them both as much as a guy like him could like anybody. But now they were the most likely way he would get identified. He couldn't let them talk. He could never trust them to keep quiet. He decided it was time for them to go.

Keri looked over and saw Mark staring at them. She didn't like the look on his face. He seemed to be lost in thought as he was looking their way.

"Mark is up to something, Kenny," Keri said.

Kenny looked over and saw Mark looking at them. But Mark didn't stop starring. He just kept looking at them with a blank look on his face.

"Yeah, I see what you are saying. I don't trust him at all," Kenny responded.

"You know I don't," Keri stated.

"I wonder if the gun is still in his pocket or the car. The last time I saw it, it was on the floor where he threw it after shooting that cop. I'm gonna walk over to my side of the car like I'm getting something and see if it is there. If it is, I'm gonna grab it. Without the gun, he ain't shit. I could kill him with my fist. You call him over here if he starts toward the car."

"Okay, be careful."

Kenny lit a cigarette and walked casually toward the car. Mark saw him heading toward the car and realized that he didn't have his gun. Mark was about 30 feet further away from the car than Kenny. He knew that if Kenny was going after the weapon that he couldn't beat him. He would have to try to pull him away from the car before he got there.

"Where ya going?" Marked asked Kenny.

"Get another shirt; this one has blood on it. Don't want to be seen with a bloody shirt."

"Come here first."

"Why?" Kenny asked as he kept walking toward the car.

"I got a plan. We need to talk."

"I'll be there after I grab a shirt."

"You don't need a damn shirt to talk." Mark stood up and started walking toward the car. But he was still more than twenty feet further away than Kenny. About that time Mark broke out in a run toward the car. It caught Kenny off guard at first, and Mark got closer to the car before he reacted.

Kenny was taller and more athletic than Mark. He took off running toward Mark. They both reached the driver's door at the same time. Mark grabbed the door handle and pulled the door open, but Kenny slammed into the door and knocked Mark to the ground at the same time.

"What the hell are you doing?" Mark yelled at Kenny while he was trying to stand up.

"Stopping you!" Kenny yelled back while bringing his left fist around and hitting Mark in the side of the head as he was getting off the ground.

Mark fell back to the ground then quickly jumped back up and charged at Kenny. He grabbed Kenny around the waist, and they both went to the ground. Mark hit Kenny in the face before Kenny could react. All Keri could do was wait and hope that Kenny won. Kenny managed to get back on his feet and kick Mark in the shoulder as he was trying to get off the ground. Mark grabbed his leg after it struck his shoulder, but his grip slipped, and Kenny brought his other foot around and kicked him in the face. Mark's nose began to bleed.

"I will kill your ass!" Mark yelled as he got off the ground and ran toward the passenger side of the car.

Kenny quickly ran to the driver's door and opened it at the same time Mark opened the passenger side front door. They both looked at the floor for the gun, but neither of them saw it. Kenny took his left hand and quickly felt under the seat, keeping his right hand free in case Mark came toward him. He felt the gun and grabbed it. As he was pulling it out, Mark jumped across the seat and lunged at Kenny. Kenny managed to get in a quick jab with his right fist into Mark's face causing the blood that had gathered around his nose to splatter.

Kenny quickly backed out of the car and pointed the gun at Mark. Mark froze exactly where he was on the car seat.

"Now, I'm making the plans. You are gonna walk out of here by yourself now, or I'll shoot you right between your stupid-ass eyes. I am so sick of you and your shit. I should just kill you now," Kenny told Mark in a calm but forceful voice while backing away from the car.

Mark remained frozen on the front seat of the car. Would he die in the same place where the guy he shot died, he wondered? He slowly lowered his head and looked down at the seat. He began to crawl out of the car after a few seconds. Kenny backed up even more away from Mark. He would shoot him if he had to, but he would rather he just left. The gun was still in the cocked position. Kenny's finger was on the trigger. The slightest pull and the gun would fire.

Keri was still watching in great anticipation of what would happen next. She was not even sure if she was breathing or not. She didn't feel any pain at the time. She was too stressed to feel anything but her heart pounding forcefully against her chest and resounding in her ears.

Mark began to laugh and said, "I planned on leaving alone."

"Yeah, I figured that you did. But I didn't like how you were planning on doing it."

"Hey, I wasn't gonna bother you guys. I wanted my gun to take with me. That's all. Why did you have to smash my face, man?" Mark asked.

"I'm not gonna argue with you. We are in a lot of deep shit here, and I don't need you around to cause it just to get worse. So get your stuff and take off. If you come back, I swear I will shoot you. I won't say nothing,' I'll just shoot your ass."

"Let a man clean his face. I don't want the cops to see blood and start razzing me," Mark demanded.

"You have got two minutes to get what you want and leave. I don't ever want to see your punk face again. I could just shoot you, and I would probably get a freaking metal! So, don't think I won't man!" Kenny told Mark.

As Mark started to walk off, Kenny spoke up.

"Wait a minute. Empty your pockets. You have friends near here. We don't. Leave the money."

"I don't have any money left," Mark answered.

"I'll shoot your ass and take if off of your dead body, so just empty your pockets right there on the blocks."

Mark thought about it for a moment. He didn't think Kenny would shoot him, but he wasn't sure enough to try him. He emptied his pockets onto the blocks and started walking without saying another word.

It wasn't long before Mark was walking out the old airport gate. He never turned and looked back at Kenny and Keri. He just took a left turn at the gate and kept on walking. Both Keri and Kenny walked to the side of the building so they could watch him leave. They sat on a stack of railroad ties where they could see the gate and kept an eye on it for more than an hour. They talked about what they were going to do. Kenny decided to wait until after dark and he would drive out of the gate.

There were some old houses and a few cars not far from the gate. He could get another tag off of one of those cars. He was hoping that if he drove at night, with a different tag, that the cops might not notice the car as much. Neither he nor Keri had a clue where they would go once they left the airport, but they knew that they needed to get away from the area.

For a brief moment they talked about turning themselves in to the cops, but Kenny decided they would never convince them that Mark had done all the damage. And besides, they were accomplices to a lot of crimes, even if they didn't know about them. They could get a long time in jail if they got caught.

Kenny took the homemade bandage off of Keri's leg to see how it was doing. The bleeding had stopped. It was very sore to touch, but she could walk with just a little limp. The bullet had sliced into the skin but did not enter the leg. Just a couple of inches lower and it may have been through the bone. Kenny had once heard that a newspaper was sterile because the paper was so hot when it was made. He found another part of a newspaper in the car, opened it to an inside section, and re-bandaged her leg.

Kenny pulled the car behind the larger hanger and away from the maintenance building. If Mark did return, he would think they had left. It would give them a chance to see him before he saw them, Kenny thought.

Keri got into the front passenger's seat and reclined. Kenny walked to the side of the hanger to look toward the gate every few minutes. Mark was still a menace, even without him being physically present.

After dark, Kenny walked out of the gate and up the road to a house. The lights were on in the house, but the car was parked in the street away from the front of the house. He took his screwdriver out of his pocket, removed the tag, and put the stolen tag back on the car. He figured if they noticed the tag gone they would report it sooner. This way, they may not see it as quickly he reasoned.

When he got back to the hanger, Keri was hiding on the ground beside the hanger where she could see the gate. She had been afraid that Mark was still out there somewhere and that it might be him that returned instead of Kenny. She was glad to see that it was Kenny.

Kenny put the tag on the car, and they slowly pulled out of the old airport. Since Mark had turned left after he passed the gate, Kenny turned right. He still did not know exactly where he was going, but he was going to try to find an interstate highway as soon as possible. He felt that gave them the best chance of getting out of the area without being seen. Once they were out of Ohio, they could figure out what they wanted to do next. Kenny knew that he had to dump that car as soon as he could.

Meanwhile, Mark had made it almost to Greenville. He caught a ride in the back of a pickup truck that took him more than halfway there not long after leaving the abandoned airport. Mark had a friend, Cody Long, who lived in a trailer south of Greenville. When the driver of the pickup had to turn off, Mark was less than four miles from where his friend was staying.

When Mark got to Cody's house, he wasn't home. So he walked to the back of the trailer and sat on the back step and lit a cigarette. He started thinking about the past few days. He began to smile as he thought about it. "Damn," he said out loud, "Not many people could do all of that in a few days." He thought of himself as some wild, bad-ass gangster from Chicago. He didn't feel any remorse. He felt a sick sense of pride.

It wasn't long until Cody pulled up. The driveway was on the side of the trailer, so as soon as he turned in, he could see someone on his steps. Mark just sat there smoking, not even looking up. His friend had been selling drugs for more than four years. He figured it was someone coming by for some dope.

"Hey, what you want?" Cody said, as he and his girlfriend, Tempest Farrell, were getting out of his old pickup.

"Some food Codhead," Mark answered.

Codhead was a name that Cody picked up in junior high school. Everyone figured it came from the first three letters of his name, but even Cody couldn't remember exactly where and when people started using it. Only a few people knew him by that name, so he was aware that it had to be someone he knew well.

"Hey man! Who is it?" Cody replied as he walked toward Mark. "Mark!" Cody said loudly. "Dang man, where have you been? I ain't seen you in forever. What ya doin' here? Where the hell have you been?"

"Been in Texas. Got back here yesterday. What's been happening around here?" Mark replied.

"Texas? What's in Texas that would make you go there?" Cody asked.

"Nothing, that's why I went there, nothing and nobody to bother me. But, got bored so I came back. Who is this?" Mark asked while looking at Tempest.

"This is my old lady. I call her Temp. She's from Chicago. We've been hanging out about a month now. Right, Temp?" Cody looked at Tempest as he finished.

"Right to what? That I'm your old lady or that I'm from Chicago?" She responded.

"All of it baby," Cody said as he laughed.

"Yeah, I guess. I don't know how long it's been, though. Seems longer than a month," Tempest said.

"It don't matter; I got it," Mark spoke up as he looked up and down Tempest's body. "You got room for me to hang here a while?" Mark continued.

"I guess. I ain't got but one bed, but you can crash on the couch," Cody answered.

"That okay with you, Temp?" Mark asked as he smiled and continued to look at her.

"I don't care; it's his place," she replied.

"Me and ole Codhead here have been sharing our stuff since we were kids. We share about everything. Ain't that right, Codhead?" Mark said with a laugh.

"Not everything," Cody replied, looking at Tempest.

"Oh man, and I thought we were best buds. Okay, dude, not everything," Mark said laughing.

Tempest just looked at him. She was not a cute girl, but she was not ugly, and she had a good figure. For Cody, she was a catch. He planned to keep her if he could.

"You got any smoke?" Mark asked Cody.

"What you think?" Cody replied.

"You ain't got none left in the bag in my purse. Hope you got some more somewhere," Tempest inserted.

"You smoke all of that already? Just gave it to you yesterday."

"You told me to split it with Debbie. Then we smoked the rest. Don't look at me like I've been smoking all your dope. I ain't been," Tempest replied.

"Oh yeah, sorry, baby, keep me straight, doll. Yeah, I got more. Let's go in," Cody said with a laugh.

The three went into the trailer. Cody pulled out two joints that he had in a pack of cigarettes on top of the refrigerator. They smoked the joints, ate some food, and talked for a couple of hours about what had been happening since they last were together. While they were talking, they also finished off a twelve pack of beer. After a couple of hours, Tempest and Cody went to the bedroom. Mark lay down on the couch. Cody walked back into the living room and threw Mark a blanket and a small pillow.

Meanwhile, Kenny and Keri had been on the road for almost an hour. They managed to get on I-70 west and were heading for Indianapolis. Kenny had only one place in mind to go. He had a cousin that lived near St. Louis. His cousin was eight years older than Kenny, but they once were pretty close. If they could make it there, he could get some money and collect his thoughts.

Now that Mark was out of the picture Keri was relaxed. They talked about it and decided that Kenny's cousin would be the best place to go. Mark had $239 in his pockets that Kenny took from him. Kenny was surprised that Mark had that much. He tried for a few minutes to figure out where he got it, but he gave up thinking about it and focused on getting to St. Louis.

It would take them about six hours to make it if the traffic cooperated. They made it through Indianapolis without any problems. They pulled off the interstate one time to get gas. While at the gas station, Kenny walked over to an all-night drug store and bought some bandages and ointment for Keri's leg. Kenny pulled into the darkest parking space available at the next rest stop. Keri went into the restroom and wrapped her leg. The bleeding had stopped, and the pain had eased up. To keep people from seeing the blood on her jeans Kenny loosely wrapped some duct tape around her pants leg. There were still some spots of blood on her jeans, but the tape covered most of it.

They drove all night and arrived in St. Louis in the early hours of Tuesday morning. Kenny did not know exactly where his cousin lived, but he had talked to him not long after Lisa was killed and he still had his phone number.

Kenny pulled into the back parking lot of a busy truck stop, and he and Keri both fell asleep. After a couple of hours, the sun was up and so were Kenny and Keri. Kenny walked to a pay phone inside the truck stop and tried calling his cousin. The phone rang several times before his cousin, Dyson Saxon, answered. Kenny told him he was in town and needed a place to stay. He said that he would fill him in when he got there. Kenny got directions to his cousin's house. His cousin told him he would meet him at a nearby store on the main highway and he could follow him from there. It took them about thirty minutes to get to the store.

After they got to the house Kenny told them everything that had happened since they left Florida. Dyson's girlfriend, Connie Pike, gave Keri some clothes and after she had taken a shower, re-bandaged her leg. Connie took Keri under her wing and assured her that it was all over. She told her that she could stay with them as long as she needed.

Kenny and Dyson drank coffee and caught up on the old days. Kenny talked about Lisa. He told Dyson that if she hadn't been killed he would still be happy in Florida. Dyson told Kenny that he had to deal with life the way it was now. After they talked for about an hour, Kenny pulled the Monte Carlo to the back of the house under some low-hanging trees.

Back in Dayton, Officer Julie Scott was out of surgery. Fortunately, the bullets did not do any permanent damage. The doctors believed that she would make a full recovery. She would not be able to speak for a week or so, but otherwise, she should heal.

The statewide lookout was still in full force, but Kenny and Keri were out of Ohio, and Mark didn't have the vehicle or the gun. Mark thought it was likely he would never get caught.

Mark decided to lay low at Cody's for a while. He had been on the run for several days. He believed he could handle lying around the house. As long as Kenny, Keri, the car, and the gun were out of his life, he was as comfortable as if nothing had ever happened.

He had plans to return to his old life around Greenville. He didn't have that many friends, but the one's he had were loyal. He felt safe. Keri and Connie talked about all that had happened.

CHAPTER TWENTY-SIX

I'm Utterly Intrigued

Thursday, June 24th 3:00 P.M.

Kent left the office early; he wanted to arrive at Holly's house promptly at three-thirty. He arrived fifteen minutes early, so he drove up the street a mile or so before heading back. He pulled in her driveway at three-twenty-six and sat in the car for a few moments, collecting his thoughts as he looked at the bewitching twentieth-century home. He had seen this home before and wondered who was lucky enough to live there. It was a house that could have been on the front page of a who's who of old-style homes. It was a beautiful Victorian Italianate home. With a nearly flat roof, extra-wide ease, and massive brackets, it was a home that took you on a historical journey at first site. It was a very rare sight in the south to see an Italianate home. Most homes like these were in the north due to the economic situation in the south after the civil war, the era when they were the most popular. The fact that he was about to walk up the sidewalk and through the large wrought iron gate and front doors of this home almost made him forget the purpose of his visit. But he was jolted back to the present when a beautiful woman stepped out onto the opulent front porch. She walked to the edge of the porch and placed her hands on the porch rail and leaned forward just a little and smiled. Kent wanted to freeze everything in place and capture it all in his mind. The gentle summer breeze caught her blonde flowing hair and tossed it in virtual slow motion against the old fuchsia colored house in the background. Even in her beige blouse and black pants, she was stunning in Kent's eyes. When she smiled, all of Kent's attention went to her lips as he anticipated her first words.

"Hello, Detective Rivers. Welcome to Mathilda," Holly said as she stepped to opened the short gate on the porch.

"Thank you. You have a beautiful place. Breath-taking. Did you say, Mathilda?" Kent responded.

"Yes, Mathilda, a nineteenth-century writer, and poet. Mathilda d'Orozco. I guess I'm a little weird naming my place, huh?"

"Oh, no, not weird at all. I think it is great, and it goes with this place. Mathilda, wasn't there a waltz named after her?"

"No. That was Waltzing Matilda, an Australian folk song," Holly said as she laughed out loud.

"Come on up; let's sit over here."

Holly led the way over to a sitting area several feet from the front door where a ceiling fan was turning slowly over an old fashion large Martini Table. On the table were an envelope, a writing pad, and an ink pen. There was a glass of ice tea sitting a wooden coaster and a bottle of water on another. The glass of tea had two slices of lemon fixed to the edge of the glass.

"I figured you for an ice tea sort of guy. Am I wrong? If so, you can have the water. I enjoy tea also," Holly said as she sat on a round stool that was sitting almost under the table.

"Yes, I am. Thank you," Kent responded as he walked over to a chair close to the table.

Between the two of them they could have come in first and second place in an beautiful eye contest; her with her gorgeous deep-blue eyes, and him with his stunning emerald green eyes. Her smooth blonde hair accented her eyes, and Kent's eyes intensified his dark hair and ruggedly handsome dark face.

After a few opening comments by each to break the ice, Holly opened the envelope and produced a letter from an attorney from New Orleans. She explained a little about the letter and the underlying situation as Kent looked intently into her eyes, listening attentively to each word.

The letter referenced an investment that Holly had made a few years ago with a person she thought she knew well. The money and the man both vanished. Now, the man wanted to return to face the music and try to go back to a normal life at some point. The letter was from the man's attorney. He had not yet turned himself into the police. The attorney was trying to test the waters to see what each victim was expecting from the prosecution of the man. He also was trying to determine if she was agreeable to a settlement that was less than the money she had invested.

Holly was seeking Kent's advice on to what would happen if she agreed or didn't agree to anything before the case went to court. She said that she wondered about her standing and what the best legal thing for her to do would be.

After hearing what his visit was about, Kent decided that she already had an attorney and already had matters well in hand. Holly was not a lady who needed guidance in her business affairs, and it didn't take Kent long to detect that fact. Could it be possible that she was just as captivated with him as he was with her? He would play the role that she had set up for him. It was something that she had put into motion. He intended to ride it out to see where it landed.

Kent quickly read over the letter. It was short and to the point.

He laid the letter down. He took a lemon from the edge of his glass and squeezed it into the tea.

"This is probably going to federal court. I'm not that familiar with the federal code covering such crimes, but I am sure the punishment would be significant," Kent said as he held the letter in his hand.

"Do you think I should accept an offer before it goes to court or wait to see what the court orders?" Holly asked Kent.

"I am sure you have an attorney to advise you on the legal aspects of this case, so I am just going to talk to you like a friend. If he goes to court he will have a lot more fees to pay and he will have a lot of time to pay you and the others. If it was me, and they offered me anything reasonable, I would take it."

"That sounds strange coming from a law officer. I would have thought you would lean toward not giving him a break and sending him to prison."

"Oh, I am for sending him for prison, and if I were investigating this case I would want you to help me send him to prison. But, like I said, as a friend, I would want my money first. Besides, it sounds like he has learn part of a lesson anyway having to beg his way back to the country. But, I would talk to my attorney before I made a final decision."

"Aren't you going to ask how much he took?"

"No, I figured that was your business."

"Two-hundred, fifty thousand dollars."

"That's a lot of money. At least to me."

"It is to me too. Part of me wants to just let him rot in jail. The other part just wants to recover what is mine; or rather my dad's. I had taken the money out of some of dad's stocks. Well, I guess I will let it stew a while. Make him sweat some too."

She thanked Kent, made a note on the notepad, put it and the letter into the envelope, and then looked quietly at Kent for just a moment. Kent was not intimidated by her wealth, but he was still star struck a little with her beauty and aura. She was a beautiful, classy lady through and through.

Kent broke the momentary silence by asking her a question.

"Does that conclude our business and the reason you called the office and invited me to come over?"

"Yes, I believe it does. Thank you," she replied. "Do you need to leave now?"

"Actually, that was going to be my next question to you," Kent said with a hint of a grin on his face. "Do I need to leave now?"

"I don't see how you could go yet. You haven't even finished the tea I made especially for you."

"And it is excellent tea, at that," Kent said. "Since we have finished the business part of this meeting, I was wondering if I could ask you something personal."

"Personal?" Holly asked as her forehead wrinkled a bit.

"Yes, well, not personal, just not business."

"Oh, in that case, I guess you can. You may not get you the answer you want or expect," she said as her forehead relaxed.

Now Kent wasn't sure that he wanted to ask his question. But he may never be back again if he didn't, he thought.

"I have this event that is coming up this weekend and I hate to go alone. Might you consider going with me?" He asked with one eye brow slightly raised.

"What kind of event? Where?"

"It is a dinner. It's with me, and I haven't decided where yet."

Kent was glad he was able to breathe now that he had asked the question.

"Now, Detective Rivers, do you ask all the ladies you help, out on a date?"

"No, just those with whom I'm utterly intrigued. And you may call me Kent now that we are no longer talking business."

"I don't know; I think I like calling you detective. Let's say it intrigues me."

"Is that all that intrigues you about me, that I'm a detective?"

"No, not really. I have to admit that your eyes intrigue me. But honestly, what goes on behind those eyes is what intrigues me the most," Holly told Kent.

She turned her eyes bashfully away briefly as she spoke, then cut them right back to Kent.

"Is that a yes?" Kent asked, without moving his eyes or even blinking.

Holly very slowly but deliberately nodded her head yes without speaking or taking her eyes off of Kent's. Neither wanted to move or even breathe for fear it would end the captivating enchantment of the spontaneous moment. They remained silent for few moments until a UPS driver spoke up.

"Hey, I hate to bother you guys, but I need a signature on this one."

Neither Kent or Holly noticed the van pull up or the driver walk up the sidewalk. Holly looked at the driver as if he were a Martian that wanted to invade her planet.

"What? Oh, hey, I'm sorry. We were talking and didn't even see you come up. Where do I sign?" Holly finally spoke up.

The UPS driver smiled as he thanked her for her signature and left. Kent and Holly looked at each other for a second then both burst out with laughter.

"Do you have to get right back to work?" Holly asked Kent.

"Not really. I planned to take the rest of the afternoon off."

"Would you like to go for a drive?"

"Sure, I can run home and get my personal car."

"No, no. We'll take mine. I want to show you something or some things. But you can shed that tie if you was like."

"That is no problem," Kent said as he pulled his tie by one of its ends, set it down on the table, and unbuttoned his shirt collar.

"Let me get my purse. Come on through the house."

Kent followed her into the house. The interior was nothing less than what he expected. He was still dazzled by the décor, paintings, and artwork. Holly grabbed her purse, which was sitting on the kitchen counter.

"This way," Holly said as she led Kent through the kitchen and out into the garage.

When she opened the door leading out to the garage, the four-bay garage lit up like a showroom floor. There was her BMW convertible that he had seen when they first met; a 1963 red and white Corvette Stingray; a black 1967 Shelby GT500 Mustang with two, six-inch red racing stripes going down the center of the car; and a white 1980 Ford F150 4 wheel drive pickup. Each vehicle was in pristine condition. On the far side of the last car was a large room. In the room was a light blue and white 1962 Harley Davidson Panhead dressed out to the max. A little past the Harley was a 1940 red-and-gray Indian Chief motorcycle.

Kent was amazed at how immaculate each vehicle appeared.

"Let's go in this one," Holly said as she walked over to the Corvette.

She reached into the seat and put on a hair scarf, smiled at Kent, and said, "Well, quit standing there with your mouth open and come on."

Kent batted his eyes a couple of times trying to believe what he was seeing.

"You have some selection," he said, as he walked to the Stingray.

"My dad left them to me. I try to keep them up the best I can, but it is a lot of work. Sometimes I just think I'll sell them, but then I vision my dad's frown, so I say, 'just kidding dad,'" Holly replied and chuckled. "I could never sell them. But the problem is, there are more in another garage. We will go there first."

Kent jumped into the front seat of the Corvette, and Holly opened the garage door and backed out. She drove up the street and got away from most of the houses. Then she pressed the gas pedal and opened up the engine and let their hair blow in the wind.

"If I get stopped by the police, are you going to help me get out of a ticket detective?" Holly yelled over the wind noise.

"Sure, I'll pay half the fine," Kent shouted back and winked.

"Oh, I see. Well, in that case, maybe I'll really open it up."

"No, no!" Kent said laughing. "I will pay it all. Just don't get caught. You may be able to outrun them in this."

"Don't give me any ideas," she came back.

They stopped by to look at the other classic cars. Kent was in awe of the collection. After leaving the garage Holly sped onto I-75 and went south into Georgia.

"You okay to be gone a while?" She asked Kent, having to raise her voice above the wind noise.

"Yes. Yes, I am," he replied. As long as you wish, he thought but didn't say.

After another half hour of driving, she pulled into a rest area. She went to use the facilities, and when she came back, she put the top up on the car. She continued into Georgia as they talked and laughed. Kent forgot about the time, the cases, and most everything else except that moment with the lovely Holly Packe.

They ended up in Atlanta. She drove to what appeared to be a hole-in-the-wall restaurant. But once inside Kent was thrilled at what he saw. The room setting and décor was that of a 1920's speakeasy. Newspaper articles and items from the 1920's and early 1930's prohibition decorated the walls. It replicated the Mayflower Club in Washington, D.C., one of the swankiest places of its time. Kent could hardly believe his eyes. As he was glaring at the various aspects of the décor, the manager greeted Holly with a hug.

"Holly, I didn't know you were coming tonight. I gave your table away," the manager said after the quick hug.

"That's okay, it was just a last-minute thought. We can sit anywhere," Holly replied. "Jim, this is Kent Rivers, a new friend of mine. Kent, this is Jim Gathers, he is the manager here, and an excellent one."

"Nice to meet you, Kent. And thank you, Holly; it's great when you hear that from the boss."

"You too, Jim," Kent said as he was trying to figure out if he had heard him right.

"Oh, Jim! You weren't supposed to tell him that!" Holly said with a scolding tone but with a smile on her face.

"The boss?" Kent repeated aloud.

"I'm sorry, Holly. Maybe you shouldn't have been so quick to say how good I was," Jim said.

"It's okay, Jim. I guess he would have found out soon enough," she replied. "Yes, Kent. I'm the owner, but Jim runs the place. I just stop by to say hello once in a while."

Kent knew Holly was unique, but he was beginning to see just how unique.

CHAPTER TWENTY-SEVEN

Fifty Miles West of Lincoln

Friday, June 25, 5:44 A.M.

It had been raining all night. Kenny sat in the kitchen drinking coffee and pondering his plight. He was mesmerized at how the light from the kitchen struck each drop of rain as it spiraled down the window against the backdrop of a dark, early morning. He had been up since five after a restless night of tossing and turning. Kenny thought it was time to leave and get further away from Ohio.

Kenny talked with Dyson and Connie about where they thought he should go. Connie told him about her uncle in Nevada.

Keri was just listening. Now that she was away from Mark she had peace, and it didn't matter where she went. She thought about her grandmother but decided she couldn't go back yet. Not just yet, she thought. Keri felt safe with Kenny. He was more like a brother than anything. Maybe she was longing for the brother she once knew.

Kenny thought that Nevada sounded great. Connie called her uncle. At first, he wanted no part of them. He spent time in the Utah State Pen on a robbery charge. He had been out six years and had come off parole the previous year. He didn't want to be involved with any troubled kids or anyone on the run from the law. But after Connie told him that they were good kids and had just gotten caught up with a bad guy, he relented and agreed to the visit. Her uncle lived in a secluded area in northeast Nevada near Deeth. He ran a small horse ranch for a wealthy couple from California, and the housing was part of his salary. The uncle had plenty of room for Kenny and Keri. He told Connie they could stay a month or so.

Keri had always loved horses and thought it would be a good place to hang out while she figured out what to do. Kenny wanted to put his time with Mark behind him, and he felt he would be able to get over Lisa easier without always having to look over his shoulder. He and Keri had not thought about being anything but friends. It continued to be that way while they were traveling.

They packed what little they had, plus the things that Connie and Dyson gave them. They left after it got dark. They would take I-70 to Kansas City, then I-29 to I-80 through Nebraska, Wyoming, and Utah. It was a long trip, but they still had some money left over, and Dyson gave them an extra $165.00.

Saturday morning, June 26, around 2:30 A.M. EST.

They were about 50 miles west of Lincoln, Nebraska when Kenny began to fight sleep. Keri had been asleep more than an hour. Kenny tried rolling down the window and turning the radio up, but nothing helped. He was afraid he was going to fall asleep and wreck so he pulled off the shoulder of the road thinking he could get a quick nap. Kenny pulled just past an overpass and into the grassy area. He quickly fell asleep. About thirty minutes after falling asleep, A bright light and a knock on the window brought Kenny out of his slumber.

As Kenny was coming to, he realized that the flashlight was not the only bright light striking his eyes. Blue lights were bouncing off of his rear-view mirror and into his face. For a split second, he thought about starting the car and taking off, but he concluded he would get stopped in the end anyway, so he turned the key and rolled down the window.

Keri was starting to come out of her deep sleep.

"I need you to step out of the car." A tall, York County deputy leaned down just enough, so he was heard through the open window.

"What's the problem, sir? I was just too sleepy to keep going," Kenny replied without moving anything but his head. Kenny noticed the officer's nameplate said Rose and was strangely distracted by a random thought of Lisa holding a rose he had given her a week before she died.

The flash of blue lights brought him back to the present reality that was starting to sink in.

"Come on out of the car, and we can talk about it out here," the deputy countered.

"You just sit tight where you are, but keep both hands on the dash. Don't take them off the dash until I tell you to. Do you understand me?" Deputy Rose said to Keri as he leaned into the window.

Keri quietly shook her head to indicate that she did.

Kenny stepped out of the car, and the deputy motioned for him to walk to the front right side of the Monte Carlo. Keri looked back at the blue lights once but kept her hands on the dash.

"Let me see your license and your registration for this car."

"Okay," Kenny replied, as he pulled out his wallet and handed him his license.

"There is something I need to tell you."

"What's that?"

"My license is suspended. I owe some fines."

"How long have they been suspected?"

"A long time. I just didn't have the money. I was only working odd jobs and didn't make enough to pay them all. I know I should have."

"Yeah, that would have probably been a good thing because, in Nebraska, we have a law against driving with a suspended license."

"So, you gonna arrest me?"

"What do you think?"

"I believe that you are probably gonna bust me," Kenny said with a small grin.

"You know any good reason I shouldn't?"

"No sir, guess not, but I would rather not get arrested."

"I'm sure you would. Who is that in the car? She looks awfully young to me."

"She is just a friend. We ain't like together or anything, I mean, we ain't havin' sex or anything like that."

"How old is she?"

"I guess she is about fifteen, sir."

"Fifteen? What is she doing traveling with you this time of night? Where does she live?

"Well, sir, it's a long story. It would probably take longer than you would want for me to explain."

"Yeah, I'm sure it will. Well, while you are explaining, why don't you explain why the tag doesn't go with this car and why there are bullet holes in your doors?"

"That's what I mean sir; it will take a long time to explain."

"It looks like we may give you a while to make that explanation. Do you have any dope or guns on you?"

"No dope, but yeah, I got a gun in my right pants pocket. I actually forgot I had it until now."

"A gun? I need you to turn around and put your hands on the hood of the car while I get that gun."

Deputy Rose had Kenny spread his legs as he did a search. He found the gun in his right front pant pocket like Kenny told him. About that time a Nebraska State Trooper pulled up behind the patrol car. The trooper saw Deputy Rose take the gun out of Kenny's pocket as he walked up on the right side of the cars. Then he noticed Keri in the front seat with her hands still on the dash. Rose placed handcuffs on Kenny and turned him around to allow him to lean on the right side of the car.

"What do you have here?" The trooper asked the deputy.

"I don't know for sure yet. This guy says he has a long story to tell. I thought maybe we should let him start telling it. Do you mind getting that girl out and take her back with you and see if she has a story to tell also?" Rose asked the trooper.

"Sure will, deputy."

The trooper opened the front passenger side door and asked Keri to step to the back of the Monte Carlo. Rose had Kenny walk to the front of the car and sit on the ground with his legs crossed and his hands cuffed behind him.

Rose walked over to the driver's side and looked through the windshield for the vehicle identification number. He told Kenny to just sit there for a while, and he would be back to hear his story.

After checking the vehicle identification number through the computer, York County communications center informed Deputy Rose that the owner of the car was a murder victim and the car was missing. Rose called to the trooper and told him to handcuff the girl. The trooper put the cuffs on Keri and walked her to the front where Kenny was sitting on the ground. He made her walk another ten feet then sit down with her back toward Kenny.

Rose told the trooper what communications had said to him. They decided to arrest the two and take them to the sheriff's office to hear their story.

The trooper advised Keri of her rights and walked her back to his patrol unit. Rose did the same for Kenny. They told them both that they could tell their stories in a few minutes at the office.

After hearing the radio traffic, another deputy and a supervisor arrived at Rose's location as an additional backup. They inventoried the car and had it towed back to the sheriff's office for processing.

Saturday, June 26, 7:22 A.M.

Rivers was taking his Saturday morning off seriously; he was sleeping-in. He had been up early and had stayed out late much of the week. His body and mind said, rest, but the phone ringing said wake-up. As usual, the phone won. It was the sheriff's department communication's office.

"Hello," he said with a little moan.

"Good morning, Chief. I hate to bother you so early, but I thought you would want to know that a deputy in Nebraska found Alex Fisher's car. York County Sheriff's Office is holding two subjects. They want to know what we want to do. Your contact person is Deputy Jason Rose. I can connect you if you want me to."

The communications officer waited for his response as Rivers paused to collect his thoughts.

"Uh, sure, go ahead and connect me."

She put Rivers on hold while she tried to get Deputy Rose on the phone. It took a couple of minutes, but Rivers and Rose were able to talk.

"This is Jason Rose, who am I speaking with?"

"This is Chief Kent Rivers of the Hamilton County Sheriff's Office in Chattanooga, Tennessee. I understand that you have a car belonging to Alex Fisher and a couple of people there with you."

"Yes sir, we do. A guy named Kenny Saxton and a young girl named Keri. She advised me that she was fifteen years old but didn't give me her last name or say where she was from. We are checking runaway reports on NCIC now. The guy stated that he didn't know her last name. I guess I believe he is telling the truth. He has been truthful the best I can tell so far. He says he has a story that he needs to tell us, but I talked with our chief, and he didn't want us talking to them until we called you guys to see what you wanted."

"Wow, that's great. Thanks. Did they say anything about another guy?"

"Not yet, but like I said, once I talked to the chief, I haven't been back there to talk with them anymore. What do you want us to do? You want one of our detectives to call you and question them?"

"Deputy Rose is it?"

"Yes, sir."

"Let me get your number, and I'll collect my thoughts and call you back in less than a half an hour. Will you still be there?"

"Yes sir, I have to do a complete inventory of the car, so I'll be at the office for a while. If I am not right at the office, they can find me."

"Okay, give me a few to think about it."

"Okay sir, talk to you in a little while."

"Yeah, thanks."

Rivers hung up the phone and sat on the edge of his bed. It would be faster if their detectives talked with them, but they do not know the case and could miss vital information. Kent determined that he needed to go to Nebraska, but this needed to happen right now. He called Chief Sal Dillard to discuss arrangements.

"Hey, chief. Good morning."

"It's beginning to sound like it may not be, hearing from you this early on a Saturday morning."

"I understand, but maybe it will be a good one after all. Nebraska is holding Fisher's car and two people: Kenny Saxton and a fifteen-year-old girl. It seems that they want to talk, but Nebraska needs to know if we want to speak with them or if we want them to handle it. I think that I need to go. The other suspect, Mark Manning, was not with them. Time may be a factor in finding him now."

"Well, what do you want me to do? What do you need?"

"I need to fly out to York Nebraska right away. I would like to call Nick Taylor and talk with him about the cost of him taking the department plane versus me taking a commercial flight. I know that the commercial flight there and back would be expensive at this late notice if I could even get a quick flight. Plus I will have to fly into Lincoln then get transportation to York County. And my other thought is, if I get there and need to go to another place to locate Manning, taking commercial flight might delay the investigation. However, I don't want to cost the county a ton of money either. I was hoping that after talking with Taylor, he could tell me if it was practical to take the department plane or not, with your approval, of course."

"You will have my approval if Taylor said the cost is comparable, but on this one, I will have to advise the sheriff."

"Okay, chief. So it's okay if I call Taylor?"

"Yeah, but keep in mind that the sheriff may have a different view, so let me see what his thinking is on it. In the meantime, you call Taylor and let him do some calculating, and Y'all come up with a plan. I have a feeling the sheriff is going to want to know exactly what your plans are."

"Okay, chief. I'll call you back in a few."

Rivers called communications to have them track down Taylor. It wasn't four minutes before Taylor was calling Rivers. Rivers gave him the complete details and the possibility of having to travel to another location after getting to Nebraska. Taylor got right on it and called Rivers back about fifteen minutes later. Taylor advised him that the cost is about the same if he included his time.

Rivers called Chief Dillard back. He had already talked with the sheriff, and the sheriff gave them the green light to do whatever he, Rivers, and Taylor felt best. Taylor headed immediately to the airport to ready the plane and charted the course. He would have to make a refueling stop along the way, so he mapped things out and made a flight plan. Rivers had the communications officer to call the Nebraska Deputy back and let him know that they were on their way to York and that he would call him before they left Chattanooga.

Rivers threw some clothes together, including a gray suit, and stopped by the office to get some files. Then he headed to meet Taylor at the airport. Along the way, he stopped by the grocery store and pick up some snacks and drinks for the five- to six-hour flight.

Taylor had the flight plane ready. He saw that York had a decent airport. York and York County were small and rural, so

Taylor was happy that they had an airport. The fact that it was in good condition was even better. It was about four miles from the airport to the York County Sheriff's Office. Hopefully, they had someone at the sheriff's office that could pick them up or at least a taxi would be available.

When Rivers met Taylor at the plane, Taylor was almost ready to leave. He had the plane out of the hanger and ready in the taxiway.

"This is getting to be a habit," Taylor said.

"Yeah, I hope it pays off."

"Me, too. It's expensive. I'm on overtime you know." Taylor said to Rivers knowing he wasn't.

"Me, too! By the time we get back, we will have cost the taxpayers a small fortune."

Rivers figured that even if Taylor was on overtime, he only said it as a dig.

"Is that everything you are taking?" Taylor asked.

"No, I have a bag of drinks and snacks in the car," Rivers replied as he laid his things in the back of the plane.

The Seneca III held a pilot and five passengers, so there was plenty of room.

"Snacks?" Taylor asked in a mocking voice.

"Yeah, unless you are serving lunch on your plane, or doing a fly by at McDonald's," Rivers countered, smiling.

Taylor just shook his head, "Come on; let's get it in the air.

CHAPTER TWENTY-EIGHT

So the girl is in Jail?

Saturday, June 26, 10:39 A.M.

It took only five minutes for them to clear for take-off. In just minutes they were in the air once again. Taylor estimated that it took about five and a half hours to fly to York, maybe less if they got a lucky tailwind. The two men started the flight just as they had the last two flight; in silence.

Rivers had the file containing most all of the pertinent information on the case. He used the next few hours to make sure he knew the case from front to back. He wasn't going to try to break any ice with Taylor. He was on a mission and appeasing Taylor was low on his list of priorities. Taylor was just the means to get him to where he needed to go. If he wanted to play junior high school, he would do it by himself.

Taylor knew the importance of this flight. He might cut Rivers some slack and try to be less hostile toward him. Each time he was with Rivers he saw less of the man who stole so much from him. But as Rivers lost the persona of Jake Long, Taylor's pride, began to push back. In his heart, he knew all along that Rivers had nothing to do with his loss. He was aware that he was holding Rivers responsible for something that was not his fault. He also knew that as long as he kept anyone the object of his hate, he would remain bitter and unable to move on with his life.

As the flight entered into its third hour, Taylor's thoughts had entirely shifted to his acidity about his broken marriage and his lost business. For the first time in a long time, he allowed his mind to begin processing the whole truth. He had always known that once he faced it all, he was be a happier and better man. But to face his bitterness head on, Taylor knew that he had to forgive the person he hated most for what had happened. The real target of his raging rancor was himself.

After Rivers had completed his review of the case file, he thought he might ask Taylor to help with the interviews. Taylor could testify when they went to court rather than an officer from hundreds of miles away.

"You awake?" Rivers asked Taylor jokingly.

"I am now. Why?"

"I thought that it might be good to have someone from our department to help me with the interviews rather than someone from Nebraska. To testify about the interviews when we go to court with this case. You game?"

"You want me to help interview these two?"

"Yeah, why not?" I've seen you talk with witnesses and suspects. I think you do a good job. Besides, you're the only one with me."

"I don't know what questions to ask. How would I be any good at it? I don't know the case. I don't mind sitting in with you, but I don't know about doing any tag team or solo interviews."

"Don't we have another few hours to go?"

"Yeah, at least two. Why?"

"I can go over the case with you. That will give you a working knowledge of it. You will be all right."

"Okay, I can do that, I guess."

After Taylor had agreed to help, they spent the rest of the trip talking about the case. By the time they landed, Taylor had the necessary information that he needed. They landed in York, and a city police officer picked them up at the airport. He took them to the sheriff's office where Deputy Rose was asleep in an empty holding cell. He had been up for twenty hours.

The city officer had been at the communications office when the call came from Rivers, so he volunteered to get them. Rose was embarrassed to be caught sleeping, but Rivers and Taylor insisted they understood and had done the same thing. After the preliminary introductions, they got right into the case.

"Thank you for holding these two. Did they say anything more since we last talked?" Rivers asked Rose.

"No, I've just left them alone. I don't know if they talked to any of the corrections officers, but I doubt it. Most of the time they just tell them to talk to one of us or a detective," Rose replied.

"I didn't know you were still here. You have been here a while," Rivers stated.

"Yeah, we had one guy that was on vacation when another guy got sick. I could have gone on home, but once I go home; it is hard to come back. You know, stick a fork in me, I'm done" Rose said with a laugh.

"I know how that feels," Taylor inserted.

"How do you want to do this?" Rose asked looking at Rivers and then Taylor.

"Let's talk to the girl first. Do you have a juvenile officer available?" Rivers asked.

"Yes, I called her this morning and told her to expect you

guys to call. She is a good lady. Her name is Micki Toolsey. I can have her come on in now," Rose answered.

"Sounds great," River said.

"Do you need one of our detectives here?" Rose asked.

"Not unless they want to be here," Rivers replied.

"No, I think they have their plates full. We have been having a bunch of burglaries lately and it's keeping them busy, but they told me to call 'em if you needed 'em."

"Thank them for me. I think we will be okay, and I want you to get some rest. I'm sure there is someone here that we could get to help us if we needed something," Rivers told Rose.

"Yeah, Della Silvers is in charge of the jail right now. She will get you whatever you need, including drinks or coffee. She said she's bringing you dinner when it's served," Rose advised.

"That's great. I certainly appreciate that" Rivers replied.

"Well, let me call Micki. She can be here in twenty minutes. I'll have Della bring the girl to this interview room here," Rose said as he pointed to a door a few feet away.

"They can access it from the jail side. Just press the button next to the door, and the tower guard will open it. They can see you on the camera. When you want out, just tell them from the intercom on the inside. They will get the girl and let you out. They won't open the door to let you out until the girl is out of the room," Rose explained.

"So the girl is in the jail?" Rivers asked, thinking that normally a juvenile is not in the same facility as the adult inmates.

"Yeah, she is down at the juvenile wing. There is a hallway that separates the jail from the youth holding area. They can't see the adult inmates or have contact with them. It is a small holding area; we don't keep juveniles here on a long-term basis," Rose replied.

About 15 minutes after Rose called the juvenile officer, Micki

Toolsey arrived at the office. Rose introduced the three and left for the day. Rivers and Toolsey talked briefly about Nebraska laws and procedures that might be applicable. Nothing was unique or different than it was in Tennessee, so it didn't take long.

Taylor, Rivers, and Toolsey went to the conference room inside the youth wing escorted by a correctional officer. Within five minutes Keri was brought in. She was still wearing a tan uniform top and pants. The uniform was part of the sheriff's office inmate clothing. The youth wing inmates wore tan, and the adult prisoners wore orange.

Toolsey had already met Keri. Keri had not given her last name or any information about her legal residence. Toolsey explained to Keri why they were there and introduced Rivers and Taylor. She explained her rights to her once again and had her sign the rights waiver form. Then she turned the conversation over to Rivers.

"Hello Keri, as officer Toolsey told you, I'm Kent Rivers, and I'm from Tennessee. We are investigating a crime that took place in Chattanooga. We are hoping that you may be able to help us. Do you want to do that?" Rivers said with a slight smile, enough to show compassion but not look insincere.

"Am I in trouble?" Keri asked in a calm, almost whispering voice.

"Keri, I'm going to tell you something that I want you to remember while you are talking to us. I'll never lie to you or trick you. If you want to know something, ask me. I promise I will tell you if I can. I don't know if you are in trouble or not. A lot of that will depend on what we learn from you. You seem to be a very pleasant young lady. If I perceive that you are in trouble, I'll let you know. How is that?"

"That sounds fair. Have you talked to Kenny?"

"Not yet, but it is my understanding from talking to the deputy who brought you in that he wants to talk to me."

"He probably does. We didn't really do anything. I mean we were around when some things happened, but most of the time we didn't even know what was going on. Not until later. This guy named Mark, he is the devil himself. I thought I was never gonna get away from him. He is the one you really need to get."

"Did you say, Mark?"

"Yes, Mark."

"Do you know where we could find Mark?"

"Not exactly, but he's in Ohio unless he left."

"How do you know he could be in Ohio?"

"That's where Kenny and I got away from him. He scared me the entire time I was with him. He tried to rape me, too. Somewhere in Georgia, in a park somewhere."

"He raped you?"

"He was trying to, and he was gonna kill Kenny if he attempted to stop him. He pulled his gun, and I was begging Mark not to shoot him. Kenny was able to stop him, but he got beat up pretty bad doing so."

"So Mark had the gun?" Taylor asked.

"Yes, a little one. Mark kept it until Kenny got it away from him later. A day or two later they had a big fight over the gun. I figured that Mark was about to kill us. So did Kenny. Kenny ran to the car and got the gun while Mark was away from it. But Mark saw him, and they got there about the same time. Kenny was just stronger, I guess. He made Mark leave. That was in Ohio. That's why I know about where he was. Mark had just shot a cop, and we got away."

"Mark shot a cop? Where was this?" Rivers asked with an insignificantly raised voice.

"I don't know; it wasn't long after we got off the interstate. I think it was near Dayton because I remember seeing Dayton signs just before it happened."

"Did he kill the cop?"

"I don't know. It is probably my fault."

"How was it your fault?"

"I mean, I was wanting to get away. I didn't know he would shoot her. I probably should have known though, cause he is mean as the devil himself. It was a woman cop who stopped us. Mark was just gonna speed away when she got to the car, but when she got close, and Mark rolled down his window, I yelled for help. That's when Mark shot her and took off."

"You yelled for help, and Mark shot her?"

"Yes. I thought it was my chance to get away, but all it did was get that cop shot. I'm such an idiot."

"I don't think you are an idiot. You obviously have been through an ordeal. We can get back to this in a minute. Why don't you tell me a little about yourself? How did you get involved with Mark in the first place?"

Keri paused for a moment and leaned back in her chair. She stared at Rivers, trying to figure out if she could trust him.

"Only if you want to," Rivers added.

"Okay, I will. I'm sorry all of this happened. I wish I had never left," Keri started, but then began crying. She laid her head down on the table and cried uncontrollably. Rivers was quiet and put his hand on her forearm and patted it gently. He left his hand on her forearm near her wrist and was still for several moments. The juvenile officer leaned forward and started to say something to her, but Rivers held up his finger on the hand that was touching Keri so Toolsey could see it. She offered Keri a tissue instead.

They all sat quietly for about three minutes. Keri slowly raised her head and looked around at everyone just sitting there waiting. All three of the adults smiled on queue as she slowly made eye contact with them individually.

"Would you like a break?" Rivers asked as he smiled and took his hand off of her arm.

Keri sat still for a little longer, not saying a word or showing many expressions. Once again she looked at each adult in the room, and once again each of them smiled at her.

"No, I'm okay. I'm sorry. I guess I'm just so lost and don't have any idea about my life now or what I am gonna do or what is gonna happen to me. I just wish it would all go away," Keri said, taking the tissue and wiping her eyes.

"Keri, it can't go away on its own. You have to make it go away. We might be able to help you make it go away, but you will have some memories for a lifetime. However, in time you can learn to use those memories instead of letting them use you," Taylor told her, just above a whisper.

"What do you mean?"

"Let's start with how you got here," River spoke up. "Then we can see where we need to go. As you do this, some of the weight of this will start to diminish and later, instead of letting this haunt you, use it to make you stronger."

Taylor nodded at her, smiled, and said, "exactly."

"Okay." Keri took in a deep breath and slowly let it out. "I ran away from home, from my grandmother in Ocala, Florida. I left with my best friend, Tiff and her boyfriend. Mark and Kenny picked us up somewhere in Florida. But when we got into Georgia, Tiff and her boyfriend were arguing and Mark kicked them out but made me stay. When we got to a park somewhere, Mark was trying to come on to me, and I tried to be nice, but I didn't want him messing with me. He got me on the ground. Then Kenny came up and knocked him off of me. That's when Mark pulled his gun. He told us that he killed his uncle before he left Florida and he would kill us both. I was so fearful. Since Mark had the gun, there was nothing Kenny could do at that moment, so he walked off, making Mark think he was going along with it.

But after a few minutes, he came back and drug Mark off of me. Mark is evil."

"What did Kenny do?" Rivers asked.

"I guess he got the drop on Mark. Mark wasn't expecting him to come back. Anyway, Kenny got the gun away from Mark and I got up and ran into the edge of the woods. But I could see what was happen."

"So then Kenny had the gun?" Asked Taylor.

"No, well, yeah, I mean for some reason Kenny let Mark have the gun back. I didn't hear everything they were saying. Kenny told me later that he was a fool for doing it. I don't know why he did. I guess he didn't know just how bad Mark was. I don't know, but he gave it back to Mark."

"What happened then?" River asked.

"Well, best I can remember Mark left and went to the car. I got up with Kenny, and we went back too."

"Why didn't Y'all just leave? Why go back to the car with Mark after all of that? Taylor responded with a puzzled look on his face.

"I don't know! Stupid, I guess. But we really didn't know what else to do right then, " Keri replied as she bowed her head and began to cry again.

Rivers looked at Taylor and shrugged his shoulders to indicate a valid question. Taylor lifted his eyebrows as if to reply, yeah, but didn't expect more crying.

"Do you want to stop for now Keri? Toolsey asked, as she lowered her head to the level Keri had dropped hers.

"I don't think so. I think I'm okay. Just talking about all of this brings bad memories. I was so scared and felt so alone. I think I would have lost my mind if Kenny wasn't there. He was good to me." Keri stated as she lifted her head. "At least what little mind I have," She said with a cute, slight, smile.

"Okay, well, I'm sure you had your reasons for going back to the car. No one here is blaming you. It's just a question we had to ask. You understand, right?" Rivers spoke up while Taylor and Toolsey nodded and smiled.

"What happened after that?" Rivers inquired.

"Well, we got back to the car. Mark was already there."

Keri paused for a moment.

"Anything wrong?" Rivers asked.

"I just want to say that I was gonna run. Me and Kenny talked about it. I don't want y'all to think we wanted to be there. We didn't. I didn't, and I know Kenny didn't, but I was scared Mark would catch me and kill me, so I just stayed. Mark said that no one would know if we didn't talk. He kept saying that. I guess trying to scare me; it worked. But Kenny was kind to me, so that helped. At first he wasn't. He didn't even want me with them; kept calling me 'jail-bait'. But after trouble started, he was on my side. You know, looking back, I didn't know where I would go. I had no money and didn't know anyone in Georgia. I was scared that I would be in trouble if the cops. Sorry, I mean, the police, caught me."

"We call ourselves cops, it's okay," Rivers said laughing.

"What happened after you left the park? Where did you go next?"

"I'm not sure where. We ended up spending the night at some place in the woods. They had been cutting down trees in the area. The car kept breaking down and not starting. We stayed that night, and it started that next morning."

"Do you know what day that was?" Taylor asked.

"Well, we left Florida that Friday, got picked up by Mark and Kenny sometime Saturday morning, so I guess it was Sunday, a week ago. I'm pretty sure anyway."

Keri began trusting Rivers and even started smiling at him. He smiled and joked with her to put her at ease.

When they took a break, Rivers told Toolsey and Taylor that Keri was strictly a victim here and he saw no reason to treat her any other way. He asked Toolsey what resources were available there to help Keri as a victim. Toolsey said she would look into it and come up with something.

With the information that was given by Keri, Rivers was able to confirm the story with Detective Pete Sanchez. A Florida deputy told the grandmother the story. A day later Nebraska sent Keri home.

After the break, Keri gave them the entire story about the woman in Georgia and that she didn't know if Mark hurt her or not. Her memory was excellent, and once she felt comfortable with Rivers and Taylor, she gave them detail after detail of what she had experienced and seen; including the Fisher murder.

When they finished the interview, Toolsey called the juvenile judge and based upon his order, Toolsey had all pending charges against her in Nebraska dropped.

Before leaving, Keri gave Rivers and Taylor a hug.

CHAPTER TWENTY-NINE

Eternal Enigma

Two correction officers escorted Kenny to the same interview room where Rivers had talked with Keri. Kenny's first question to Rivers was about Keri. Once Rivers told him what had happened and that she had given them all the details, Kenny was totally honest and didn't leave out any details.

The statement of Keri and Kenny matched other than a few minor details or time frames. The complete interview was recorded and later transcribed into eighteen pages. Based upon what Kenny and Keri had told the investigators they were able to verify the shooting of the officer and the circumstances surrounding the shooting. The wounded Ohio officer was able to give a full written report. Her report was consistent with Keri and Kenny's statements. Nebraska did not pursue charges against Kenny. He waived extradition and was soon on his way to Chattanooga to stand trial for his part in the Alexander Fisher murder and the theft of Fisher's car.

Kenny Saxton had given Rivers enough information about Mark Manning and his hometown of Greenville, Ohio that Rivers felt comfortable about pursuing him in Greenville. Rivers called the Darke County Sheriff's Office in Greenville and had the on-call detective call him back. It took about thirty minutes, but Detective Steve Winn called. Rivers filled him in on what he needed help with and asked permission to come into their jurisdiction to try to locate Mark Manning.

Steve Winn had no problem with the team coming to Darke County. However, since it was a homicide case and the suspect could have already shot an Ohio officer, he took it to his supervisor, who in turn took it to the sheriff. It wasn't long before Sheriff Les Parker called Rivers. Rivers gave him all the details he gave Detective Winn. The sheriff gave his permission and full support for the team to come to his county.

In the meantime, Parker had one of the detectives start running down leads on Mark Manning's whereabouts. Also, Sheriff Parker called the chief of police in Brookville, and advised him of what he had learned, and invited him or someone from his department to meet with them once Rivers was in Greenville.

Rivers and Taylor flew to Greenville. They found a hotel and spent the night. A Darke County deputy picked up Rivers and Taylor at the hotel and took them to the meeting. Everyone involved met at the Darke County Sheriff's Office at 8:00 A.M. The investigators started putting together the information they had on possible locations of Mark Manning.

After Rivers had given the group some background on the case and what he knew about the other cases, they compiled a list of possible locations. The list contained past contacts they or some of the road deputies had with Mark Manning and his friends.

Rivers teamed up with Darke County Detective Mike Fellows. Taylor went with Detective Billy Upton. The first person that the detectives attempted to contact was Mark's mother, Delores Ward. DeSota County, Florida investigators, had already reached

Delores about her uncle, Tom Shelton, so she was aware that someone would come looking for Mark. She had not seen or heard from Mark since he left for Florida. Both Rivers' and Taylor's groups went to the mother's house. A uniformed deputy went to the back door along with Upton and Taylor.

Delores Shelton Ward was at home when Detective Mike Fellows knocked on her door. She came to the door and invited Rivers and Fellows into the house. Fellows opened the back door after cautiously walking through the house and let the other lawmen in the house. Fellows, the uniformed deputy, and Upton searched for Mark with Delores' permission. Rivers remained with Delores and engaged in small talk while the others searched.

Mark wasn't in the house, so Upton, Taylor, and the deputy left the area. Rivers and Fellows remained at the house and collected information about Mark. They were aware that their presence was creating anxiety for Ms. Ward, so out of respect, they allowed her to process the reality of her uncle's death as they listened.

Ms. Ward was contemplative as she was trying to remember things she had deliberately not thought about for a while.

"I've not seen my son in over a year," she murmured, struggling to find the words. "My uncle allowed Mark to come down there to stay, even though he didn't truly know Mark. He did it as a favor to me." She nervously straightened her blouse with slightly trembling hands. Then she took a deep breath and continued.

"I am heartsick because of what happened to my Uncle Tom. I feel responsible." She looked at the floor and slowly shook her head back and forth in disbelief.

"I'm sure that's quite normal," assured Rivers. "But you must know that you are not responsible for any of this. Your son is an adult, making his choices."

"I know. But I can't help but wonder if there was something

else I could have done; or not done. I ask

myself over and over; was there something I could have done differently?"

At that moment she looked across the room, and something on the back wall caught her eye. She glared entranced for a brief moment at the collage of family photos displayed there. She fixated on one particular photo. It was a portrait of a little boy about six years old. He was standing on the front steps of a porch, smiling and waving at the photographer.

Delores Ward fell back into an overstuffed chair, buried her head in her hands, and began to weep violently. Rivers and Fellows looked at each other solemnly. Rivers gently patted Ms. Ward's hand as they listened to her anguished discourse about her only son's gradual transformation from an innocent, sweet child into a person she no longer knew and sometimes even feared. She talked about the abuse of his alcoholic father and the hardships they both faced during long periods of her husband's absences. She told them that in spite of how things were that Mark loved his dad and longed for his attention. She then revealed something that surprised the two investigators. She told them that when Mark was 12 years old, his father had hung himself in the garage and while looking for his dad to play ball with him, Mark was the one who had found him.

They knew that her real loss had happened long ago. She and Mark had dealt with their grief in different ways. Because she had never given up hope on her son, she had never really grieved the loss of her family or that innocent child she had once held tenderly in her arms. She knew she had lost him forever. She realized it all now, and there was nothing anyone could say that made it any better, and for that matter, any worse either.

After allowing Ms. Ward time to collect her composure, they were able to obtain some friend's names and general locations of the friends, but she told them they were old friends from high school, and she did not have a clue about his other buddies. Mark had only come to see his mom when he needed something, so she had little up-to-date information on where he could be. But Fellows took what she had and went back to the sheriff's office to plan the next move.

The names that Mark's mother was able to put together were, David Brewster, Kevin Hammons, Katie Bells, Jesse Walker, and some guy they called Codhead. Fellows gave the names to the correction's office and the clerks at the detective's office so they could start running down more information on the names.

Darke County had begun building an intelligence data system several years ago. Every time someone was booked into the jail, or interviewed by a patrol deputy, or questioned by a detective, a trusted clerk entered the information into the system. If someone had contact with a member of the Darke County Sheriff's Office, they would be in the system. Hopefully, one of the names Ms. Ward had provided would be in the system.

Taylor and Upton went to several of the known hangouts, but it was still too early on a Sunday morning for many to be out and about. Fellows and Rivers went back to the detective's office to help research the data banks. A couple of other Darke County detectives had met in the field with the uniformed patrol deputies and also with some of the nearby city officer trying to get information about those on the list.

No one from the drug enforcement unit was working that Sunday morning, but Fellows did talk one of them into coming to the office to research the drug unit's intelligence information.

In the meantime, Mark Manning was getting restless. He had been sitting around the house with Cody and his girlfriend for days. The events of his recent past had given him an adrenaline rush, and he needed another fix.

The part of town near Cody's had fallen on hard times as people and businesses relocated to the north side of the city. In place of the dress boutiques, sports stores, and specialty shops, there were now pawnbrokers, tattoo shops, a few secondhand stores, and a convenience market. Not far from where Cody lived was such a strip mall; Nellie's Tattoos, Jimbo's Gun and Pawn, and Harry's Food Market were open for business. There was also a Salvation Army thrift store in the plaza.

Late on the same Saturday night that Rivers and Taylor had flown into Greenville, Mark had broken into Jimbo's Gun and Pawn. Mark didn't attempt to open the large firearm safes, but he managed to find a Gerber Combat fixed-blade knife and a .38 Smith and Wesson five shot snub nose revolver. The revolver had the grips and rear sights replaced.

The owner had been interrupted before fixing the gun and had set it aside and carelessly left the gun out of the safe. Mark found a box of shells on the shelf behind the cash register. Inside the cash register was seventy-three dollars in one's, five's, and ten's. No one had ever broken into the pawn shop in Jimbo's eight years as owner. So Jimbo had gotten a little sloppy about protecting his valuables. He had left cash in the drawer to keep from running to the bank before he opened each morning and he had not repaired the alarm system that had been disabled by an electrical storm.

The pawn shop closed on Sundays, so it would be Monday before the owner discovered the burglary. Mark left with the knife, the gun, the cash, and a pocket full of shells. He decided he would steal a car, rob a store, and leave Greenville. He didn't know where he would go, but he would steal enough before he got out of town to stay at a campground somewhere for a while.

Mark took the loot from the pawnshop and headed back to Cody's through a wooded area. It was after two in the morning when he got back. Cody and Tempest were asleep. He had gotten the adrenaline rush he wanted. He ate chips and watched TV until it wore off and then fell asleep on the sofa.

Drug unit supervisor Sergeant Clint McDaniel had found information in his system on two of the names Delores Ward had provided. Jesse Walker and Codhead. Jesse Walker was in the Montgomery County Ohio jail at the time, so the focus was then on finding Codhead. The filed information showed that the suspected marijuana and cocaine dealer lived on the south end of Darke County. The system did not show an address, but it did show a name of someone who had purchased cocaine from Codhead.

Jay Glover was a small-time thief and drug user that had been in and out of jail. His last arrest was three weeks prior, so they had a current address for him. Rivers, McDaniel, and Fellows went to the address given in Glover's last arrest report. By this time it was a little past noon.

Glover was still in bed when Fellow's knocked on the door. Glover was reluctant to say anything about knowing a Codhead or buying drugs from him, but McDaniel convinced him that he already knew he had bought from Codhead. He threatened to check him daily until he was either clean or went to jail. Glover gave them what he knew about Codhead. He said that he believed that his real name was either Colby or Cody, but he wasn't sure. He was aware that he had a girlfriend named Tempest. He remembered it because the name was distinctive.

As it turned out Glover had bought pot from Codhead on Friday night at Codhead's trailer. Glover reluctantly rode with a detective to show him Codhead's trailer. Other investigators were able to verify some of the information that Glover had given them about Codhead, so they were able to get a search warrant for

Codhead's trailer.

The investigators on the case met back at the sheriff's office while McDaniel prepared the search warrant and located a judge to issue the warrant. Once McDaniel had the search warrant in hand, he met the others at the sheriff's office. Fellows and Rivers had been working on a plan to execute the warrant. The main goal was to find drugs on Codhead and give him an opportunity to flip and tell what he knew about Mark Manning.

McDaniel, another drug investigator, and Don Akers, would knock on the door. Taylor and Upton would hide behind an old car that was about fifty yards from the trailer on the front side of the property. Fellows and Rivers would go to the rear of the trailer behind an empty trailer that was about forty feet from the target trailer. The element of surprise would be conditioned on McDaniel getting the door open quickly.

A drug raid seldom goes as planned.

As McDaniel pulled in front of the trailer, someone believed to be Codhead was getting into a pickup. McDaniel decided to pull to the rear of the trailer and behind the pickup before it could get out onto the road. The driver of the pickup stopped as the old beat up undercover pickup pulled in from behind. McDaniel got out, leaving the pickup running. His partner, Don Akers, got out and went to the passenger side door. McDaniel identified himself as a detective asked the driver his name; he told him, Cody Long. He asked Cody if anyone was in the house because they had a search warrant. Cody glanced at Akers, then back to McDaniel. He chose to not attempt to flee at that moment.

Cody knew that he had two pounds of marijuana and three ounces of cocaine in the trailer. He was nervous and started to show it. McDaniel picked up on the fidget actions of Cody, so he placed handcuffs on him. He put his hands where one was through the stirring wheel and one outside the stirring wheel to reduce the chances of him running.

"No one is in the trailer. I was just leaving to go get my girlfriend from her mom's. There sure ain't no drugs, that's for sure," Cody responded to McDaniel's question.

"You're lying," McDaniel flatly told him while looking him straight in the eyes.

"About what?"

"Everything. You're lying. What's going on in the trailer?"

"Nothing's going on."

"Don, we're going to have to do this the hard way," McDaniel spoke across the truck to Don Akers.

"There's nothing going on, but okay, I lied about going to get my girlfriend. She's in the trailer with her cousin. You guys just scared me and I got nervous."

"Why would you get nervous?"

"Hell man, everyone gets nervous around the cops."

"I don't"

"Of course not, but others do."

"So, answer my question."

"What question?"

"What's going on in the trailer. I know that something is."

"Just what I told you. My girlfriend and her cousin are in there. Probably watching TV. But no one is doing anything wrong."

"Who is your girlfriend's cousin?"

"We call him, Jimbo, but I'm not sure if that's his real name or not."

"What does he look like?"

Cody gave a general description that matched that of Mark Manning. At the time, Cody figured that the detectives were only there to search for drugs. He knew that Mark might be wanted but didn't imagine that they

McDaniel decided to let Cody open the trailer door with his key. He took off the handcuffs just in case Manning was in the house. As McDaniel and Akers walked Cody toward the door, Rivers and Fellows stuck by the original plan and made their way to behind Cody's pickup.

As Cody unlocked the door and opened it about an inch, he pushed McDaniel and bolted away from the door. The force of the push was just enough to cause McDaniel to trip backward over a small shrub.

Akers took off running after Cody. Rivers and Fellows had already closed in on the house and were close enough to take control of the front door. McDaniel got on his feet and ran to assist Akers. Fellows cautiously entered the door; unaware the noise had awakened Mark Manning. Manning was now armed and alert. Manning's first thoughts were that someone was trying to steal Cody's drugs, but he quickly dismissed that notion.

Blankets hung over the windows causing the living room to be dark. As Fellows entered the room, the light coming from the open door lit up his profile. Fellows' eyes had not adjusted to the dark. He could not see much in the room other than the areas near the windows where a dim light made its way pass the blankets.

Manning had the revolver raised and pointed at him. Almost immediately Manning saw the badge on Fellows belt. Manning took aim at Fellows and pulled the trigger. The round struck Fellows in the right shoulder causing him to fall onto an end table and onto the floor.

Rivers was just a few feet behind Fellows but was not instantly noticed by Manning. Manning re-aimed the revolver at Fellows laying on the floor and was about to shoot him for the second time when he saw Rivers. Rivers quickly moved to his left after hearing the shot. His eyes were not yet adjusted, but they were working hard to find the shooter.

When Manning saw Rivers coming into the room he took aim at Rivers and fired one shot. Rivers' eyes immediately caught Manning's motion and dropped to the floor just as Manning fired. The round went about a foot above Rivers' head. Rivers swiftly recovered and fired three hurried shots in the direction of the motion and faint muzzle flash.

All three bullets found their target. Manning was struck once in the hand that was holding the gun, once in the left upper chest, and the third pushed through the middle of his chest less than an inch from his heart. Manning's body collapsed onto the sofa. He slowly slid off the couch onto the floor face up. There was little blood; most of the blood was from his wounded hand.

With his eyes wide open and a look of disbelief and shock, he took short, labored breaths. Rivers rushed to retrieve Manning's revolver on the floor. He then squatted close to Manning, looking into his dark, brown eyes. Manning blinked rapidly as his eyes met Rivers'. It was indisputable that Manning was no longer a threat so Rivers holstered his weapon.

McDaniel and Akers had come rushing into the room right behind Rivers. They saw that Rivers had control of Manning, so they turned their attention to Fellows. Akers advised the Communications Center of the situation. It wasn't long until emergency medical care units were on their way. Fellows was sitting up and talking but was losing blood. They had him lie on the floor while they tended his wound in an attempt to stop the bleeding.

Rivers knelt on one knee alongside Manning as he observed him struggling for breath. He didn't know
everything Manning had done, but even if he had, he still would have compassion on a dying soul. Rivers couldn't help but think about Mark's mother and the things she had told him

earlier. He remembered the picture of the young boy smiling and waving and wondered what kinds of choices it took to bring Mark to this place and time. It was surreal to be experiencing the final realization of Mark's mother's fear and grief.

Manning never took his eyes off of Rivers. He tried to speak a couple of times, but couldn't manage any words. Rivers looked at his wounds and took a nearby towel and wrapped it around Manning's bleeding hand.

"There is an ambulance on its way. They should be here soon," Rivers announced in a hushed voice.

Manning's expression didn't change, and neither did his focus on Rivers. It was like he was trying to size up the man who had just fatally wounded him. His breathing became more difficult with each passing moment. Rivers pulled a blanket off the sofa and laid it across Manning's body.

Since he was breathing and there was not much blood, there was little that Rivers could do to save his life at that point. Rivers knew enough about where the wounds were located to know that his chances of survival were slim. All he could do now was be there, so Manning would not die alone.

"You may want to make your peace with God now. It's not too late," Rivers told him looking him in the eye.

Manning managed to raise his left hand a little toward Rivers. At first, Rivers wasn't sure what he was doing or what he wanted. But Manning looked at his hand to signal Rivers to take it. Rivers slowly placed his hand in Manning's. Manning softly gripped Rivers' hand and then let it go.

Was Manning congratulating him for catching him? Was he reaching out for a final human touch? Rivers wondered silently. Perhaps he is letting me know that he made peace with God, Rivers thought. Manning's hand dropped quickly to his side and remained still. He refocused on Rivers' eyes once more, took a shallow breath, and escaped into an eternal enigma.

Rivers, still kneeling, looked at Manning's face of death, let out a faint sigh, and gently shook his head. There was no final message from Mark's face of death, Rivers thought, only the ending of a sad story.

As the first medical personnel entered the room, they attended to Detective Fellows. Once they saw that the bleeding had stopped, they turned toward Manning. Rivers was standing as they got to Manning's side.

"I think he is gone," Rivers told the emergency responders as he walked away.

CHAPTER THIRTY

Half Moon Horse Farm

Tuesday, June 29th

Keri Mendez was welcomed home with a home-cooked meal, a gentle hug from her grandmother, and her favorite flower-yellow daisies, on her bed. Keri had been to hell and back. Home took on a different look and feel; and meaning. It was friendly, warm, and kind. In the coming days, she grew close to her grandmother. As she turned sixteen and got her driver's license, she took her grandmother to the store and other places that she wanted to go. She became very respectful and kind to her grandmother.

Keri seldom saw Tiff Todd or Jimmy Singleton after her ordeal. Tiff came over a few times, but Keri had moved on and grew-up in so many ways that they shared little in common anymore. Keri enrolled at the local community college to get her high school diploma.

Keri loved animals and became interested in horses. With the help of an instructor at the college, she was able to get a job at one of the world-renowned Ocala horse ranches. She started by cleaning stables and learning to care for the horses.

Her grandmother died six months after Keri received her high school diploma. It broke Keri's heart to know that she had lived so many years with her grandmother without showing love and respect. But, it gave Keri comfort realizing that they had spent the last part of grandmother's life enjoying each other and sharing an affectionate love.

Keri inherited the house and her grandmother's possessions, including the car. She sold the house and bought a trailer closer to the horse ranch where she worked. She had found her passion working with the horses and being on the ranch. She seldom dated, but she did enjoy going out with friends on occasions. She had also developed a special friendship with a co-worker, Tony at the ranch. Tony was almost ten years older than she was, but they came from similar backgrounds. He was raised by an aunt near Orlando and had gotten into trouble as a teen. He was sent to the Florida Sheriff's Boys Ranch to help him straighten up and it worked. When they each had some free time they would sit and talk for hours. Keri had a lot of confidence in Tony and said many times that he had been put in her life by "God Himself." They were never romantically involved, but were the best of friends. Keri was good for Tony also.

Kenny Saxton pleaded guilty in the criminal court of Hamilton County, Tennessee, for theft of an auto, accessory after the fact in the murder of Alexander Fisher, and conspiracy to commit a felony. He received seven years in the state penitentiary. He was given credit for the eighteen months he was in jail waiting for trial. He served eleven months after his sentencing and was released on parole. He kept his nose out of trouble and was considered an excellent inmate.

The DeSota County Florida State's Attorney did not have any evidence that Kenny played any role in the murder of Tom Shelton. The State's Attorney and the Sheriff's Office closed the case.

Spalding County, Georgia filed charges for the murder of Mrs. Beasley, conspiracy to commit first-degree murder, and robbery charges against Kenny. He was taken to Georgia to face charges while still in custody in Tennessee. There was little evidence that he took part in any crime or had direct knowledge of any crimes in Georgia. He did know about the stolen things from the Beasley home. But Georgia decided to drop all but one charge against him in exchange for a written statement of what happened while he was passing through the state of Georgia. He pleaded guilty to accessory after the fact to theft charges. Kenny Saxton received a three-year sentence. He served the Georgia sentence on inactive probation after he served his time in Tennessee.

The state of Ohio never placed charges against Kenny in the shooting of the Brookville officer. The officer's statement put the blame on Mark Manning. Eventually, the District Attorney closed the case. Officer Scott made a full recovery and returned to regular duties four months after the shooting.

Since Kenny had no known relatives or a place to go in Tennessee, he was allowed to transfer his parole to Arcadia, Florida. On his first day back in town, he visited Lisa's grave. He knelt by her grave for a few moments, touched her name on the headstone, and let a few teardrops fall on the blades of grass that covered her grave. He wondered for a few moments how his life would have been different if she had lived. She was the only person he had faithfully loved or felt had loved him. His heart was still heavy as he leaned his head against the marker and just rested quietly.

He stood up after about fifteen minutes. He touched the top of the tombstone, whispered "goodbye, Lisa," turned and started walking to his car. He paused for a moment and let his eyes follow a squirrel to the top of a tree. He thought about turning around to look at the grave one last time. He glanced up as the squirrel jumped to another tree. He continued walking to his car. He never returned to Lisa's grave.

Kenny soon found a job at an oil lube shop and moved in with a co-worker who needed a roommate. He made a decision to stay in Arcadia.

JoBeth and Bo had parted ways about a year before Kenny returned. Bo had moved to Plant City to work with his uncle. JoBeth had started going to a small Baptist church a mile from her trailer, and Bo wanted nothing to do with her new-found religion. When Kenny came to visit a few weeks after he was back in town, she apologized for her behavior on the day he left and invited Kenny to go to church with her. .

On a sunny Sunday morning, a little less than six months after he had returned to Arcadia, Kenny pulled into JoBeth's driveway. He went to the door carrying three red roses that he had bought at a grocery store on the way to see her. She was surprised but happy to see him so early on a Sunday morning. He agreed to go to church with her under the condition, that she would began to date him. She agreed, and he started to go to church with her that morning. Three months later Kenny was promoted at the oil and lube company and made assistant manager.

They continued to date and let their relationship grow slowly. Kenny told JoBeth that she was the only person alive that really cared about him. They were married at their church a year to the day that Kenny returned to Arcadia.

★

Five years after the nightmare with Mark had ended,Kenny and JoBeth drove to Ocala in an attempt to find Keri. It didn't take them long to find her at the Half Moon Horse Farm. She had grown into a beautiful woman. She was still single, attending classes, and working toward her degree in animal science from the University of Florida. Half Moon Horse Farm had given her a scholarship, and in return, she agreed to continue her work there for at least four years after graduation.

She didn't recognize Kenny right away. He had put on a few pounds, had shorter hair, and was clean shaved. There was something about him that had aged beyond his years, but when she heard him speak she knew right away it was Kenny. She gave him a long, hard hug. They talked for a little while but never about the days had they spent on the road with Mark.

Kenny had known of her love for horses, so he brought her a gold belt buckle with a small, silver horseshoe, engraved with her first name. They caught up on some of the events of each other's lives for the past few years. They laughed, ate lunch, and exchanged contact information. They promised to keep in touch as Kenny and JoBeth drove away.

Keri stood along the gravel drive and waved. She thought about how Kenny had saved her during those crazy few days that seemed like a lifetime ago. She smiled slightly as the car drove out of sight but felt a deep ache in her heart. She reflected on the bond of trust they had shared through the difficult circumstances that had brought them together. She felt sad at the grim loss Kenny had suffered and the harsh price he paid for the choices he had made because of it. She felt a twinge of loss herself as he drove away. She smile at the fact that he came to see her. It brought her comfort just to know that they both were finally at peace. Remembering that she did have peace in her life caused a big smile to take over her face. Even though she realized their lives were on different paths, she knew Kenny would always be her hero.

Kent Rivers began to see Holly Packe on a regular basis. They traveled together quite often, and even flew to Rome one spring week. They didn't talk much about marriage. It was not a question of love, they loved each other, but it was a matter of lifestyle. Kent wasn't sure he wanted to live her life of luxury or be the one that married into money. Kent wondered if he was just being proud or if he feared he would change if they got married. The thought also crossed his mind that he might not be able to take another loss like he had with Adelicia. The lack of a marriage license didn't stop Holly and Kent from sharing a special kind of love.

It was Super Bowl Sunday, a year and a half after the Fisher murder. Kent and Holly were together with some of their friends at his place when he received a phone call.

"Hello, this is Kent Rivers."

"Hello sir, I'm sorry to bother you, but Detective Nick Taylor asked me to give you a call. He is on the scene of a missing person, and he thinks you should meet him," the communications officer said.

"A missing person? Did he say why he needed me?"

"No sir, he just called in on the radio and asked if you was come to his location."

"Okay, where is he?"

"He is at the home of State Representative Bobby Owens."

"Bobby Owens? Who is missing from Bobby Owens'house?"

"His wife."

"Okay, I'm leaving now."

Rivers hung up the phone but kept his hand on the receiver for a moment while he tried to collect his thoughts about what he had just heard.

Bobby Owens was a former Chattanooga police sergeant, a successful businessman, a popular state representative, and a friend to almost every cop in town. Why was his wife missing? Was it a domestic situation where she just left to cool off? Did someone kidnap her? This situation was very troubling to Rivers.

"I'm sorry everyone, but I'm going to have to leave for a little while," Rivers announced to the friends in the room. "I want everyone to make themselves at home. I should be back soon."

"Oh, Kent, do you really have to go? You have been looking forward to today," Holly said as the two walked out on the front porch.

"Yeah, it's weird, Holly. Bobby Owens' wife is missing. Nick thinks I should meet him. You know Nick; he is not an alarmist. I'm not sure if he is just making certain that we are covering all the bases for Bobby or if there is something big going on, but I should be back soon; Hopefully," Kent replied as he leaned in to give her a kiss.

Holly pulled him by his shirt to a corner of the porch that could not be seen from inside the house.

She smiled really big and said, "You better get back here. We have some celebrating to do after the game, no matter who wins."

She pulled him in and kissed him on the lips for several seconds.

Kent grinned, "Don't worry; I love celebrating with you. I will be back soon!"

Taylor was standing by his car outside the home of Bobby Owens when Rivers pulled up. He didn't give him a chance to get out of the car before he walked over to Rivers' door and motioned for him to roll down his window.

"What's up Nick?"

"I think Bobby Owens killed his wife."

★ ★ ★ ★ ★

**Another *Kent Rivers* book by Anthony Benefield
was released in 2015.**

"Crimsoned Corruption" gets into the lives and time of the Dixie Mafia, a loose-knit group of thugs, drug lords, and killers.

A Preview of Crimsoned Corruption:

Bobby Owens was a well known, well respected, and well-liked member of the State House of Representatives in Tennessee.

When his wife, Patricia, unwittingly discovers his connections to the Dixie Mafia, her life changed forever. She decided that it was too dangerous to remain in her home, so she vanished without telling a soul.

Her worse fears came true when she realized the magnitude of the far-reaching power, and resources of the Dixie Mafia. Patricia reached out for help to Chief Kent Rivers from Chattanooga.

Rivers and his investigators are frustrated when Patricia is kidnapped right from under their noses.

Things seem to get worse before they get better for the crime fighters. They learned just how willing, ready, and able the Dixie Mafia bosses were to resort to violence.

Patricia Owens found herself alone, and face to face with cold blooded - hardened criminals. As she faced certain death, Patricia found an unlikely ally, but would the help be enough to save her life?

Get it at www.kentrivers.com or asked for it at your bookstore.